What Scholars Say about *Whose Development?*

'This is a book which moves beyond the conventional deconstruction of development, and its simple and dualistic conceptions of power, towards an understanding of social action at development interfaces in which people (in development agencies and in local 'communities') shape processes and outcomes in ways that are creative as well as constrained. It is a book which stimulates new, relational ways of thinking about development and which will find a central place in the reading of students, practioners and researchers.' *Cecile Jackson, School of Development Studies, University of East Anglia*

'Revisioning international co-operation is a key task for the 21st century, but reforms must be based on a clear understanding of why our current development efforts fail so often. *Whose Development?* provides a rich picture of the complexities and power relations involved in foreign aid. This book will be a valuable reference for students and an important resource for practitioners. It deserves to be widely read.' *Michael Edwards, Senior Policy Advisor, NGO Division, World Bank*

'A fine grained ethnography of aid ... showing well the context sensitivity of all participants in development projects and their multiple identities and shifting roles.' *Frédérique Apffel-Marglin, Smith College, USA*

## About the Authors

*Dr Elizabeth Harrison* is a lecturer in social anthropology at the School of African and Asian Studies, University of Sussex and currently co-directs the master's programme in gender and development. She has carried out research in Sub-Saharan Africa and Sri Lanka, and advised multilateral and non-governmental development organizations on gender and natural resource management.

*Dr Emma Crewe* is a researcher at the Department of Anthropology, University College London. She has carried out research in South Asia, East Africa, and Europe, mostly while employed by the British development agency, Intermediate Technology. She has also worked for governmental and non-governmental organizations, including the UK National Lottery Charities Board, and continues to advise UK grant-making institutions.

# Development and environment studies titles from Zed

Zed has been a leading publisher of an exceptionally innovative and wide-ranging variety of books in Development Studies. Our specific lists in this area include:

- Globalization
- New Development Paradigms
- Experiences of Grassroots Development
- Studies in Structural Adjustment
- Sustainable Development in the North
- Environment and Development
- Gender and Development
- Urban Development
- International Health Policy and Practice
- Studies in Conflict and Violence in Society

In addition, Zed has published a number of key student texts in Development Studies. Recent titles include:

John Martinussen, *Society, State and Market: A Guide to Competing Theories of Development*

Ronaldo Munck and Denis O'Hearn (eds), *Critical Development Theory: Contributions to a New Paradigm*

Majid Rahnema with Victoria Bawtree (compilers), *The Post-Development Reader*

Gilbert Rist, *The History of Development: From Western Origins to Global Faith*

Wolfgang Sachs (ed.), *The Development Dictionary*

Frans Schuurman (ed.), *Beyond the Impasse: New Directions in Development Theory*

Visvanathan, Duggan, Nosonoff, Wiergersma (eds), *The Women, Gender and Development Reader*

For full details of these titles, our various Development Studies and Environment lists, as well as Zed's other subject and general catalogues, please write to: The Marketing Department, Zed Books, 7 Cynthia Street, London N1 9JF, UK, or e-mail:

sales@zedbooks.demon.co.uk

Visit our website at: http://www.zedbooks.demon.co.uk

# Whose Development?
## An Ethnography of Aid

*Emma Crewe and*
*Elizabeth Harrison*

Zed Books

LONDON AND NEW YORK

*For Nicholas and Paddy*

*Whose Development? An Ethnography of Aid* was first published by
Zed Books Ltd, 7 Cynthia Street, London N1 9JF, UK and Room
400, 175 Fifth Avenue, New York, NY 10010, USA in 1998.

Distributed exclusively in the USA by St Martin's Press, Inc.,
175 Fifth Avenue, New York, NY 10010, USA.

Copyright © Emma Crewe and Elizabeth Harrison, 1998

Cover designed by Andrew Corbett
Set in Monotype Dante by Ewan Smith
Printed and bound in the United Kingdom
by Biddles Ltd, Guildford and King's Lynn

The right of Emma Crewe and Elizabeth Harrison to be
identified as the authors of this work has been asserted by them
in accordance with the Copyright, Designs and Patents Act,
1988.

A catalogue record for this book is available from the British
Library

Library of Congress Cataloging-in-Publication Data
Crewe, Emma, 1962–
    Whose development? : an ethnography of aid / Emma
Crewe and Elizabeth Harrison.
        p.    cm.
    Includes bibliographical references and index.
    ISBN 1-85649-605-8 (hb). — ISBN 1-85649-606-6 (pb)
    1. Applied anthropology—Asia.  2. Applied anthropology–
–Africa.  3. Rural development—Asia—International
cooperation.  4. Rural development—Africa—International
cooperation.  5. Rural development  projects—Asia.
6. Rural development projects—Africa.
I. Harrison, Elizabeth, 1963–   . II. Title.
GN397.7.A78C74    1998
301—dc21                                        98–42003
                                                   CIP

ISBN 1 85649 605 8 cased
ISBN 1 85649 606 6 limp

# Contents

# Preface

Following in the footsteps of other anthropologists of development, we aim in this book to explore the social relationships and political processes underpinning the aid industry in South Asia, Sub-Saharan Africa, Europe, and the United States of America. We do not, however, make explicit policy recommendations about how aid should be reformed. This does not imply aloofness on our part. We are keenly aware that we are part of development. We have been employed by the Food and Agricultural Organization (FAO), Intermediate Technology, and a wide range of other development agencies, while carrying out and writing about our research. We recognize that a detached high ground is not tenable.

We critically reappraise some of the policies and practices we have observed within international development agencies, so it might seem natural to make suggestions for the future. However, to resort to simple prescriptions for the whole industry can create new misconceptions and stultify creative thinking. In other contexts our involvement in the world of development has involved (and does involve) making policy recommendations. In this book, we are suggesting something rather different: a need to reflect on moral and political assumptions, and to reconsider how one's own position may influence these. We hope the book will interest development studies theorists, teachers, researchers, and students as well as development practitioners and policy-makers.

We are indebted to many people. We would like to thank Robert Molteno (Zed Books) for his encouragement and comments. Ralph Grillo (Sussex University), Andrew Scott (Intermediate Technology), and Helen Pankhurst (ACORD) made invaluable comments on the final draft, for which we are extremely grateful. Any inaccuracies remain entirely our responsibility.

Elizabeth Harrison would like to thank the Department for International Development for funding her research with FAO; Arne Andreasson, Uwe Barg, Boyd Haight, Andreas Jensen, and Manuel Martinez (FAO); the staff of the Department of Fisheries in Luapula Province, Zambia; the farmers of Monga and Chibote, especially Abraham Kasongo and Annie Mwenya; James Muir and Alan Stewart at Stirling;

and Jock Stirrat and Ann Whitehead at Sussex. Emma Crewe would like to thank the Economic and Social Research Council for funding her research with Intermediate Technology; Caroline Ashley, Tammy Flavell, Ian Grant, Tim Jones, Pete Watts, and Pete Young (Stoves and Household Energy, Intermediate Technology); development workers, potters and stove-users in South Asia, East Africa and Europe, especially B. Somapala and K. B. Chandrawati; Tony Good at Edinburgh University; Uma Kothari at Manchester University; and Nicholas Vester.

# Abbreviations and Acronyms

| | |
|---|---|
| ALCOM | Aquaculture for Local Community Development |
| APO | Associate Professional Officer |
| ARECOP | Asia Regional Cookstove Program |
| ARPT | Adaptive Research Planning Team |
| AT | Appropriate Technology |
| BTO | back to office report |
| CBO | community-based organizations |
| CEB | Ceylon Electricity Board |
| DAC | Development Assistance Committee |
| DAWN | Development Alternatives with Women for a New Era |
| DFID | Department for International Development |
| DGIS | Directorate General for International Cooperation |
| DoF | Department of Fisheries |
| ESMAP | Energy Sector Management Assistance Program (World Bank/UNDP) |
| ESRC | Economic and Social Research Council |
| EU | European Union |
| FAO | Food and Agriculture Organization (UN) |
| FFF | Fuel For Food |
| FINNIDA | Finnish Development Corporation |
| FSR/E | farming systems research and extension |
| FWD | Foundation for Woodstove Dissemination |
| GAD | gender and development |
| GID | gender in development |
| GTZ | German Agency for Technical Cooperation |
| HE | home economist |
| HQ | headquarters |
| HUM | home unit manager |
| ICLARM | International Center for Living Aquatic Resource Management |
| IDEA | Integrated Development Association |
| IDS | Institute for Development Studies, University of Sussex |

| | |
|---|---|
| IFAD | International Fund for Agricultural Development |
| IMF | International Monetary Fund |
| IRSEPS | Imperfectly Rational Somewhat Economic Persons |
| ITDG | Intermediate Technology Development Group |
| JFS | Joint Funding Scheme |
| JICA | Japan International Cooperation Agency |
| KENGO | Kenya Environment and Energy Organizations |
| LIMA | Learned Improved Methods of Agriculture |
| MIS | Management Information System |
| MoA | Ministry of Agriculture |
| MPE | Ministry of Power and Energy |
| NGO | non-governmental organization |
| NLCB | National Lottery Charities Board |
| NORAD | Norwegian Agency for Development |
| ODA | Overseas Development Administration |
| OECD | Organization for Economic Cooperation and Development |
| OVR | overseas visit report |
| PCRU | Policy and Country Representation Unit |
| PFDO | Provincial Fisheries Development Officer |
| PRA | participatory rural appraisal |
| REM | Rational Economic Man |
| RRA | Rapid Rural Appraisal |
| SADC | Southern Africa Development Community |
| SEWA | Self-Employed Women's Association |
| SIDA | Swedish International Development Agency |
| SNV | Dutch Volunteer Agency |
| TCP | technical cooperation project |
| UN | United Nations |
| UNDP | United Nations Development Programme |
| UNICEF | United Nations Children's Fund |
| UNIP | United National Independence Party (Zambia) |
| USAID | United States Agency for International Development |
| VSO | Voluntary Service Overseas |
| WAD | women and development |
| WID | women in development |
| WWF | Worldwide Fund for Nature |

# CHAPTER I

# Development Aid: Successes and Failures

Is development a failure? Critics argue that development projects regularly fail to meet objectives and, more fundamentally, that the whole enterprise of development has failed. However, one person's failure can be another's success – an obvious point, but one that is seldom adequately recognized in the critical literature. In this book, although we do critically reappraise some of the policies and practices of development, it has not been our intention simply to denigrate the development industry or to explain failure. Rather, we aim to look constructively at the complicated interactions involved in the processes of development aid to see how different people and groups are constrained by, yet able to subvert, the objectives of others – and why they are motivated to do so.

Such an examination shows that people working in development aid often overestimate their own importance. It is easy to forget that, for many intended to be on the receiving end, the effects of what developers do are peripheral or even entirely irrelevant. At the same time, the pressures placed on developers are often overlooked by critics – pressures of time, the need for accountability, an obligation to show expertise, and pressures faced by partner organizations who need to retain and pay staff. Partly to cope with these demands, assumptions are made to ease and speed the process of decision-making and to account for unpredictable results. Such assumptions involve simplifications of complex social constructions – for example, about what is modern and what traditional. Failure may be accounted for by blaming the traditionalism of an ill-defined, but convenient, idea of 'culture'. Success may be seen as people responding to simple economic incentives or being attracted to modern technology. Closer scrutiny reveals other dynamics at work.

The processes described in the following two stories are central to this book.

## The failure of fish-farming?

In an international development organization in Rome, Jeanne works late, ploughing through project reports. She has a lot of work to catch up on. 'Too much time travelling, not enough in the office,' she thinks. A report on a fish-farming project captures her interest: she was involved in the preparation of the project some years ago. 'A number of improvements to fish-farming practices have been observed, and adoption rates are becoming more and more encouraging, including among women,' Jeanne reads. 'However, the poor management problems persist. Furthermore, the project has been hampered by a lack of cooperation from government agents. The objective of the project – improved nutrition through small-scale fish-farming – remains the same.'

In rural Zambia, Moses Chiluba is proud to be associated with the development project. When the vehicle comes, he is always on hand to greet visitors and answer their questions. He has dug many fish-ponds and hopes they will bring him a good income one day. This year, though, his maize must take precedence. Perhaps he can persuade his wife to work on the fish-ponds? He hopes to trade river-fish for cigarettes in town and then sell the cigarettes in the village. He wonders if perhaps the project could assist him with transport.

On the other side of the village, his cousin Rosemary has dug her own fish-pond. She has never been visited by the project, but has heard about it from other women. The banks of her pond collapsed and she lost all the small fish. She thinks maybe it would be better to concentrate her efforts on beer-brewing.

In town, extension workers hang around the fisheries office, waiting for the project vehicle to take them to the villages. They are worried about the delay – if they don't get going soon they could lose their daily subsistence allowance. At least Moses Chiluba usually gives them a warm welcome. The boss emerges from his office looking disgruntled. 'How will I ever get my work done with all these distractions?' he asks crossly: yet another team is coming from the capital to look at the project.

Back in Rome, Jeanne stows the reports in her filing cabinet. She is worried. A lot of money has been spent and she can't really tell if it has been any use. 'Maybe I should go and work for an NGO,' she thinks.

*The success of stoves?* Jim, a young energy expert from a British NGO, gets out of his Land Rover. He is committed to his work and hopes it will improve the lives of poor people. The superintendent courteously conducts him round the Sri Lankan tea estate. Women on their way to work stop and gather round. To their astonishment he quite suddenly walks into one of their houses, which happens, at that moment, to be empty. The interior is dark. He side-steps a pile of washing and two string beds, ignores the family photographs and finds his way to the kitchen. It has not occurred to him to ask anyone's permission.

The superintendent has asked his organization for advice about cooking stoves. After a moment, his eye lights on something unusual: the smoke from the stove is directed up a chimney by a hood. In most homes in the area chimneys are unknown: smoke slowly and with difficulty leaks out of the narrow gap under the eaves of the corrugated-iron roofs. Living in such a house may be the equivalent of smoking several packets of cigarettes a day.

Jim draws the superintendent's attention to the hood and the owner of the house is found. She tells them that it was her own invention, and made by herself out of thin sheet-metal. Jim congratulates her, sketches it and continues his tour. Back in the office, he composes a funding proposal for the World Health Organization, in which he proposes to use 'traditional indigenous technology' to reduce indoor air pollution. WHO's priority area is Bangladesh so Jim suggests piloting the scheme there. WHO consents; Jim's NGO starts field-trials. In the trials, the Bangladeshi users are polite about the new sheet-metal hoods, complimentary even, but it is observed that in daily life they almost never use them.

Jim and his local counterpart conjecture that the hoods are not used because they interfere with a 'cultural' function of the traditional fires. They decide to develop an appropriate modern stove, which, being new, they believe will not have 'cultural significance' and with which, therefore, the hoods may be accepted. After trials, a survey shows that 73 per cent of users prefer the new stoves to fires, and the local partner organization begins to distribute them nationally. It becomes obvious that the hoods are too expensive for users to buy and they are dropped from the programme, but 10,000 new stoves are sold to middle-income households within two years.

Jim writes a report justifiably claiming success for the stove project, and also a manual explaining how to make the hood. His organization is pleased to accept it as a success, too. The director of the partner organization is reasonably pleased, mostly because the project has paid the salaries of three staff members for two years, and the staff members themselves are satisfied as they have become known as experts in stove dissemination. The people who bought the stoves find them useful: they consume less fuel, even if the majority who cannot afford them are left out.

The World Health Organization is less satisfied. It is disappointed that, since most stoves were sold without hoods, the reduction in indoor pollution for which they thought they were paying has been much less than they hoped.

Meanwhile the originator of the hood, the tea-worker in Sri Lanka, has designed an improved version, made of stronger materials, which has been widely copied in her area without the help of any aid agency.

The contrast between success and failure in development is often over-simplified. It is one of a number of paired opposites upon which both observers and practitioners rely to explain a complex world. In the critical literature and development policy documents, simple dichotomies oppose, for example, developers and developing, donors and beneficiaries, rich and poor, rural and urban, Third World and First World, indigenous and Western. The stories above indicate that such polarities may be misplaced – social reality is far more complicated. But for development policy-makers, such simplifications are the basis for action.

This is obviously problematic in itself. Even for those consciously wishing to deconstruct the development process, such dichotomization sits rather oddly with a stress on nuance and complexity. For example, Ferguson (1990) and Escobar (1991, 1995a) have made influential contributions to the anthropology of development. They have moved beyond a view of anthropological engagement with development as being simply 'cultural brokering'. Nevertheless, as we discuss later, an opposition between 'us' and 'them' recurs even in their work. In this book we hope to offer a less polarized and, perhaps, less essentializing view of development intervention. We want to show that development practice is influenced by ideas and assumptions about what development is or should be, but that this does not take place in a predetermined way.

While it is necessary to avoid over-simple stereotypes, it would be wrong to go too far the other way and suggest that no patterns exist. People behaving differently from one another often reflect different experiences. More specifically, the experience of power influences action in subtle and complex ways and sets limits on what people can do. This experience of power is clearly linked to social and material conditions structured by, for example, class, gender, and race. Just as gravity takes water down a river rather than up its banks, people tend to act within boundaries defined by power differentials. Banks may shift and boundaries may move – neither are inevitably insurmountable. Furthermore, since people do not live in one fixed position in one power structure for more than a moment, they are restricted by different boundaries and create different power dynamics within each relationship over time. Thus the same person behaves differently in different situations.

Discussion of detailed ethnographic material at several levels can provide a nuanced picture of how the interface between different actors in the development process combines with the structural and historical specifics of their institutional location. Whether one is a senior planner, a junior researcher, a man, a woman, Sri Lankan, Zambian, or British, these are all aspects of this location. This creates a messier view of reality than many of the 'deconstructors of development' appear to imply, but arguably a more accurate one.

These observations arise from our personal experiences of international development. In this book we are explicitly drawing on fieldwork with the Food and Agriculture Organization (FAO) and Intermediate Technology (formerly Intermediate Technology Development Group – ITDG), but also more widely from our separate years of experience with development practice and from research carried out by others. FAO is well known as part of the United Nations, and Intermediate Technology is a British charity founded in 1966 by Fritz Schumacher, an alternative economist who was an adviser to the British National Coal Board (1950–70). Our inclusion of research on both a multilateral development agency and a non-governmental organization (NGO) is important. Although similar assumptions are made by those working in both, their institutional situation and structures of accountability are very different. While multilateral agencies (for example, specialized UN agencies, the World Bank, and the International Monetary Fund) are meant to be accountable to national governments – that is, their donors – NGOs have tended to rely on direct financial support from the public, the private sector, and charitable institutions in addition to governmental sources. NGOs, in theory at least, derive their legitimacy from the claim that they serve or represent sections of the public. This role has been complicated by their increasing dependence on government for funding.

Over the past few years the quest to 'get development right' has been associated with a great proliferation of development NGOs. For many they epitomize greater sensitivity and an ability to embrace the needs and aspirations of their intended beneficiaries (or 'partner' organizations) in Africa, Asia, South/Central America, and the Caribbean. The state, on the other hand, is increasingly viewed as inefficient, wasteful, and ineffective and is increasingly sub-contracting its service provision to NGOs. There is a growing literature that weighs up their comparative advantages in relation to government-instigated development (Fowler 1988; Edwards and Hulme 1995). Increasingly, governments prefer to work through NGOs and in many circumstances the latter are taking over roles previously performed by government. Today there are an estimated thirty thousand international NGOs (Stirrat and Henkel 1997), and an uncounted number of local, community, or grassroots organizations. But the proliferation of NGOs cannot be assumed to be evidence of widespread opposition to the state and multilateral agencies. Rather, we have found that in the case of Intermediate Technology, many of the assumptions and ideologies that permeate its practices have notable similarities to those of FAO and other official development agencies.

At the same time, within our case studies of FAO and Intermediate Technology, we do not represent one development discourse or ideology; such things do not exist in the singular. We describe certain aspects of practice, ideology, and social relations which, we propose, are indicative of wider patterns. We look at how different people relate to each other and how that relationship is mediated by their relationship to the material world. An aspect of this is an apparent disjunction between the ideas and concepts of one set of actors – the personnel in international development organizations, and another – their supposed beneficiaries. But importantly, we also want to show that neither development organizations, nor the communities with which they work, are monolithic.

## An ethnography of aid

Ethnography in a conventional anthropological sense once meant a detailed description and analysis of an apparently discrete and bounded community. It is now widely acknowledged that 'communities' are constructed through social relations and largely bounded only in a conceptual sense. More recently, too, ethnographers have begun to observe social relations within organizations and wider groups. Since ethnography is inevitably partial, it will not necessarily be more complete if a smaller number of people or a particular locality are chosen. The study of only one small group is the ethnographer's interpretation of no more than a tiny number of interchanges, actions, words or artefacts. An ethnography of aid, therefore, is less problematic than it may appear, or at least no more fraught with problems than any other ethnography.

Our description and analysis is ethnographic in the sense that we are presenting our interpretation of patterned social relations within a conceptually bounded group of people. That group may be large, those working in the 'aid industry' as planners, advisers, project staff, beneficiaries, and so on, but the relationships between these groups are distinctive. We undertook research in different countries and, for much of the time, on different continents. Even so, the patterns in our separate observations are so complementary that taken together, we argue, they constitute an ethnography.

This study focuses on particular locations within Western Europe, the USA, Sub-Saharan Africa, and South Asia. Other places, of course, are as relevant to aid processes; most obviously, Japan is the largest bilateral aid donor and many countries within Southeast Asia and South and Central America are also donors. The arguments we will make about the intellectual heritage of development clearly exclude, for example, Japanese ideologies about aid or the extent to which these may overlap with those of Europe and the USA. Our emphasis emerges from experience of practices and ideas in particular places and we do not claim that patterns are identical elsewhere.

Although our observations will be predicated on broader experience and illustrated with a wide range of case studies, we will introduce our two main ones – fish-farming in FAO and stove development in Intermediate Technology – separately and in some detail. We intend to introduce both the sectors and the organizations, and also to indicate some of the similarities and differences between these by exploring how success and failure are judged.

Our two case studies concern limited areas of the work of Intermediate Technology, FAO and their partners. We do not try to provide a broad comparative overview of all the activities of both. Cookstove development in Africa and Asia has been seen as a failure by many energy experts in large donor agencies, but as a success from the perspective of a few European agencies, many national experts, producers, and users. Intermediate Technology and FAO are both unusual in continuing to support cookstove programmes. In parallel, fish-farming development in Sub-Saharan Africa is a failure in the eyes of many but has, once again, a more ambiguous status when seen from different viewpoints. In each case, we trace perceptions and assumptions at headquarters through to relationships with 'partner' agencies (both governmental and non-governmental), to the supposed 'beneficiaries' and others affected by the project. We suggest that despite the differences between the two organizations, patterned assumptions and practices emerge that have broader relevance. Our aim is not to arbitrate between these groups and decide upon either success or failure, but to comment on what the perceptions about good or bad programmes reveal about the workings of development.

## Fish-farming and FAO

'Aquaculture' is the 'cultivation of animal and vegetable life in water' (Maar and van der Lingen 1966). While this covers a wide range of activities from large-scale salmon-farming to the raising of fish in earthen ponds, it is the latter that has been the focus of development assistance. Small-scale aquaculture has been promoted in Sub-Saharan Africa since at least the 1940s. Colonial, and later donor, aspirations for the technology centred on its potential to improve nutrition, generate income, and diversify livelihoods. The most common model was one in which farmers were encouraged to dig ponds and to stock them with 'seed' produced in government hatcheries. Between 1972 and 1985, over US$150,000,000 of international donor money was spent on the promotion of small-scale aquaculture (Kent 1988). Among donors there has been a strong perception that these efforts were largely wasted. There was a series of failures associated with aquaculture development projects: people not building ponds, or building them and then abandoning them, and extension services collapsing on the departure of donors. Where aquaculture was sustained, indications are that it has contributed little to most people's livelihoods.

By the late 1980s, disenchantment with the results had led to a reduction of support to small-scale aquaculture, and in particular an avoidance of the large infrastructural projects of the 1970s. As is the case with many aid interventions, failure has been attributed to an overly technical focus and a failure to understand the needs and motivations of the intended beneficiaries. The disproportionate expenditure on natural science research, combined with apparent technical failure, had led to a prevalent view that missing explanations could be found within rural communities. The intended beneficiaries of the technology were not behaving as expected. The greatest gap in knowledge concerned the beneficiaries themselves: why they did what they did and, importantly, what aspects of their 'culture' were resistant to the innovation.

FAO has been at the forefront of aquaculture promotion in Sub-Saharan Africa. It has implemented more projects than other donors and spent the most money over the last twenty years. By the mid-1980s, it too was concerned to understand more about what had gone wrong. In 1986, FAO initiated a fish-farming programme in the Southern Africa Development Community (SADC) region that aimed to learn from the lessons of the past. Aquaculture for Local Community Development (ALCOM) also reflected the growing interest among some donors in taking a more iterative, participatory, and 'bottom-up' approach to development. Its experimental nature meant that rather than introducing infrastructure and extension packages, or trying to persuade people to farm fish, the programme's focus, especially at the beginning, was on studies. The rationale was that the results of these studies would then be field-tested in a series of 'pilot projects' throughout the region. These were to be part of a process of 'methodology development', through which ALCOM would assist host governments to test and demonstrate methods and approaches for aquaculture development. The idea was that these methods would then be more widely applied, not by ALCOM, but by governments themselves or through externally assisted projects.

The official British aid agency, the Department for International Development, DFID (or the Overseas Development Administration, ODA, as it was then) was also concerned to understand more about the barriers to aquaculture development. In 1990 it funded a collaborative research project between the University of Sussex and the Institute of Aquaculture, Stirling. The aim of the project was to look at aquaculture development in action through detailed field research. Elizabeth Harrison was the principal researcher on this project, working with Jock Stirrat at Sussex and Alan Stewart and James Muir in Stirling. At this time, DFID had no functioning aquaculture projects in the region but a visit to FAO headquarters in Rome resulted in a suggestion that ALCOM should host the research. It was agreed that ALCOM and FAO would provide Elizabeth with access to their activities and a degree of logistical support, while she would feed the findings of her research into their programme.

Although ALCOM was based in Harare, Zimbabwe, the research team decided to focus on a pilot project in Luapula province, Zambia. Luapula showed, according to people in Rome, an extraordinary case of fish-farming success. In the space of a few years, many people had dug fish-ponds, apparently with little advice, assistance, or encouragement. The knowledge of numerous ill-fated attempts to promote fish-farming in completely unpromising environments also suggested that Luapula would be a good place to work. However, it was a priority that the research should consider not only the activities of the farmers, but the relationship between these and local extensionists, project workers, and ALCOM people in Harare and Rome. This meant fieldwork in several diverse sites. During 1991 and 1992, Elizabeth Harrison divided her time between two villages of project activity in Luapula province, Monga and Chibote, and the provincial town, Mansa. She also attended ALCOM's six-monthly staff seminars in Harare and returned to Rome to discuss findings as they emerged.

The Luapula pilot project, initiated in 1989, had two main aims: the consolidation and improvement of existing fish-farming in the province and the strengthening of the local Department of Fisheries (DoF). Over four years a great deal of activity took place including on-farm trials, studies, extension, and farmer training. Three expatriate workers were employed, initially an aquaculturist and a sociologist, then another aquaculturist. With only one paid worker, a four-wheel-drive vehicle, and basic operating costs, the pilot project was clearly relatively small by the standards of many development projects.

When it was wound up in 1993, a review in Harare suggested that despite the best efforts and considerable energy of the staff the major objectives of the pilot project had not been achieved. Impact on farming practices had been minimal and pre-existing weaknesses in the department had not been improved. Fieldwork observations pointed to great discrepancies between the aspirations and aims of the ALCOM personnel, the local staff, and the farmers of Luapula. The planners' assumptions, whether about motivation for fish-farming and local social relations or the priorities and commitment of the department, had been fairly wide of the mark. People were farming fish for a range of reasons that did not meet the planners' expectations about economic rationality. Furthermore, there was a clear divergence of interests and assumptions between the department and the project workers. Critically, there was a failure to take on board the impact of earlier intervention by ALCOM and others.

An evaluation of the overall programme in 1994 suggested that although much work had been done, especially with regard to the collection of information, substantive evidence of either improved fish-farming practices or strengthened institutional capacity was thin on the ground. ALCOM is by no means one of the pariahs of development that many of the industry's detractors love to hate, and it is unlikely that any poor farmer was seriously harmed by the programme. But it does illustrate a number of factors apparently common to development 'failure'. Most importantly, perhaps, the programme as a whole is an example of the expenditure of large amounts of money with little evidence that the supposed beneficiaries were benefiting. On the other hand, in this particular case it would be difficult to see what would constitute evidence of either success or failure because the objectives were sufficiently loose for their attainment to be hard to spot. The programme produced a great number of reports and studies whose relationship to better fish-farming practices is not easy to trace.

The problem of ascertaining whether or not the project really was a 'failure' is crucial to the attempt to understand it in other ways. If people have different priorities and interpretations of what would constitute success, then the attribution of failure can make sense only in a very limited context. And the identification of this context cannot follow neat dichotomous boundaries between 'us', the developers, and 'them', the recipients. On the face of it, we are considering an FAO project with FAO employees, and their interaction with their 'hosts', Zambian and other African government employees. Clearly in some ways the 'hosts' could be said to be part of the development bureaucracy. In other ways, they are not: ALCOM was conceived in Rome, not Harare or Lusaka. The choices of different individuals were constrained and shaped by diverse factors – position in the hierarchy, vulnerability, nationality, and age, to name a very few. Exploration of these issues may enable us to say more about the 'failure' than is usual.

## Improved stoves and Intermediate Technology

Improved stoves were first put on the agenda of planned development in the 1950s and many international agencies became involved during the 1970s. Half the households in the world use stoves to burn biomass (wood, charcoal, or organic residues), principally for cooking. National governments and international agencies decided that the existing stoves, most commonly three stones arranged in a triangle, were wasteful of fuel. In the 1970s the oil price hikes, and alarm about the depletion of resources (most influentially spread by Meadows et al. 1972), combined to create a perceived 'woodfuel crisis'. Following this, a series of misplaced assumptions about household or domestic energy, deforestation, and biomass fuel evolved in most international development agencies during the 1970s and 1980s (Leach and Mearns 1988). 'Experts' mistakenly thought that people routinely cut trees to get fuel for domestic consumption and deduced that a decrease in domestic fuelwood consumption would reduce the rate of deforestation in areas of scarcity. The orthodoxy also stated that domestic fuelwood consumption increases proportionately with population growth and that both are directly related to deforestation (Cline-Cole et al. 1990: 514).

Widespread deforestation was undeniably taking place. But timber-logging, land clearance for agriculture, and charcoal-making were all far more significant than woodfuel consumption as reasons for tree-cutting. Even so, the reaction to the predictions of catastrophe was woodfuel-related intervention on an enormous scale. Planners in donor agencies hoped that fuel-efficient stoves would save trees through reduced wood consumption. The claims about deforestation, and availability of funding, influenced national governments to concentrate on disseminating vast numbers of fuel-efficient stoves very quickly. Quality was often sacrificed on the altar of quantity. The technical performance of stoves was measured in relation to fuel consumption, despite the fact that in many places the stove-users were more interested in saving time than in saving fuel. The unpopularity of most new stoves was attributed to the cultural conservatism of their users. By the late 1980s Africa, Asia, and South/Central America became littered with abandoned 'improved' stoves. As a result, after around $20 million was spent on 137 stove programmes over five years up until 1991 (ESMAP/UNDP 1991), energy departments in many major donor organizations dismissed stove programmes as a failure and cut their funding completely.

While most European and American donors have deleted stove programmes from their menus of technology development, national governments and NGOs in many Asian and African countries (and a few in Europe) have continued to support them. By 1993 over 165,000,000 improved stoves had been installed in kitchens worldwide, mainly in China, India, Sri Lanka, and Kenya (Crewe 1993: 112–13). These stoves have mostly been very popular with those who have purchased them.

Some of the most successful stove programmes have been supported by Intermediate Technology. The recent introduction of wood-burning stoves in Sri Lanka was initiated by the NGO Sarvodaya Shramadana Sangamaya in 1979. In 1980 Intermediate Technology staff visited Sarvodaya and began to advise on design. In 1984, the president of Sri Lanka made national conservation a high priority as a short-term means of slowing the pace of deforestation and, as a consequence, a production and dissemination strategy for a stoves programme was developed by the Ceylon Electricity Board (CEB). Potters were trained to make the pottery liners designed by Sarvodaya, and these were then purchased and sold at a subsidized price by government officials. In most areas, the subsidy was funded by agreements between foreign governments and the CEB. By the end of 1987, there were seventy-five potter households making and selling stoves.

It was at this point that a concern developed within Intermediate Technology that the programmes were driven by environmental and technological, rather than social, objectives. In cooperation with the University of Edinburgh, Intermediate Technology secured funding from the Economic and Social Research Council (ESRC) for research into the socio-economic impact of new technology on its producers, in this case potter communities in Sri Lanka. Emma Crewe carried out this ESRC-funded study in twenty-two villages in 1988. She observed that the stove-producers were becoming surprisingly wealthy, which caused considerable tension within relatively egalitarian potter communities; that women's workload had been increased by their role in stove production; and that it was men alone who received the training and retained control over the production process, the marketing, and the income gained from their new stove-making businesses.

Emma Crewe returned to Sri Lanka in 1989 to explore the programme's impact on one potter village in more detail. As interesting as this was, Emma realized that she was not in the right place to carry out an ethnography of development. It was observation of all the groups involved in a project, rather than just the beneficiaries, that seemed necessary. So she accepted the offer of a job working as a social scientist in Intermediate Technology's stoves department based at its headquarters in Rugby, the UK.

While she worked for Intermediate Technology between 1989 and 1993 Emma was responsible for 'social science' inputs into the work of the stove team. Social scientists were seen as 'experts' in so-called 'project cycle methodologies' (that is, planning, feasibility assessment, implementation, monitoring, and evaluation of projects). She was employed to undertake, or to train 'project partners' to carry out, socio-economic and economic fieldwork, including an investigation of the marketing aspects of programme work. This job took her mainly to East Africa and South Asia. She worked on a regular basis with staff in five main project partner agencies in Sri Lanka, India, and Kenya: one government, three small NGOs, and one networking NGO. These were: the Ceylon Electricity Board and Sarvodaya (Sri Lanka); the Centre for Appropriate Technology and the Gandhiniketan Ashram (India); and the Foundation for Woodstove Dissemination (Kenya). In Kenya, she advised the Intermediate Technology project staff employed by the 'in-country' office who were based in Kisumu in western Kenya. Emma also worked regularly with expatriate donor representatives, technical 'experts', researchers, and consultants working from France, Germany, the UK, and the USA.

During her time at Intermediate Technology Emma watched the Sri Lankan stove programme thrive. By 1990 230,000 rural households had a new Sarvodaya stove and 28 per cent of Colombo households had a portable equivalent. By 1993 40,000 stoves were being sold per year. Increasingly her job involved lobbying donor organizations; despite the success of some stove programmes, they were no longer a priority for most European and American donors. A World Bank-funded study carried out by the East-West Center argued the case for stove programmes (K. R. Smith 1992). Donors remained unconvinced, however, because what had emerged as the most substantial benefit, reduction of women's unpaid labour (as opposed to their preconceived agenda of woodfuel reduction), was deemed to be insignificant as an energy issue.

So how should success or failure be judged? Most energy experts in donor agencies claim that stove programmes have failed because they have no measurable beneficial impact on national economies, forests, or levels of global pollution. Meanwhile, gender analysts claim that the programmes have failed because they do not challenge gender inequalities – although time-saving stoves may reduce women's unpaid work, they do not lead directly to more equal control over resources on the basis of gender. On the other hand, many African and Asian energy experts in national NGOs argue that stoves can generate income, relieve the pressure on biomass resources, alleviate women's workload, and point the way to an alternative, more environmentally sustainable energy strategy for their country (e.g. Davidson and Karekezi 1993; Asia Regional Cookstove Program 1995). Some producers have become significantly wealthy through participation in many stove programmes, while millions of users signify their popularity by buying them. Plainly stove programmes have both succeeded and failed in different ways and from different perspectives.

These case studies form the basis for much of the rest of the book. Our analysis of them has been influenced by specific changes in anthropological thinking about development. It is these that we outline below.

## The deconstructors of development

Development intervention has been widely criticized. There is both statistical and visible evidence of increased poverty, environmental degradation, and inequality in many parts of the world (Simmons 1995). If reducing these is an aim of development intervention, then, many argue, it is not working. At the same time, the history of development aid is apparently packed with a series of costly project failures. The shortcomings of the development 'industry' itself are increasingly well publicized. Overpaid expatriates are imposing inappropriate schemes on helpless 'locals' while aid processes in general are riddled with corruption and plagued by inefficiency. Aid, many claim, is geared towards satisfying donors' rather than recipients' interests.

The nature and direction of these criticisms are far from simple. This is partly because development is understood in two very different ways, and these meanings are often employed interchangeably. On the one hand, development intervention involves a set of institutions, policies, and practices with an identifiable history. In this sense, development has sometimes been characterized as an industry. The activities of organizations like the World Bank, United Nations, bilateral donors, and NGOs are described as 'development'. Many date development in this sense from post-war decolonization. On the other hand, development is clearly also an ideal, an objective towards which institutions and individuals claim to strive. This aim is seen as inherently good, implying a positive change, but its content is not necessarily specified. Embodied in this is the notion that certain countries and regions are less or more developed than others, and critics of development practice do not necessarily challenge this ideal.

From within the industry itself, in response to continual criticism of development processes there are attempts to make agencies more effective, even if the need for the aid industry itself is rarely questioned. Accounting for failure and improving practices usually entail looking to the recipients, the supposed beneficiaries who are not behaving as expected. It is common within aid agencies for advisers or planners to emphasize the need for better consultation with and understanding of intended beneficiaries. The current preference for participatory approaches can be seen as exemplifying this view, as can the desire to employ anthropologists and other social scientists to ease the development process (see for example Grillo 1997; Gardner and Lewis 1996).

When development flounders, self-criticism is often limited to an acceptance that insufficient attention has been paid to the recipients of aid. Implicit in this, however, is a tendency to root explanation in the culture of the recipients. Colonial denigration of the 'customs of the natives' may be long gone, but the reification of culture as a 'barrier to development' is still common. Indeed, in DFID there has been a proliferation of Social Development Advisers whose role is to mediate, translate, and explain, but always with the long-term objective of rational development planning. Even the stress on 'participation' and the widespread adoption of participatory research approaches, such as participatory rural appraisal (PRA), seldom escape such assumptions. They also implicitly suggest that earlier approaches to development made mistakes because they failed to consult with or understand 'them': 'beneficiaries', 'farmers', and 'local communities'. Participatory approaches are often no more than a tool to do this more effectively. Those who argue for self-reflection and a change in professional attitudes tend to acknowledge that developers have made serious mistakes, but rarely question the project of development itself.

Arguably, reformers within the development industry remain entangled in the principles and ideas upon which it was founded. These include a series of related assumptions, with their origin in the European Enlightenment, in which rationality, the search for objective truth, and a belief in a movement towards modernity are paramount. This point about reformers has also been made by those who distance themselves from the development industry and take a more radical line, arguing that the assumptions on which the industry are based are inherently problematic (Escobar 1984, 1991, 1995a; Esteva 1992; Ferguson 1990; Crush 1995; Marglin and Marglin 1990; Sachs 1992). The 'deconstructors' of development have argued that a tendency for over-systematized and simplifying models misinterprets and misconstrues the nature of social action and, relatedly, that the diverse motivations and perspectives of different actors in the development process are overlooked. They rightly assert that more sensitive translation and interpretation will not resolve these divergences. These critics also observe that developers are predisposed to find a uniformity and predictability within the communities with which they work that does not exist in reality. Furthermore, there is an implied compatibility, or even confluence, of interests between different people that should be explored rather than merely taken for granted. These more radical theorists see development itself as a Western-generated idea that has served to perpetuate relations of subordination in its creation of the 'Third World' as the underdeveloped 'other'.

These two broad lines of critique could be characterized as illustrating the difference between 'development anthropology' and 'the anthropology of development' (Grillo and Rew 1985). Development anthropologists are among the reformers who, from the inside and through processes of translation and communication, try to make development better. Anthropologists of development hope to stand outside and to comment on the discourses and practices of the 'machine' (Ferguson 1990), usually as analysts rather than developers. There are some anthropologists, of course, who swing from one role to the other at different times or in different contexts. Furthermore, both kinds of critique are also pursued by those associated with other disciplines or interests.

Development anthropologists have been accused of failing to acknowledge the relations of power within which they are embedded, in particular the links between colonial history and present-day political processes. For example, Escobar argues that the 'discourse of development' has its roots in colonialism and modernization theories and that 'development anthropologists choose to remain blind to the historically constituted character of development as a cultural system' (1991: 676). Building on the writings of Foucault, Escobar argues for an analysis of how 'certain representations become dominant and shape indelibly the ways in which reality is imagined and acted upon' (1995a: 5). He argues that a certain order of discourse, in this case created through the post-Second World War 'consensus' in the West about the existence of 'underdevelopment', creates and moulds particular permissible ways of thinking and being while excluding others. Escobar examines the establishment and consolidation of this discourse in the development industry. He sees development as both an instrument of economic control and an invention and strategy produced by the 'First' World about the 'Third' (1995b: 212). Institutional practices and professional discourses permeate this, and relationships between different actors are mediated by it. He suggests that the constitution of certain people and countries as 'underdeveloped' and 'poor' has acted as a form of silencing of alternative representations, discourses, and knowledge.

Ferguson's (1990) work on the World Bank in Lesotho has also been influential and is broadly within the same vein. His argument is that the way the Bank represents Lesotho as 'underdeveloped' and backward is an aspect of a wider process through which international donor development discourse serves to depoliticize the process of intervention, while simultaneously bolstering bureaucratic state power. Many consequences of development projects are unintended, but nevertheless sustain specific interests; aid-givers reproduce themselves and recipient governments perpetuate bureaucratic procedure. Similarly, a collection edited by Crush (1995) focuses on the texts and words of development to reveal 'the power relations it underwrites and reproduces' (1995: 3). They aim to expose the conceptual problems behind what is taken as self-evident, and to show how the language of development perpetuates its practices.

Discourse analysis is clearly a favoured tool for the deconstructors of development. However, as Apthorpe and Gasper (1996) note, the terms discourse and discourse analysis have been used in a great variety of ways, and not always consistently. The dictionary definition of 'discourse' is quite limited, referring simply to 'talk, conversation, dissertation, treatise, sermon' (as quoted by Apthorpe and Gasper 1996: 3). Discourse is an extended stretch of language or a debate, and discourse analysis involves deconstruction of both speech and texts. But much wider understandings of the term have evolved. For some theorists, 'discourse' means an intellectual framework and is comparable with 'paradigm'. Others, among whom are many deconstructors relying on Foucault's ideas, have a still wider understanding in which 'discourse' is a combination of both practice and the thoughts, ideas, and assumptions that shape such practice.

The danger with such a broad view of discourse is that it is possible for all things to become labelled as discourse, which diminishes its use as an analytical tool. Also, referring to the 'discourse of development' imbues development with an artificially unified and monolithic character.

The conception of development as an idea and essentially a 'good thing' becomes subsumed beneath the presupposition that it is synonymous with the development industry, and that this industry is the single most significant powerful entity to be deconstructed. Des Gasper (1996) accuses both Ferguson and Escobar of essentialism in their portrayal of the dominant power of the development industry – which is, however, illustrated by very different sets of evidence by the two writers. (Ferguson extrapolates from the discourses of one donor to make statements about the development machine, while Escobar focuses principally on North American discourses about South/Central America and the responses to these (Gasper 1996: 169).)

While deconstructors of development claim to eschew polarized, dichotomous views of the world, there appears to be an overwhelming pressure to return to them. Abandoning simple dichotomies between 'us' and 'them' is not easy or straightforward. As Gasper (1996) points out, for many authors the temptation to specify a singular 'development discourse' remains irresistible. Escobar argues that the development encounter should be seen not so much as a clash between two cultural systems as an intersection in which people and social situations are seen and represented in different ways. Although Escobar's call for both reflexivity and scope for 'their' voices to be heard is coherent, they are still 'them'. He argues that we need to understand local forms of 'resistance' to development and his solution to the problem of 'imagining a post-development era' is to support 'new social movements' (1995b). However, Escobar's implicit assumption is that developers develop, while local people resist, and arguably that this resistance is the most important part of their lives. Developers remain at the centre of the analysis while other people's actions are read merely as responses to the fixed centre, rather than as formed and influenced by all sorts of circumstances, many of which will be unconnected to development activity. Conscious resistance may be easy to spot, but how is it possible to distinguish between unconscious resistance and action that is independent of developers?

Other writers are more explicit in their maintenance of the dichotomy. Hobart writes in the introduction to a collection of papers on the anthropology of development: 'just how separate and indeed incommensurable are the respective discourses of developers, developed and governments, is a striking feature of many of the essays in this volume' (1993: 12). There is no scope within Hobart's perspective for an analysis of how everybody uses, interprets, and is differently incorporated into different 'discourses of development'. These are some of the processes that we aim to describe in this book. To fail to do so, and to adhere to certain categories of actors as if their characteristics were known and fixed, means that power becomes reified in a deterministic way, which serves to perpetuate a view that nothing can change.

Clearly, people can be and are identified with particular social groups. However, to assume sharp division and simplicity in what makes 'us' us and 'them' them may result in an incomplete account of agency. A fuller exploration of how the boundaries between one apparent category of social actors and another are bridged, transformed, and shifted is needed. Recently, this has come in the form of ethnographies and analyses that explore the complexity and multi-level nature of development processes (for example, Long and Long 1992). Interventions are seen not as the simple outcome of a value-free and linear planning process, but rather as the changing and negotiated manifestation of diverse and sometimes competing interests. The image of intervention as a discrete project in time and space with a clearly identifiable beginning and end is replaced with one of intervention as a 'set of social practices arising out of the interlocking of actors' strategies and intentionalities' (Long and van der Ploeg 1989: 237). Rather than homing in on the perspective of one set of stakeholders in development (the developers or the beneficiaries, for example), it is more useful to look at the relationships surrounding intervention practices as they actually take place. This involves examining the 'interface' between many different groups of actors – for example, the relationship between planners, project personnel, extensionists, groups within local communities, and so on. Our intention in this book is to offer such an examination. Before we outline how we have organized this examination, we will draw attention to the challenges posed by joint authorship.

## Writing the book

Many would agree that it can be important to contextualize observations within one's own personal and social history. While the novelist should leave much to the imagination of the reader, the ethnographer should leave as little as possible to guesswork. In ethnography, cultures or societies are described with the author's own moral, ideological, and cosmological perspective implied throughout the writing (Clifford 1986: 98). Where possible, these perspectives should be made explicit, since the partiality of a 'textual stance' does not invalidate the author's insights, but situates their statements (Rabinow 1986: 244). To allow some reflexivity and accountability we will briefly describe the process of joint authorship, highlight similarities and differences between us, and account for some of the key themes selected in the book.

The fact that we have written as if we were one author is a reflection of the large areas of overlap in our experience. The book is the product of a dialogue between two anthropologists, where the most significant shared analytical viewpoints are given prominence. Our arguments are jointly made and yet our own judgements are at least partially reflections of different kinds of involvement with development practice. While Elizabeth Harrison spent most of her research living with 'beneficiaries', farmers in Zambia, Emma Crewe carried out most of her research working with 'developers', principally NGO project staff and advisers in the UK, Sri Lanka, and Kenya, but also did fieldwork in a Sri Lankan village.

The relationship with informants and responsibilities to them were different as well, although sometimes only in degree. Emma Crewe remained an outsider in the Sri Lankan village, clumsy at speaking Sinhala, a source of information about exotic places such as London, and a particular cause for concern during unstable times. Elizabeth Harrison in some ways carried out more 'conventional' anthropological research through her residence in Luapula, but this was also partial and fragmented, particularly as it became clear that what she observed there was only one part of a complicated process that itself needed examination – hence time spent in Rome and Harare. For both of us, these relationships contained significant power imbalances. Money has often been relevant. Most of the people with whom we spent time assumed initially that, like most white development agency staff, we would bring financial assistance. When we proved hopelessly stingy as far as money was concerned, because we had no control over funds, and it was obvious that we were not even technical experts, the difficult question of what we could offer arose.

Elizabeth Harrison's position within ALCOM was one of semi-autonomous insider: not on the payroll, but nevertheless commenting and advising on the programme's work. In Mansa, the aquaculturist was both a colleague and a subject of enquiry. The Department of Fisheries personnel found her position similarly ambiguous: clearly associated with the programme, but disappearing for weeks on end into 'the bush' and making various attempts to distance herself from ALCOM. In Mansa, the difference between the expatriate community and Zambians was marked, most obviously by a white/black division mediated partly by money. Even the lowliest VSOs were better off than the Provincial Fisheries Officer. As a white researcher with her own motorbike, Elizabeth Harrison was clearly one of 'them'.

Emma Crewe became so thoroughly socialized within Intermediate Technology that her identity as a researcher dissolved and she became one of the 'developers'. For long periods, her worldview was shaped by assumptions shared between Intermediate Technology workers; detachment was almost impossible. Her job entailed mostly working with people whose posts were formally ranked higher than her own. In informal terms too, as a female social scientist working with technical experts, her social position was relatively low. Another social scientist warned when she arrived: 'You should not try to fight for power but prove your worth and persuade the technical people to listen to you. We have to accept that we are in a technically based organization, so we have to play a secondary role to the technologists.'

Emma Crewe's relationships with staff in partner agencies in different countries were constituted in very different ways. In Sri Lanka, her relationships with middle-class Sri Lankan project staff were characterized by apparent equality from her perspective. Although she was a young unmarried female student or low-grade project officer, her white, European background placed her in a position very roughly equal to middle-class professional Sri Lankans. This was not always true in relationships with project partners in Kenya. As Elizabeth Harrison found in Zambia, her relationship with urban-based, middle-class Kenyans was often negotiated at first through the medium of race, since there appeared to be a more explicit power imbalance constituted by being white/black than was the case in Sri Lanka. An African colleague noted that an important lesson learned from working with white development experts is that the racist stereotypic image of whites as efficient, honest, competent professionals often collapses.

Since our work with Intermediate Technology and FAO, we have both continued the study of various actors involved in development through teaching, consultancy, and our continuing contact with FAO and Intermediate Technology (for example, Emma Crewe has recently been made a Member of Intermediate Technology). This work has ranged from designing policy for grant-giving organizations to inspecting the social aspects of sustainably managed forestry and fundraising for UK NGOs. We are clearly part of what we write about.

Even if differences in our experience are evident, we share an alertness to particular kinds of social relations. Our own social positioning, as white, middle-class anthropologists, has plainly inclined both of us towards a particular shared intellectual disposition. The most significant shared area of experience relates to gender: few women social anthropologists are immune to feminism. As we are specialists in social relations, and identify ourselves in some senses with women as a subordinate group, our interest in gender is not surprising. More specifically, we have both moved within the male-dominated world of international technology development and, conversely, the women-dominated world of thinking on gender. While the practice of technology development marginalizes women and exacerbates gender inequalities, gender policy development has tended to simplify both the analysis of, and solutions for, such problems. We both see the need for a more nuanced analysis of the workings of gender relations in development.

We have also both become aware of the contrast between the prolific debates about good and bad gender policy and practice on the one hand, and the silence about race on the other. Development institutions have struggled with women/gender in development for over twenty years, but scarcely mentioned racism in policy documents, project plans, meetings or even informal conversation. And yet racism – in different guises – rears its ugly head at the very core of political relations within development. It is predominantly white planners in aid-giving countries who determine how aid is spent. Racist stereotyping, although different according to who is constructing and being constructed, underpins much development policy and practice.

In this book we are most importantly trying to confront inequalities in power and wealth. As we explain in Chapter 4, the language of 'partnership', which currently pervades much development policy, is oddly blind to the unequal basis on which such aid partnerships are formed. Inequalities in wealth, relationships of exploitation, and conflicting interests are, of course, based on gender, class, race, ethnicity, age, and so on. We do not want to argue here for the analytical priority of one of these, but assume that they intersect and are mutually con- stitutive of one another. When we focus on one or another form of subordination in particular parts of the book, it is because it has been relatively neglected in the literature.

## Summary of the book

This book is about ideas, relationships, policies, and practices in international development. In this chapter we have introduced ideas about development derived from academic research and policy debate, particularly those ideas explored by anthropologists. We have tried to build on the work of those researchers who have eschewed an essentialist conceptualization of power relations in development, and it has been our aim to achieve a contextual and relational understanding of develop- ment processes. At the same time, we have tried not to lose sight of material realities, especially the inequalities that aid does not appear to challenge.

The next chapter deals with some underlying ideas that subtly prevail in the development industry. These are often contradicted by explicit policy and planning aims, some of which are explored in Chapters 3 and 4. Also, chasms exist between ideas and policies and the actual behaviour of the groups and individuals involved in development. These are examined in some detail in Chapters 5, 6, and 7.

In Chapter 2 we explore a range of overlapping intellectual and moral systems of explanation that are prominent in the industry. The assumptions upon which these paradigms are founded, which we have looked at in detail and challenged, include the notions that development is an evolutionary and civilizing process; that culture is possessed by 'locals' in remote places (but not, apparently, by developers) and often impedes progress; that technology alone solves poverty, is morally neutral and is man-made; and the idea derived from neo-classical economics that economic exchange is individualistic and value-free rather than embedded in, and constrained by, morality and political relations. These ideas tend to be taken for granted, rather than explicitly articulated by those who hold them.

In contrast to these unspoken ideas, Chapters 3 and 4 focus on explicit areas of development policy: those relating to gender and partnership. We look at how discussion about, and action on, these areas often glosses over conflict and inequalities. We argue that the reason for this can be found partly in the political structures out of which the discussion arises, and in which the action takes place.

In Chapters 5 to 7 we explore the validity of the assumptions out-lined in Chapter 2 by looking closely at how people actually behave. We give a chapter each to technology, money, and culture. Chapter 5 considers some prevailing ideas about technology, gender, and expertise, and examines how these simultaneously both shape, and are con-founded by, practice. We argue that technology and expertise are often valued according to whom they are associated with, rather than by their utility. Chapter 6 builds on our critique of neo-classical economics: we suggest that people are not necessarily motivated by culture or by material gain, that economic exchanges within the aid industry are far from morally neutral, and that interests, priorities, or control are not evenly shared within or between households. In Chapter 7 we re-consider ideas about culture and cultural barriers. We illustrate how culture, contrary to assumptions made by many development workers, does not determine practice in a simple way. Furthermore, we show how cultural rules and practices are refashioned or invented within development organizations with just as much creative vigour as they are within 'communities'.

Chapter 8 challenges the idea that the recipients of development are invariably either passive or resisting. We show that these clichéd alternatives present an over-determined view of what 'local people' do, which serves among other things to put developers at the centre of the analysis. The supposed 'misbehaviour' of development interventions, we argue, may be only the result of differences in the way that people selectively internalize ideologies.

In the final chapter the intellectual cohesion of the development machine is questioned further by showing how different people interpret discourses in various ways, create room for manoeuvre for themselves, and continually cross 'them' and 'us' boundaries. It becomes clear that 'developers' and 'beneficiaries' are fluid, fragmented, and unstable categories. Finally, to avoid becoming lost in a post-modern maze we try to grapple creatively with the politically paralysing nature of deconstruction, acknowledging that while diversity must be recognized, it remains possible to make some generalizations. While we have found strict binary oppositions in development to be artificial and misleading, we still propose that some consistent patterns can be found of which the dominance of certain groups is a feature.

We argue that people use ideology to explain their past and make sense of their present. When those in a position of power in a particular context represent the past or present with themselves at the centre, they consolidate their power in that context. Through various development rituals, such as participatory rural appraisal and project evaluation, the legitimacy of donors as powerful but benign benefactors is reinforced. Behind this process, however, is not simple passive dependence on the part of those thus characterized as powerless. They too have a (largely unheard) account in which they are at the centre, which contributes to the unpredictability of outcomes. All actors are constrained, and power is not a commodity invested in people but more a description of an unstable relationship between people in a particular context.

# CHAPTER 2

# An Intellectual Heritage
# of Development

## Silent traditions

In this chapter we highlight some of the intellectual constructs that
have gained prominence in the diverse institutions of development. We
focus on a series of related ideas that overlap, are expressed in different
ways, and are surprisingly persistent. The first of these concerns
evolution. Social evolutionist paradigms, which imply that societies
progress through stages and, for example, that development means
movement from 'tradition' to 'modernity', recur in various forms. More
specifically, technological evolution is an essential part of development,
an apparently neutral, scientific process, yet invariably treated as if it
were in men's, and not women's, domain. Another set of ideas relates
to money, which is seen as the key variable in measuring people's quality
of life; its acquisition in greater and greater amounts is portrayed as
automatically progressive. All humans are (or at least should be if
'modern') motivated by rational, self-interested acquisitiveness. At the
same time, if any household member increases their income, it is
presupposed that all members will benefit because equality exists within
households. If new technology and increased income are made available
to 'developing' people, why then does the process of modernization
sometimes falter? We look at one evolutionist explanation: traditional
culture acts as a barrier. Culture is often reified as a collection of rituals
and customs exhibited principally by the less evolved, at times to be
celebrated and at other times to be overcome.

These constructs do not determine behaviour in a direct or lineal
way. Rather they are used by individuals within development institutions
to plan the future and make sense of the past. They give meaning to
representations of reality and lend shape to the way people re-create
their past experience of the world. They are revealed sometimes in
speech, and sometimes in action, but mostly they are assumed, implicit,
and taken for granted. They are in a constant state of reproduction or

revision by individuals or groups, are fragmentary within one institution, and are certainly very different between institutions. Identifying the constructs is, therefore, an inherently contentious process. We can cite what people write and what people say in an unproblematic manner. But it is equally important to consider what is left unsaid. For example, with respect to one area we will focus on – perceptions of economic motivation – there is some written evidence of assumptions in research findings and in project documentation, even if they are usually implicit rather than explicit. Assumptions about motivation are also revealed in informal conversation, meetings, discussions, speeches, and so on. But many interesting assumptions are neither written nor spoken about because, as Bourdieu puts it, *'what is essential goes without saying because it comes without saying*; the tradition is silent not least about itself as a tradition' (1977: 167, original emphasis).

So how do we identify what 'goes without saying'? We can deduce assumptions from observing the practices of individuals and groups: from what they do, how they relate to each other, and the ways in which they organize their work. No one explicitly says that there is equality within households, for example, but by organizing projects around the person they see as the household head (nearly always a man), and claiming that whole households will gain, equality is assumed. It is also people's silences, what they do not say, write, or do (for example, the fact that planners do not debate with farmers about motivation), that are in themselves revealing:

> The endless cycle of idea and action,
> Endless invention, endless experiment,
> Brings knowledge of motion, but not of stillness;
> Knowledge of speech, but not of silence;
> ...
> Where is the knowledge we have lost in information?
>
> (Eliot 1940: 77)

The conceptual threads we outline in this chapter are made up of numerous assumptions. They are not free-floating but are connected to particular kinds of social and political relations and can, therefore, be described as ideologies. Identifying threads of ideology is, to an extent, an arbitrary process. We have chosen to explore why it is often assumed that development is evolutionary, technology is man-made, material gain is the driving force in 'economic rationality', and culture preserves innocence or holds people back, but these notions are clearly linked and could be substituted by other equally interesting ones.

Development institutions operate with assumptions, values, and concepts, which are shaped in conjunction with historical and material forces. These are not comprehensive, monolithic, or held equally by all. Institutions are conglomerations of individuals and groups with varying interests, histories, and capacities for agency; they diverge in their particular reinterpretation of ideologies. At the same time, it is possible to identify those that prevail and chart how they have changed. This is the aim of this chapter.

## Development as evolution

The idea that development involves evolution of one sort or another has a complex heritage, reflecting some very different political perspectives. Both neo-liberal and Marxist theories rely on evolutionist assumptions. Neo-liberal evolutionism can be traced from current manifestations of modernization theory, back through the writings of Rostow, and Talcott Parsons, to early evolutionists such as Morgan and Tylor, and to Herbert Spencer, the first to apply Darwinian theory to societies. Radical critiques of modernization theory, particularly the work of dependency and underdevelopment theorists, such as André Gunder Frank, have their intellectual origins in the writings of Marx and Engels. Their fiercest criticism, however, is not that modernization is evolutionist; they too attach value to the differences between more and less developed societies. In fact, Mouzelis (1988) has pointed out that much of Frank's work is a mirror image of the modernization theory he criticized, with its presentation of an extremely schematic and simplified picture of the chain of exploitation between core and periphery and a clear delineation between development and underdevelopment.

So, these very different theoretical perspectives share evolutionist presuppositions about historical progress, whether this entails movement from homogeneity to differentiation (Spencer, Parsons), from savagery to civilization (Morgan and Tylor), from static to economically growing societies (Rostow), or from tribalism through feudalism to capitalism and then socialism (Marx). In all these cases, technological change is seen as a central aspect of evolution.

Social evolutionism has been effectively questioned, for example by anthropologists such as Boas, for over fifty years (Sanderson 1990: 36). Critics point out that if a writer reconstructs the history of one place and contrasts this with their own society, then, not surprisingly, claims for universality will be unfounded. In particular, the supposition that all societies share inevitable natural historical laws is not borne out in reality. As Mudimbe puts it: 'evolutionism, functionalism, diffusionism – whatever the method, all repress otherness in the name of sameness, and thus fundamentally escape the task of making sense of other worlds' (1988: 72).

Whichever political theory accompanies it, evolutionism has rhetorically justified intervention in 'backward' countries since European colonization (and, of course, other previous or concurrent forms of imperialism), through the presupposition that the influence of more advanced outsiders will enable traditional societies to catch up with them. Stephen Gould reminds us that early anthropologists in the nineteenth century represented the white race as biologically ahead of blacks and hence the latter as being in need of help (1977: 214): 'modern science had shown that races develop in the course of centuries as individuals do in years, and that an underdeveloped race, which is incapable of self-government, is no more of a reflection on the Almighty than is an undeveloped child who is incapable of self-government' (Strong, as cited by S. Gould 1977: 218–19).

Since 'they' were incapable of self-government, the compassionate Christian solution was to take control of the responsibilities of government on their behalf. Early anthropologists like Strong, it has been argued, thus indirectly contributed to maintaining the power structure of the colonial system (Asad 1979: 92). Although their influence may have been limited, Asad accuses them of being agents of imperialism by using evolutionary schemes as a justification for colonizing primitive societies. This continued during the heyday of functionalist anthropology, with Malinowski arguing that 'the practical value of such a theory is that it teaches us the relative importance of various customs, how they dovetail into each other, how they have to be handled by missionaries, colonial authorities, and those who economically have to exploit savage trade and savage labour' (1927: 40–1).

The tarring of all subsequent anthropologists with the Malinowski brush has been challenged (Kuper 1983; Asad 1973; James 1973). Indeed, Malinowski's relationship with his colonial funders has been shown to be much more strained than the quotation above might imply. On the other hand, the fact that neither he, nor many of those that followed, were willing to be the tools of imperialism must be counterbalanced with their undeniable dependence on colonial funding. Whatever the verdict, the continuing involvement of anthropologists in development and their implicit acceptance of evolutionist schemata have often been closely linked with their historical relationship to colonialism (Escobar 1991; Grillo and Rew 1985). Evolutionist development paradigms may use culture, technology, and economics as their reference points, rather than the more ancient biological ones, but they are still hugely in-fluential.

While ideas about pre-modern societies requiring assistance have gained hegemony, they do not constitute the only form of evolutionism. In European populist traditions, the pre-modern society is not neces-sarily perceived as inferior. Often its people are seen as remote from corrupting influences, living in harmony with each other and their environment, and holding great stores of practical wisdom. Such a perspective has ancient roots: Homer and Pliny idealized the Arcadians and other 'primitive' groups, while in the romantic writings of the eighteenth and nineteenth centuries, 'noble savages' were glorified, most notably by Jean Jacques Rousseau. Of course, talk of 'primitives' or 'savages' has become unacceptable, but just as ecologists have tended towards a over-romanticized view of 'primitives' nurturing nature around them (as pointed out by Ellen 1986), many working in develop-ment assume that 'local communities' protect their environment. For example, Niamir argues that 'pastoralists have devised techniques for managing (harvesting, improving, protecting and regenerating) natural resources. Rules and regulations enshrined within the traditions of society ensure the smooth functioning of the system' (1995: 255).

Meanwhile, a shift in the intellectual climate has shaken the certainties of grand theories such as Marxism and modernization theory. Norman Long (1992) has labelled this 'paradigm lost'. Populist development theorists have responded to this new climate by stressing the need for reversals in attitudes and an examination of 'Whose Reality Counts' (Chambers 1996). 'Indigenous knowledge' is, meanwhile, to be dis-covered, celebrated, and used rather than denigrated (Brokensha et al. 1980; Hobart 1993; Richards 1985; Warren et al. 1995). This call for greater respect for indigenous people is to be applauded. It challenges the assumption that people in all societies should assimilate to the most 'civilized' model embodied by Western capitalism, and it encourages greater tolerance for difference. On the other hand, the local, indigenous, or poor people are still 'them'. Chambers, for example, advises that 'outsiders should not assume that they know what poor people want', but makes sweeping generalizations about their behaviour: 'the poor, contrary to popular belief, are able and willing to make longer-term investments for lesser rewards' (1988: 10). Who are these 'poor' people, exactly? The categories vary, and great confusion about who is local, indigenous, or poor abounds, but it remains clear that it is 'they' who have the problems. These words, although not derogatory in themselves, can thus become euphemisms for tabooed words such as primitive, savage, or native.

So, for those working in development, whether they seek modernity or greater respect for local people, 'primitive' has been replaced by 'traditional' or, more recently, indigenous and local, and 'civilized' by 'modern'. Hierarchical connotations persist. 'Locals' are problematized, portrayed as deficient in various ways, and this deficiency is referred to when legitimizing the intervention of expatriates. Locals are seen as lacking in skills, corrupt, uneducated, or tradition-bound. As one radical ecologist colleague put it: 'It is very difficult to shake off the idea that we know more than them and accept that we might even learn from them.'

Images of people vary, of course, according to their identity and that of the beholder. The 'irresponsibility and corruption' of African men is often highlighted. African women, in contrast, are often assumed to be honest, hardworking, and altruistic, even if they are relatively out of touch with the modern world. While large regions of Africa, or even the whole of Sub-Saharan Africa, tend to be homogenized, racist images of Asian women and men are usually attached to particular countries or ethnic groups. We have heard development workers describe Indian men as devious and hopeless with finance, Sinhalese people as impossible to get close to or trust, Pathan men as fierce and women as conservative, and Nepali men as friendly but lazy. Of course such racist stereotyping is not the preserve of white Europeans or Americans alone. Indians have been known to complain that Africans are unreliable as workers. Kenyans have talked about some whites as efficient in presentation of their knowledge but deceitful and humourless. And so on. Our intention is not to survey racist representation, but to point out that such stereotypes circulate within development agencies. Biological racism has been largely rejected, but it has been replaced by private conversations about the cultural differences between groups. More specifically, it is often traditional culture that apparently accounts for the slow progress of some groups in embracing modernity (as we explain later in this chapter). And it is new technology and money that are the most potent symbols of modernity.

## The technology ladder

If 'traditional' culture is perceived as static and unchanging, or as Kirk puts it 'preserved in the timeless aspic of tradition and custom' (1983: 32), then where do the concepts of social change and development enter into this scheme? There are two perceived engines for progress: technology and money. The importance of technology in European images of modernity cannot be overstated. Non-European civilizations were measured according to their knowledge of European science and technology as far back as the seventeenth century, according to Adas (as cited by Hess 1995: 85). Just as Europeans could point to their superior technologies, particularly in the areas of warfare and navigation, as justifications for the civilizing mission of the 'white man's burden' three centuries ago, they rationalize their role in aid with reference to their more advanced technology and technical expertise.

Utopian visions based on scientific discoveries, as anticipated by Francis Bacon (Hess 1995: 83), are alive and well as a central part of modernist philosophy. Both Marx and Rostow depicted technological development as a necessary precondition for social progress. Illich has pointed out that despite the evidence to the contrary, the Western belief in medical science, technology, and experts is so strong that it is assumed that there are no limits to their potential curative power (1976). Many ecologists claim that environmental damage has been caused, but could also be reversed, by 'Western' science and technology (for details see Redclift and Benton 1994). It is not surprising, then, that technological advances are still seen as a vital key to development or even synonymous with it. For example, the Brandt Report states: 'The sharing of technology is a world-wide concern ... But clearly it is most important to the developing countries; and it can even be argued that their principal weakness is the lack of access to technology, or of command of it' (1980: 193).

Technology, it is often assumed, can tame and protect the 'natural' environment as well as act as a catalyst towards a more productive economy. It is therefore seen as a key to poverty alleviation or reduction. Technology development has been the most important activity in at least four out of seven of DFID's priority objectives, including: enhancing productive capacity; direct assistance to poor people; human development through health and children by choice; and tackling environment concerns (ODA 1995b: 55–61). For DFID, project workers are 'technical cooperation officers'. Although FAO is not an aid agency as such it undertakes 'technical cooperation projects' through the UNDP and stresses the technical expertise of its personnel as a principal attribute. Among its functions, 'technical advice and assistance' are important. The organization stresses its 'normative function', providing guidance through the collection and dissemination of information. The idea of value-free neutrality is central to this and equated with the technical.

Intermediate Technology has similarly constructed the concepts of intermediate and appropriate technology as if they are value-free, politically neutral global developmental ends in themselves, and it goes without saying that technology improves people's incomes and access to resources. Its mission statement is as follows: 'Intermediate Technology enables poor people in the South to develop and use skills and technologies which give them more control over their lives and which contribute to the sustainable development of their communities' (Intermediate Technology 1997a). 'High' (or capital-intensive) technology is attacked on the grounds that it is expensive, encourages unemployment, and damages the environment; the alternative – intermediate or appropriate technology – is seen as intrinsically beneficial. For example, intermediate new stoves are described generically as 'improved' before they have even been tested by cooks. Although it is acknowledged that matters such as who has access to and control over technology and who decides what is appropriate are relevant to the work, these are peripheral to the central aim: the widespread promotion of technology as a catalyst to development. If a technology development project does not meet its objectives, the local people's attitudes, environmental problems, or project management may be scrutinized to account for the failure; the need for technology is not, however, questioned. Just as the Azande in East Africa attribute inconsistent results of divination to a faulty application of the procedure, but not to divination itself (Evans-Pritchard 1937), so too Intermediate Technology staff members do not question the magical power of technology.

Intermediate Technology Headquarters' Operations Division is organized into technology departments with technical experts within each one: building materials and shelter, disasters mitigation, energy, food production, food-processing, manufacturing, mining, and transport. It is, therefore, inevitable that Intermediate Technology makes partnerships, seeks opportunities for work, and plans its work in response to a perceived need for technology. The flexibility of each department is severely limited because projects are organized around a particular technology and links between departments tend to be weak. When links are made, between housing and stoves for example, it is often as a result of a rapport between two experts in the different departments rather than the outcome of policy decisions. Since the 1980s social scientists have joined the technicians, and brought with them the means for consulting with 'communities' more thoroughly. However, they have not dented Intermediate Technology's technology-driven focus. In the vast majority of projects the only possible intervention is a technical one.

Intermediate Technology has expanded its Communication and Policy Divisions, partly because it recognizes that its impact on poverty will be negligible unless it influences the policy and practice of others. There is a concern, shared by many British NGOs, to multiply or 'scale up' impact. But Intermediate Technology staff rarely question the potential positive effect of technology itself – for example, it can expand economic infrastructure (Intermediate Technology 1997b) or improve people's capabilities to cope with change on a macro-level. On a case-by-case basis, Intermediate Technology staff make it clear how appropriate technology can enhance people's lives. As examples, better storage of food means that people can wait for a higher price for their products, better stoves save money, and more productive farms raise incomes. So, piecing together the broader picture, the implication is that poverty is caused by technological gaps and solved primarily by technological improvements. We do not claim that no link between poverty and technology exists. Improving access to intermediate/appropriate technology has alleviated poverty for some on a micro level, even if it does not permanently reduce national or regional levels of poverty. As part of a wider development strategy too, technology can have a place in enabling people to gain control over their lives. Intermediate Technology's work clearly shows, however, that the obstacles to such a process cannot be overcome with technology alone (see Chapter 5).

Informally, many of those working in Intermediate Technology explain that poverty is caused by economic and political inequalities. Why is the work, then, not planned to respond to this analysis? Perhaps it is because social relationships are much harder to change directly than skills and machines. It is for this reason too that some development projects perform delicate political operations under the cover of apparently neutral technical missions (Ferguson 1990).

The assumption that technology brings progress and requires assistance from Westerners is in part a reinterpretation of statements made in the past. In the case of Intermediate Technology, its founder Fritz Schumacher is especially influential. Although he is famous for his opposition to the transfer of Western 'modern' technology, his argument is that traditional technologies are from an earlier stage of development: 'we develop technologies which are very much better than the decayed, mediaeval technologies of the poor' (Schumacher 1975: 10), and 'their technological backwardness is an important reason for their poverty ... their traditional methods of production, in their present condition of decay, lack essential vitality' (Schumacher 1971: 88). His solution was to give knowledge: 'the gift of knowledge makes them free' (Schumacher 1973: 165). Underlying the two components – first, 'we' have knowledge to give and, second, knowledge makes people free – is an implicit assumption that 'they' are ignorant.

Even though some writers have challenged the perception of local people's ignorance, many still assume oppositions between indigenous knowledge and science by assuming that the latter is in some sense more 'theoretical'. In reality, everyone is concerned with practical matters, and practice is meaningless without theory or explanatory schemes. Bourdieu points out that even though practices are not the straightforward product of explicit, consciously formed principles or laws, theories accompany even the most 'automatic' practices. The teaching of tennis, the violin, or chess may consist of explaining individual moves, but the practice integrates 'all these artificially isolated elementary units of behaviour into the unity of an organized activity' (Bourdieu 1977: 18).

Despite the conceptual problems with assumptions about indigenous as opposed to technical or scientific expertise, the perceived need for technology transfers remain uppermost in development agendas. Technology has become so bound up with ideas about professionalism that 'soft' scientists such as economists, market researchers, planners, and social anthropologists imitate scientific styles. Models, matrices, numerical calculations, and typologies proliferate in training manuals, policy and planning documents, and development studies literature (for example, the use of Logical Framework, cost-benefit analysis, and methods for environmental impact assessment). As these relatively new domains become technicalized, the supposed need for them to be transferred also gathers steam within development agencies.

Technology is also gendered in its invention, use, production, and distribution. Past studies have shown that technological change has been mainly, although not always, relatively detrimental to women (Ahmed 1985; Stamp 1989). We will explore further the empirical evidence that technology is not neutral in practice in Chapter 5, but at this stage we argue that impact is not indicative of qualities intrinsic to the technology itself. Rather it is the product of relationships between people, in this case as structured by gender inequalities. Thus, when technology has been useful to women 'the miracle of technology lies not in its physical attributes but in its enlightened application' (Stamp 1989: 53).

In the invention and development of technology, women's technical expertise has been displaced with particular efficacy. In much development thinking science and technology are defined as male domains while women's equivalent concerns are relegated to the category of culture. For example 'improved' stoves designed by men are categorized as technology, while women's fuel-conservation strategies, employed when using their so-called 'traditional' stoves (usually a three-stone fire), are referred to as 'cultural practices'. Messing around with a three-stone cooking fire is not real technology if you define it as being equated with equipment, machines, or 'hardware'. After all, cooking involves manipulating materials (the fuel and stones) but not necessarily creating new appliances, and the absence of new equipment leads some to suppose that there is no innovation in the process. There is, however, another, more convincing way of looking at the use of three-stone fires. The fuel and stones are materials in one context, that is, when they are not being used for a purpose. They are transformed into equipment, on the other hand, once the cook has arranged them for a task. Innovation can be involved either in developing new equipment or creating ways of arranging equipment. Thus, Bush is right to distinguish between: (1) tools, such as appliances or equipment; (2) techniques, that is methods or skills for using tools; and (3) technology, which is the organization of tools and techniques for the performance of tasks (1983: 155). If the boundaries of what constitutes technology were changed, then women's technical expertise might be recognized.

Ironically, it is not male technicians alone who perpetuate such assumptions. The link between men and technical expertise has received a boost from some feminist thinkers who point to science and its technical applications as the cause of women's oppression. More specifically, ecofeminists connect the domination of women by men with the exploitation of nature through their separation from each other, and some assert that it was the European scientific revolution and its technical applications that began this misogynist and destructive process (Merchant 1980). Technology was not only 'man-made', it was used by men both to subdue the chaotic forces in nature and to control irrational women. This project continues through the modern capitalist system, which colonizes the 'South' (Mies and Shiva 1993). Western science, according to some ecofeminists, is shaped by invasive and reductionist masculine principles, leading to such evils as the destruction of natural resources, control of women's fertility, and disruption of rural people's subsistence economy. The feminine principle, in contrast, is associated with a loving, nurturing, holistic, non-violent attitude, and is naturally suited to the anti-market, anti-technology, subsistence perspective that the 'South' enjoyed before colonialism.

Ecofeminism has had a considerable influence over development agencies. It has generally been accepted that investing in women's projects could be a 'win–win', cost-effective strategy that simultaneously advances gender and environmental goals. This is problematic for a number of reasons. First, inequalities between women, and even between women and men, are glossed over; second, it is implied that women have the responsibility of setting the world, especially the natural world, to right; third, a reactionary position, ascribing caring but unrewarded roles to women, could be strengthened.

The idea of women's special relationship with nature, and correspondingly men's with culture, is undermined by historical and cultural diversity. We have seen that women's fuel-conservation techniques are labelled as 'cultural'. The world is not divided into nature and culture in all societies (McCormack and Strathern 1980). Also, when people do use these concepts, interpretations vary enormously because culture is a framework for interpreting the world, while nature is given its meaning through the cultural categories. Moreover, in some cultures it is men who are associated with nature, at least part of the time. The biological determinism underlying ecofeminism, whereby women's reproductive functions make them closer to nature, creates an undifferentiated category of women that cannot take account of differences across time and place. Finally, as Jackson (1992) points out, romantic assumptions about how women are naturally disposed to be custodians of the environment are not borne out in practice.

The ecofeminist claim that science has been used to dominate both women and nature is too conspiratorial and simplistic. Nevertheless, it is undoubtedly true that because of the existing gender division of labour and its affinity with assumptions about gender and expertise, development is perceived as men making machines for progress.

## Rational Economic Man

So far in this chapter we have looked at how people are placed into evolutionary schemata and how supposed technological expertise is more closely associated with men than with women. These are processes that lead to social differentiation, reaffirming existing social hierarchies. Assumptions about economics, which we consider in this section, have a parallel effect but rely on a process of universalizing about human motivation by assuming that individuals, households, and communities make rational decisions based on economic interests. Household decision-making is also equated with male decision-making. As much as the beneficiaries may be impeded by 'culture', the ideal from which they supposedly stray is construed as its opposite: economic rationality. Analysis of whether or not farmers will be willing to adopt a technology does not always take place. When it does, however, one analytical perspective dominates in many contexts: this perspective is rooted in neo-classical economic theory.

The dominance of neo-classical economics in both the theory and practice of development has been widely noted (for example Markoff and Montecinos 1992). In FAO, for example, 'economist' is often taken as substitutable for 'social scientist'. The majority of the few 'non-biological' experts in the Fisheries Department are economists. Further-more, the language of economics permeates FAO publications and in many a number of the simpler axioms of neo-classical theory are accepted with little sense of the problems entailed by them. Recurring terms in ostensibly non-economic publications include 'cost-benefit analysis', 'utility maximization', 'economic rationality', 'profitability'. Behind these concepts is the idea that people are 'utility maximizers', making decisions according to a weighed analysis of options. In its simplistic form, utility maximization focuses on cash or material gain. From this axiom, formalization and modelling of the decision-making process naturally follow. For example, an FAO publication considering the reasons people choose to adopt fish-farming makes the following argument:

> To what extent the farmer goes in for fish farming will depend on how much it will benefit him. He has to weigh the costs and benefits of various options on the use of his resources. In particular, the costs of various inputs for each option and the prices he can charge for the outputs. On the basis of this assessment, he may opt for fish farming plus one or more farm crops, or he may not opt for fish farming at all (ALCOM 1992a: 16).

Arguably, this view of economic behaviour no more reflects African farmers' calculations than it does ours. An element of calculation exists, but this is based on a pre-defined set of parameters and a stock of knowledge that is partial, fragmentary, and provisional. The constituent parts of the calculation are therefore subject to change. There is also no reason to expect that material or cash gain are the most important motivators. As Cancian argues: 'we seem to believe that people generally act on knowledge – that they use this knowledge to calculate, and having calculated, act. The fact of the matter is that they very often are called upon to act before they can know' (1980: 174).

Within Intermediate Technology, social scientists now outnumber economists but material gain is also often assumed to be the primary motivation for 'poor producers' to engage in development. For example, an evaluation of the Sri Lankan Urban Woodburning Stove Project focused on rising fuel prices and the low payback period of the new fuel-economic stoves as key factors influencing whether people purchased them or not. Payback periods are explained as follows:

> The payback period of a stove is determined by the relationship between the price paid by the user and the money value of fuelwood savings which result from its use. The lower the price and the greater the money savings,

the shorter is the payback period and the more attractive is stove purchase (Aitken et al. 1989: 40).

Similarly, it is assumed that artisans will agree to make stoves only once they have calculated the financial risks of starting a new business. In practice, many have reported that they did so because they 'trusted' the project staff or simply because 'development is a good thing'. The focus on economic motivation, which gathered steam during the 1980s and persisted during the 1990s in Intermediate Technology, did not depend on the presence of economists. It was a response to the neo-liberal intellectual climate where multilateral and bilateral donors gave the impression that hard-headed, monetary cost-benefit analysis in planning and evaluation documents was indicative of professionalism.

Economic power is often perceived by 'developers' as the biggest step on the path to development. Where does this idea come from? For Sahlins, 'money is to the West what kinship is to the Rest' because they have parallel organizing functions, classifying the 'entire cultural super-structure' (1976: 216). And yet, as Bloch and Parry argue, the meaning of money and exchange is determined not by its function but by a particular 'world view' (1989: 19). Transactions need to be anchored in their social context. On the one hand, what are viewed as gift exchanges are not necessarily as innocent and non-exploitative as they are construed to be. On the other, in many cases, money itself conveys the moral qualities of those who use it. Bloch and Parry argue for the need to uncover the diversity of meanings which can be attached to both gifts and commodities (1989).

It is misleading to assume that the meaning of a transaction can be simply read from the action itself according to invariant criteria. Instead of transparency, there is a complex and largely obscured background to the transaction, involving the biographies of the parties involved and their relationship with each other. As Andrew Long maintains, all trans-actions, both material and non-material, form part of a process of symbolic communication in which there is no separation between economic and social exchange:

> Two partners, even when engaged in what we might regard as an 'economic' transaction, are simultaneously involved in exchanging deference, affection, information and negotiating the meaning or value of the good. Hence the notion of exchange itself is replete with a multiplicity of meanings that can be exploited by the transactors themselves (A. Long 1992: 152).

Male fishworkers in Sri Lanka conceive of money as unclean and a potential threat to the correct order of caste relations and so do not handle it directly (Stirrat 1989: 99). While market relations in Fiji are seen to be morally neutral, morality and order are tied up with exchanges between kin, so that, for example, to refuse a request from a relative for money or goods, if you can afford it, would incur disapproval (Toren 1989: 151). In Madagascar money is morally neutral and can even be given to a lover after sexual intercourse without bringing to mind any uncomfortable associations with prostitution (Bloch 1989b: 166). In contrast, in Britain money is perceived as impersonal, and associated with business, and so it is usually highly inappropriate as a gift between lovers. It is especially revealing to look at the moral concepts that make sense of money within the context of relationships, rather than the social purpose of exchanges. As Bloch and Parry point out:

> Regardless of cultural context and of the nature of existing relations of production and exchange, it is often credited with an intrinsic power to revolutionize society and culture, and it is sometimes assumed that this power will be recognised in the way in which the actors themselves construct money symbolically ... Money, we believe, is in nearly as much danger of being fetishised by scholars as by stockbrokers (1989: 3).

This perception of the intrinsic power of money plainly circulates within the world of government and aid as much as it does in centres of learning and finance. There are many representations of money and morality within Western Europe, but the two most potent ones are still associated with Marx and Adam Smith. Both assume not only that society can be radically transformed through changing the relations of production and exchange, but also that the motivating premise is one of material interest. This materialism is described rather differently by each. Within capitalism, for Marx, material interest is expressed in terms of class, while for Smith, society's needs are met through the economic self-interest of individuals, so that 'it is not from the benevolence of the butcher, the brewer, or the baker that we expect our dinner, but from their regard to their own self-interest' (quoted by Bloch and Parry 1989: 17).

An emphasis on the individual, on wealth creation, and on small enterprise development became popular in development planning during the 1980s. In aquaculture development, an emphasis on government hatcheries and extension has been replaced by a stress on the need to privatize as much of the productive process as possible: 'it becomes more and more evident that the best chances of success lie in the development of a private sector, economically sound and technically independent from government support for most of its needs' (Coche et al. 1994: 50). The use of subsidies in stove programmes became unfashionable at the same time, and the commercialization of both production and marketing became an aim of almost all aid-funded initiatives.

The neo-classical economic theory permeating developers' understandings of motivation also tends to be implicitly gendered, based on a mythical 'Rational Economic Man' (dubbed Mr REM by Nancy Folbre):

> His tastes and preferences are fully formed; his personal and financial assets are given. He is a rational decision-maker who weighs costs and benefits. He processes perfect information perfectly. All his decisions are motivated by the desire to maximize his own utility – to make himself happy. In the competitive market place where he constantly buys and sells, he is entirely selfish, doesn't care at all about other people's utility. In the home however, he is entirely altruistic, loves his wife and children as much as his very self (Folbre 1994: 18).

Individual motivation is thus quite different inside and outside the household. The kind of rational behaviour in the marketplace outlined above is replaced by selfless altruism within the household. The corollary of this assumption is that intra-household relations are unproblematic because interests are shared: Mr and Mrs REM want the same thing.

The household as an empirical and analytical category has, of course, been frequently contested. First, household form and structure are not straightforward. Neo-classical ideas of 'the household' embody a picture of a domestic group based on a conjugal relationship that is clearly bounded and separable from the rest of the economy. Such a picture has little empirical validity in any context; in some it is entirely inappropriate. For example, in Sub-Saharan Africa, generalized models of households as discrete units of residence, production, consumption, and reproduction are inaccurate (Guyer 1986; Whitehead 1990). Kinship, marriage, and economic relations influence household form, making identification of the household unit complicated. Thus it becomes important in any particular case to specify the forms that household organization takes or the basis on which any particular entity is judged to be a household.

Importantly, too, the tendency to treat the household as a black box of joint utility is unwarranted (Kabeer 1991; Evans 1989). The household contains a variety of interests, not all of which are concerned with material welfare, and not all of which can be equated with those of one individual. One response to this might be to define a person's interests in such a way that no matter what he or she does, he or she could be seen to be furthering those interests (Sen 1979). The sacrifices that mothers make for their children are defined as 'maternal altruism', which is unproblematic because it is assumed that they are happy to make them (Whitehead 1981). They are maximizing their utility. Folbre notes that in response to criticisms of joint utility models, Mr and Mrs REM revised themselves into Imperfectly Rational Somewhat Economic Persons (IRSEPs). Economists adapted and widened their models. Thus Becker argued that: 'the economic approach is not restricted to material goods and wants or to markets with monetary transactions, and conceptually does not distinguish between major and minor decisions or between "emotional" and other decisions' (1981: ix). Significant problems remain in the circular definition of interest in terms of utility: how are preferences and wants formed? How is the shifting coexistence of apparent selfishness and altruism accounted for?

These debates have largely bypassed international development agencies, including FAO and Intermediate Technology. Although there is ample evidence to show that household decision-making, labour supply, and control, and allocation of resources are both contested and influence the outcome of outside interventions, they are seldom examined. Notions of household decision-making or household motivation tend to anthropomorphize the household, implying that it thinks and makes decisions rather than recognizing that certain people within households make decisions, reflecting different forms of power, cooperation and conflict. This may be because, as Guyer (1986) argues, there is a feeling that intra-household control issues may be too complex to understand in a limited time period or too sensitive a topic for enquiry.

Although development agencies may note the need to differentiate between household members, there is a consistent tendency to return to a simple, undifferentiated model of 'rural households', run by people bearing a strong resemblance to REM at the least. The undifferentiated picture of household structure and functioning is accompanied by a number of assumptions about farmers (or other 'beneficiary' group) and their relationship with other members of their family. First, the farmer or carpenter or entrepreneur is a man. (Although Intermediate Technology avoids words that exclude women completely, such as fishermen, there is a tendency to specify gender only when the group concerned are female.) The man then makes decisions on behalf of his family, who contribute work as part of the joint interest of the family. Benefits from this and other activities are distributed to the mutual satisfaction of everybody. The evidence of this kind of approach to decision-making is widespread throughout development bureaucracies. For example, FAO's *Thematic Evaluation of Aquaculture* states that:

The small-scale isolated farmer sees aquaculture above all as a way of spreading his risks. Before launching himself into aquaculture (most frequently the culture of fresh water fish), he assesses the likelihood that aquaculture will help him obtain a higher aggregate output from land, water, agricultural by-products, and his own efforts. He is concerned about feeding himself and his family. He produces more than he can use, that is perfectly acceptable. He will then barter, or sell, the surplus (FAO/NORAD 1987: 10).

The undifferentiated picture is also illustrated in FAO's commitment to the 'farming systems' approach, which is seen by many as an antidote to top-down, transfer-of-technology models of rural development. Farming systems research and extension (FSR/E) developed during the early 1980s and gained popularity by the middle of the decade, but has faced a crisis of credibility because of an apparent failure to 'come up with the goods', perhaps created by unrealistic expectations (Norman and Baker 1986). Multi-disciplinary adaptive FSR/E teams are no longer seen as the cure-all alternative to technical fixes. Nevertheless, the underlying theoretical notion, the idea of a 'farming system', has survived. It is the mainstay of two of the biggest aquaculture projects in Africa in the 1990s, ALCOM and the International Center for Living Aquatic Resource Management (ICLARM), which is based in the Philippines but has a project in Malawi. FAO has claimed that the 'farming systems development approach' emphasizes the understanding of the interrelationship of farms and communities with their wider environment as a basis for planning and complementing development interventions (FAO 1989).

The appeal of the approach lies in its aim of discovering and building on farmers' own knowledge, rather than devaluing and ignoring it. Recognizing that what people work out for themselves is likely to be more appropriate than plans imposed from outside, the approach has considerable value. But there are difficulties, too. As Gatter (1993) points out, although it seems reasonable to see agricultural activities as related systematically in aiming towards a number of goals, there is a problem in assuming that farmers' activities are related by them in a body of agricultural knowledge. Also, the focus on crops and productivity creates an impression that farmers operate outside any political or social context.

The very idea of a farming system assumes a uniformity that simply does not exist. It is as if it is possible to join neat boundaries around this identifiable system and then proceed to analyse it. The reality is, of course, that people's access to resources is variable and negotiated and that they act in response to the actions of others they are in contact with. This occurs within households as much as between them.

## Culture is a barrier

While rational motivation is assumed to direct people towards maximizing gain, there is a prevalent view that 'traditional culture' relies on something far less reasonable. The idea of traditions holding people back has a persistence across the development industry. 'Developers' talk and write about the traditional way of life, the traditional relationship between husband and wife, traditional skills, the traditional three-stone fire, and traditional farming practices. This traditionalism is partly attributed to economic or ecological conditions, but is often conceived of as being linked to a psychological or cultural disposition that is in some sense backward and prevents people from embracing modernity. For example, an FAO Chief Technical Adviser writes:

> Unfortunately, many of the factors which determine the ability to climb up the ladder are largely beyond the scope of specific energy development progammes. Among these are household income and size, climate, settlement size and – let's be realistic – culture and tradition to a large extent (Hulscher 1997: 12).

Another FAO study describes the process of modernization in rather more complex terms:

> Such changes have affected urban life in many countries far more directly than rural society. The capitals are already integrated into the world economy. Their rural hinterlands depend on them for imported commodities and for centralized services based on export revenues. However, the villages are often far behind, not only in economic benefits, but also in the change in value-orientations that characterize what may be called a modern society. This is not because villages are isolated. Nor does it mean a breakdown in social integration between urban and rural members of families ... But a differentiation is taking place between people of more modern orientation, with more education and/or ambition, and those with less (Hayward 1987: 3).

This characterization of culture implies stasis, unless a culture is influenced by 'modern society'. Other cultures are portrayed as absolute and given, and their characteristics subject to identification and possibly subsequent modification. Kinship, 'norms', 'taboos', and other aspects of social relations are treated as fixed, often in relation to 'modern' and flexible values. Echoing Malinowski's claim that anthropologists can help colonialists (1927: 40–1), social scientists are still used by development agencies to understand and then handle cultural and social factors. For the promoters of technologies, such as fish-farming or improved stoves, the practices associated with them are influenced by a social context that can be delineated and separated from the particular entity we (they) are interested in. The perception involves a simple process and unidirectional causation: cultural rules drive practice. In this way, gaps in knowledge, social obligation, reciprocity, and levelling mechanisms are seen as factors that influence whether or not the technology is 'adopted', rather than mental constructs developed partly by the 'developers' themselves. It is true that beneficiaries give expression to such ideas, but they are in part a reformulation of the developers' ideas about cultural rules.

So, 'local' people in Africa and Asia are seen as slow to adopt new technology partly because of 'cultural barriers'. These are portrayed in two ways: (a) as barriers derived from ignorance, and (b) barriers created by cultural rules. The following explanation by a technician stresses ignorance:

> An evaluation indicated that the replacement of the traditional ovens did not work successfully, basically because of social barriers. The new oven design worked well in the laboratory and was easily constructed by traditional oven builders, who supplied most of the households with ovens. However, despite many promotion activities, there was no awareness and concern about the need to save fuel and the new oven was not utilized economically (Usinger 1991: 7).

It is, therefore, natural to argue that it is the role of the promoters of the technology to assist in filling the knowledge gap. Although difficult to overcome, the problem is seen as essentially a technical one. Its solution is found in developing appropriate extension methods and technologies suitable to local conditions. If ignorance of the 'locals' is stressed, an aspect of this barrier is also acknowledged to be a failure on the part of the 'developers' themselves. For example, there have been attempts to introduce aquaculture to environments where people are not used to or are not keen on eating fish, or to introduce new stoves that burn fuel not available in that area. Attempts to improve understanding often entail an appreciation of the need to avoid earlier blunders.

The second category of barriers, those created by cultural rules, is seen as much more immovable. Broadly speaking, it is about the role of 'social control': this may include social obligation, reciprocity, and levelling mechanisms. In this sense, culture is a barrier to development in much the same way as it was when the language of 'primitive customs' was current. The potentially inhibiting role of cultural rules concerning accumulation, reciprocity, and appropriate behaviour has been widely noted (Ruddle 1991; Nash 1986; Hayward 1987). It is suggested that 'in many societies worldwide, levelling mechanisms are fundamental in controlling the individual and in functioning to maintain social status ranking' (Ruddle 1991: 12).

In 'developing' or 'traditional' societies, such mechanisms are expected to be particularly influential. Thus an individual who invests too much time and energy in economically productive activities as opposed to meeting social obligations is likely to be regarded as a deviant who must bear social costs. The nature of the costs will vary from theft and social ostracism to witchcraft accusations. The net result, however, is perceived to be the same: reluctance to adopt new technologies and inability to continue using them after adoption. For example, aqua-culture, with its potentials for accumulation and image of modernity, is thought to be subject to such pressures. A frequently cited example comes from Malawi, where apparently belief in witchcraft is so strong that small-scale farmers, including fish-farmers, dare not produce more than their peers for fear of being bewitched (ICLARM/GTZ 1991). In these accounts, 'traditional' and 'modern' are regularly contrasted. Particular beliefs and behaviour are presented as being internal to the village and in opposition to those from outside, and standing independ-ently of people's interpretation and use of them. Little or no attention is paid to explaining why and how in particular situations beliefs and actions are labelled by actors themselves as traditional or modern.

This outlook is not really surprising. 'Tradition' and 'culture' are associated in people's minds with anthropology, and as an anthropo-logist you are expected to understand them. As Holy and Stuchlik (1983) point out, however, the assumption of norms having a compelling effect on behaviour is still implicitly entertained in many anthropological analyses, despite the common phenomenon of people violating rules to which they verbally subscribe. They argue that social life should not be treated as an entity with a definite (though changing) form. Rather, analysis should focus on the ways in which norms are given force when people invoke them or disregard them in their actions: 'the basic ques-tion is not whether the action is norm conforming or norm breaking, but which norms, ideas and reasons were invoked by the actors for the performance of the action' (Holy and Stuchlik 1983: 82).

'Culture' as a barrier is not, however, always seen as an impediment to be circumvented. Development workers, expatriate or national, some-times explicitly state that they should not interfere with the 'traditions' of a culture. Within some agencies, this is particularly the case when it comes to gender relations. It is often argued that by challenging gender relations, outsiders disrupt the 'traditional' ways of an alien culture. The imposition of their values could possibly precipitate an unacceptable social upheaval. In some contexts, the social order within 'traditional' cultures is implicitly perceived to be closer to nature than 'modern' societies, and therefore governed by what some would describe as natural laws, which might include male dominance. Certainly it is often deemed to be inappropriate to question a gender division of labour where tasks such as fuel provision and cooking are designated as female, even when this critically affects the outcome of a fuel conservation or stove project. In the next chapter we take a closer look at resistance to gender-sensitive policy, but we note here that there are some unlikely alliances between such views and those of opponents to the supposed imposition of Western feminism from within these countries.

The idea that culture is worth protecting when gender is involved is inconsistent when set beside other social transformations brought about by development. It is taken for granted by many that development rearranges class relations – the purpose of many projects is, rhetorically at least, to make poorer people richer. Even caste relations, which tend to be portrayed as a traditional cultural system, can be fair game. For example, Intermediate Technology project staff have related with pride that one project in Sri Lanka challenges the caste system because lower-caste potters employ higher-caste labourers. They dismiss gender concerns, in contrast, as cultural and irrelevant to their work with technology.

If the simplistic traditional culture versus modernity dichotomy is misleading, why does it survive? In some ways it is useful for development planners. It conceals many social processes – for example, how social phenomena are continually re-created, negotiated, and changeable. Nevertheless (or maybe therefore), it does help provide a framework for making difficult decisions. With limited resources, both project staff and development planners are increasingly faced with a dilemma. Given that you are unable to work with all farmers, which ones do you work with – those who are poorest or those who are more likely to make a 'success' of whatever venture is being promoted? The distinction between tradition and modernity thus fulfils two functions. It is a simplifying device for those who identify themselves with mainly technical issues and require a straightforward explanation of failure. It is also potentially a tool for overcoming the tricky problem of choosing which farmers to work with.

## Conclusion

In this chapter, we have described strands of development ideology almost as if they stand apart from the social and political relations that surround them. But we recognize that ideas would have no potency at all if they existed as mental frameworks alone. Evolutionary schemata, for example, are sustained by the international political and economic systems that affirm in people's minds the 'Third World' and its populations as backward while the 'First World' is advanced. Technology and economic growth remain as the twin engines and symbols of development partly, though not entirely, because technologists and economists predominate within the institutions of the 'development industry'. Male-centred technology development is partly the product of male control of planning and decision-making within development institutions. The idea that money automatically confers power on people is apparently reflected in the control that aid donors have over aid recipients. Traditional culture is reified partly because it is associated with the 'beneficiaries', while the 'developers' ally themselves with modernity.

It has been well documented that these political structures in development aid reflect gender and class. Control over how aid is spent is disproportionately in the hands of men in bureaucracies, communities, and households. But what about race? Racial identity, although rarely mentioned directly within development agencies, is certainly relevant to development. Within development studies in British universities black academics are rare and authors tend to rely on other white authors (Saha 1998). Racism also underlies some of the public rationalization of intervention and the private stereotyping of large populations ('African men are lazy').

Relating these stereotypes to racist structures is fraught with complications. On the one hand, many bilateral donor agencies and international NGOs employ very few black staff. Most positions of power in international development bureaucracies are held by white people and anti-racist strategies are tokenistic, if they exist at all. On the other hand, it is not the international development bureaucracy staff who necessarily control how aid is spent and on whom. Development projects are not simply in the hands of white people because, in practice, the 'developers' and 'beneficiaries' in aid-receiving countries, most of whom are black, accumulate considerable control over project resources even if it is not always recognized by their benefactors. Since much of this process goes unnoticed, it rarely challenges those in positions of formal power. Many apparently powerful white 'developers', meanwhile, may have the false impression that some of their stereotypes of Africans or Asians are legitimitized by the supposed subservience of the latter.

Thus it is the link between practices, ideas, and structures in the past and present that partially accounts for the continuing prevalence of all three. We do not suggest that they determine each other in any inevitable manner. Rather, there are symbiotic relationships between the practices, ideas, and social structures. Other ideologies and practices would be compatible with the current social structures but there are affinities between these particular ones so that they nurture one another: a survival of the fittest affinities.

In this chapter, the assumptions that we have questioned are often fluid and overlapping. Notions about technology are intimately tied to those about gender and money; evolutionism implies particular notions about culture, technology, and gender, and so on. Equally, the social structures from which they arise comprise both overlaps and discontinuities. In one particular context or at one moment, gender, race, and/or another social differentiator may have particular salience.

These assumptions are not usually publicly articulated. In fact, there is a chasm between the notions described in this chapter and the policies of most development bureaucracies. Despite the gender blindness we have highlighted, gender is apparently central to the rhetoric of development of many agencies. And despite the prevalence of racially based inequities, the language of equal partnership is pervasive. These paradoxes are explored in the next two chapters.

CHAPTER 3

# The Gender Agenda

Discussion of gender relations has become an essential and, for some, incontestable component of the development agenda. For this reason, many might take exception to our claim in the previous chapter that male perspectives dominate many development discourses. It might be retorted that if a tendency to misunderstand gender relations persists, this should be set against efforts to take development practice in the opposite direction. We acknowledge that attention to gender relations and awareness of feminist arguments are at least nominally prevalent in development organizations. The United Nations supported the Fourth World Conference on Women in Beijing, many agencies employ individuals or create units with specific responsibility for making sure gender is taken seriously, and few development interventions pass without some scrutiny of their possible impact on gender relations. DFID demands consideration of gender in all its projects and Britain's second largest funder of UK development NGOs, the National Lottery Charities Board (NLCB), gives priority to work that benefits women.

We do not want to ignore or belittle these changes; they are at least partially the result of an improved understanding of gender relations. But they take place within a circumscribed context, an interplay of both ideologies and material conditions that influences power relations and sets limits on possible change. We suggest that the changes are, for the most part, shallow. Within both FAO and Intermediate Technology gender sensitivity is taken seriously but within the context of an impoverished understanding of the interests of and power relations between women and men. For example, a document written by Intermediate Technology policy staff in 1993 accounts for women's disadvantaged position by saying that they 'may be subject to cultural and religious constraints which affect their lives' (Intermediate Technology 1993: 1). A few staff have expressed a desire to be 'more radical', for example by acknowledging political and economic gender inequalities, but they worry that their analyses or recommendations would be dismissed as too negative or threatening.

Structural factors could be acknowledged only if there were a political will to reverse inequalities. On the one hand, silence about such factors could be construed as a naivety regarding conflict and contestation. More cynically, it appears as if people are replicating and perpetuating material conditions in which the choices and voice of women are inevitably limited, curtailed, or silenced. We argue, however, for a contextual rather than conspiratorial account of people's actions. Neither ideas nor material interests determine or even influence people's behaviour in a simple causal manner. Ideas are selectively used by 'developers' to make *post hoc* rationalizations of the practices in development that create and re-create gender inequalities, despite the policies that often aim to empower and enrich women. At the same time, they can be used as effective rationalizations only because the ideas have a powerful affinity with existing structures of gender relations.

Within the development industry, gendered structures exist within myriad other cross-cutting political, social, and cultural influences, whether formal or informal. People involved in development belong to different regions, nations, areas; various ethnic, community, and kinship groups; groups based on gender, race, religion, age, and class; institutions, professional associations, and government bodies, and so on. People's identity is always made up of an affiliation to more than one of these. Some might define themselves in relation to a wide range of them. We recognize, therefore, that our particular emphasis on gender in this chapter, and on race and nationality as illustrated through the rhetoric of partnership in the next, refers to only a part of people's identity; nevertheless these divisions are critically important to the production and reproduction of power relations and have been relatively neglected in the study of development organizations.

Development organizations are, of course, characteristic of bureaucracies more generally. From Max Weber onwards, certain aspects of bureaucratic form and functioning have been held to be archetypal: rationality; a stress on modernity; hierarchy. Until recently relatively less attention has been given to the way that bureaucracies are gendered (for exceptions, see Collinson and Hearn 1996; Morgan 1996). Weber himself did not question the predominantly male nature of bureaucracies in terms of both form and functioning, or their tendency to reinforce masculine values. Subsequently, although many studies have looked at the exclusion of women from or within bureaucracies and the way in which men operate within them, few have tried to understand the ways in which they are systematically gendered.

## An overview

Over the last thirty years or so, feminist analyses have apparently influenced both thinking and practice in international development agencies. The language of gender and development has been widely adopted; checklists and gender officers proliferate. The evolution from 'women in development' (WID) to 'gender and development' (GAD) has been widely documented (Moser 1993; Kabeer 1994; Razavi and Miller 1995; Young 1993). This evolution reflects parallel and not always compatible influences. On the one hand, feminist scholars have drawn attention, not only to the invisibility of women's labour (Boserup 1970; Dixon-Mueller 1985) but to the socially constructed nature of many of the differences between men and women and to the unequal power relations these reflect. Analyses in terms of women's subordination in the development process have conflictual implications; acknowledging difference to be the result of systematic power relations clearly potentially threatens these power relations.

On the other hand, mainstream development has taken on board and incorporated much of the empirical information provided by these feminist scholars. Awareness that women's work and responsibilities had been overlooked then gave rise to calls from within the development industry itself for better integration. Many argued that a valuable resource was being wasted. A DFID report states, for example: 'improving the status of women is a necessary precondition for sustainable and equitable development' (ODA 1995a: 183). The United States Agency for International Development (USAID) made the premise of its policy clear in its 'Gender information framework': 'the key issue underlying the women in development concept is ultimately an economic one: misunderstanding of gender differences, leading to inadequate planning and designing of projects, results in diminished returns on investment' (USAID 1982). For the OECD, evidence for the need for gender sensitivity is threefold: investment in the education of girls yields high rates of return; women are disproportionately affected by poverty; and women are key in environmental management (OECD 1998).

Such arguments have been characterized as the 'efficiency' approach to women in development (Moser 1993) where, as Kabeer suggests, the emphasis was on what development could get from women, rather than on what women could get from development (1994). However, the focus on women's productive capacity neglects their reproductive work. It also fails to scrutinize the role of men in development, even if many acknowledge that gender encompasses relations between women and men. Despite changing its form at various times, this approach still characterizes much of the work now described as gender and development.

Most recently, the goal of using women to make development more efficient has, in name at least, been supplanted by that of 'empowerment'. This shift has a mixed history. In part, the concern with empowerment arises from the activities and arguments of feminists worldwide, many of whom challenge mainstream development intervention. Debate has taken place in an environment of increasing focus on identity politics. Awareness of the differences between women, particularly how gender subordination may be less significant than that of race or class, has given rise to discussion, sometimes acrimonious, about the role of Western feminists in setting the agenda. This has been a regular theme at the UN World Conferences on Women. For example, at Beijing in 1995, acceptance of the term 'gender' was challenged by some delegates because of its association with Western feminist arguments about the relations between men and women (Goetz and Baden 1997). Mohanty has argued that in much of what has been written about women in development, there has been a tendency to portray 'Third World' women as passive victims, with little consideration of either their diversity or their agency (1988).

Along with these divisions, alliances have also been made between feminist groups worldwide who have found common cause for solidarity. Issues such as male violence and common economic subordination have been central. Overshadowing these debates, however different their political implications may be, has been a sense among those active in them that women have been finding ways of taking greater control of their lives – or 'empowering' themselves. Examples are widespread, from the much-cited Self-Employed Women's Association (SEWA) of Ahmedabad in India, to less well-known cases of women organizing together around common interests (see Basu 1995, for example).

What makes this 'empowerment' is a moot point and one that is often overlooked in the popular use of the term. Most simply, to be empowered is to gain power, but this begs a number of questions. Power is not an object or commodity and does not have fixed quantities. It describes the relationship between individuals or groups. The process of gaining power implies a change that is in some person's or people's interests but not those of another or others. Is it therefore possible for some to be empowered without disempowering others? Is it also possible to determine what people's real interests are without imposing our own normative frameworks? These questions have to be addressed before empowerment can be understood.

Kabeer has explored such questions, drawing on the work of Lukes

(1974), by distinguishing between three different dimensions of power: 'the power to', 'the power over', and 'the power within' (Kabeer 1994). The first, she argues, underpins much of WID literature, which tends to focus on the capacity of individuals to make decisions and act. However, 'the power to' dimension fails to take account of what has been excluded from the observable decision-making process – that is, the way that institutional factors may succeed in excluding certain issues from the agenda. A second dimension tries to take this into account, and looks at how institutional rules and procedures (including those of the household) may succeed in suppressing conflict. What Kabeer calls 'the power within' applies Lukes' third dimension of power, which acknowledges not only that conflict may be suppressed from the decision-making agenda, but that individuals or groups themselves may not be aware that their interests are in conflict.

Recognition of 'the power within', she argues, can deepen people's awareness of conflicting interests, however problematic and piecemeal this may be (Kabeer 1994: 229). This involves the disempowered gaining greater knowledge of the conditions of their subordination and taking action to change it. She gives examples to show how collective action may reveal needs that were not initially evident (for instance, SEWA in Gujarat, India, the Grameen Bank in Bangladesh, and SUTRA in Himachal Pradesh, India). Other feminist analyses, such as the work of Development Alternatives with Women for a New Era – DAWN (Sen and Grown 1985), also stress both the cultural specificities of women's experience and the need to find a common platform for organization.

These contributions could be extremely useful. Those using 'empowerment' as a development objective seldom take on board the political implication – that is, that conflict is accompanied by resistance, and that the process of empowerment is therefore not necessarily 'win–win'. It is important that the meaning of empowerment encompasses the potential conflict between people's real interests, even if this conflict is only latent. At the same time, people's real interests should be seen as existing on analytical or theoretical levels and as therefore not ascertainable in empirical reality. Thus any assumption that some people may be unaware of their interests is problematic. Just as those advocating false consciousness tended to portray the exploited as passively accepting their own subordination (Scott 1985), the ignorance and acquiescence of women are often overemphasized.

Despite the fact that it is now very difficult to find development policy documentation that does not have the empowerment of various specified groups as a key objective, its meaning is taken for granted rather than explored. Depending on the orientation of the organization or department, the groups may be 'the poorest', 'women', 'labourers', 'fish-farmers', 'potters', and so on. The empowerment of women was a stated aim at most of the UN Conferences in the 1990s – not only the Beijing Women's Conference. The Platform for Action from Beijing was subtitled 'An Agenda for Women's Empowerment' (UN 1995). The National Lottery Charities Board adopted the language of women's empowerment when initiating a new international grants programme for UK NGOs working internationally. However, this was later moderated by the phrase 'where appropriate' (NLCB 1996).

The adoption of empowerment as a development objective by donors coincides with a general questioning of the role of the state and an emphasis on both individual self-reliance and the capacity of NGOs to facilitate this. At the same time, because empowerment has been said to have its origins in the South, it is a plausible response to the charges of cultural imperialism that many donors wish to avoid. (The same could of course be said of 'participation', which is closely related to empowerment.) The use of the term has, therefore, arguably evolved somewhat from its radical origins: when used within international donor agencies it usually refers to the individual capacity to act ('the power to') rather than to a collective challenging of structural inequality. Such an interpretation allows an evasion of the problem of ascertaining people's interests.

According to Lukes, real interests are what people would choose if they could have perfect knowledge (1974). Although this may be reasonable as an analytical definition, it does not help to define the content of interests in a specific empirical context. With regard to gender, the understanding of interests has been advanced by Maxine Molyneux (1985), and subsequently modified by Caroline Moser (1989, 1993). Molyneux distinguishes between practical and strategic gender interests. She argues that practical gender interests are 'generally a response to an immediate perceived need and do not necessarily entail a strategic goal such as women's emancipation or gender equality', while strategic gender interests are 'derived from the analysis of women's subordination and from the formulation of an alternative, more satisfactory set of arrangements to those which exist' (Molyneux 1985: 240). Moser's definition differs in that she refers to practical and strategic gender needs. The former relate to those needs that 'women identify in their socially accepted role in society', while the latter are 'the needs women identify because of their subordinate position to men in their society' (Moser 1993: 40, 39). This distinction has been adopted widely by international development organizations including FAO and DFID, perhaps partly because of its simplicity and potential for universal application. DFID's *Checklist for the Participation of Women in Development Projects* (ODA 1992) relies on it as a central analytical distinction.

As a model for analysis, the strategic/practical needs polarity is open to question. Needs are so obviously relative, subjective, and contextual that distinguishing between practical and strategic needs for women collectively is difficult. Many actions may fulfil both practical and strategic needs at the same time, or one after the other, and it is unclear as to how they should be valued by development planners. Wieringa (1994) has argued that in practice the distinction is hierarchical and top-down, and that it denies the diversity and complexity of women's interests. People experience power and powerlessness in diverse and complicated ways: as result of their gender, class, ethnicity, age, and so on. What happens when these differences overlap or conflict? Furthermore, if the distinction were taken to its logical conclusion, it would threaten male and institutional interests – a point that is not really addressed by the numerous agencies so willing to adopt it. Indeed, the twin concepts of empowerment and participation are antithetical to the top-down nature logically inherent in the concept of 'planning'. A useful theoretical framework becomes a rather blunt tool in the hands of planners and other development personnel. But it is precisely because it is such a blunt and simple tool that it has such an attractiveness – a point we will return to later.

The rhetoric of empowerment has become widespread, especially with regard to gender and development. However, the misbehaviour of projects for women noted by Buvinic in 1986 is now replicated by the tendency for 'gender planning' to slip subtly and imperceptibly into the much older 'projects for women'. A relational approach to gender is replaced by a focus on women, while male gender identities lie un-examined in the background. The problem of institutionalizing gender analysis, making it more than a nagging concern on the margins, is as acute as ever: 'despite the energy and resources allocated to this work for more than a decade, WID still most frequently remains an "add-on" to mainstream policy and practice' (Moser 1993: 4). The commitment to gender analysis only rarely becomes gender-sensitive practice. More frequently it is translated into 'targeting women' and gradually ex-changed for the practical exigencies of project reality. Arguably, some of the explanation for this lies in the ideologies and assumptions prevailing in the development bureaucracies themselves.

Much analysis of what happens to gender and development planning has focused attention on the 'intervention' end – what happens to projects, the intended beneficiaries, and so on. For example, some very useful empirical work has explored the impact of credit programmes, which are favourite tools for empowerment (Ackerly 1995; Goetz and Sen Gupta 1996; von Bulow 1995). This work has provided valuable information in support of a more nuanced understanding of what empowerment means 'on the ground'. The authors show that reading 'empowerment' from the success of credit programmes may not always be justified; the wider ramifications of control and social cost also need to be explored. It is not, however, our intention to contribute to this literature here. Rather, we are interested in exploring how the gender and development agenda sits within the broader institutional context of development organizations, specifically Intermediate Technology and FAO. These organizations are, of course, themselves gendered. The way in which 'gender planning' is incorporated (or not) is clearly closely related to gendered dynamics within the organizations – a point we will return to in the final section of this chapter.

## Gender mainstreaming: still swimming against the tide?

Gender mainstreaming is now widely accepted as the appropriate alternative to the marginalization that accompanied the creation of women in development (WID) units in international development bureaucracies (Jahan 1997; Razavi and Miller 1995). Jahan identifies two approaches to mainstreaming: the first 'integrationist' (not changing or challenging dominant paradigms) and the second 'transformationist' (reorienting the nature of the mainstream itself) (Jahan 1997: 312). A number of recent analyses (for example, in Staudt 1997) have questioned the prospects for transformational mainstreaming, given the prevailing resistance and the gendered nature of the organizations themselves. Despite trends in the opposite direction, there has been an apparently substantial effort in many agencies, including FAO's fisheries department and Intermediate Technology, to include gender analysis in their work. It is the provenance, and the response to and by whom, of this effort that we consider below. We explore what happens in practice once gender mainstreaming is, at least nominally, on the agenda.

The first, most striking, tendency we have found is the persistence of the assumption that gender analysis and sensitivity are only about women – and particularly about women 'out there'. This is perpetuated by men and women alike and reflected in the overwhelming dominance of women in positions of responsibility for dealing with issues of gender. Second, action to promote gender equality has been largely in the realm of information collection, the development of checklists and guidelines, and the formation of sub-groups. While we do not question the need for many of these activities, it is also true that they are often explicitly depoliticized and do not confront the contentious nature of what they are revealing. This is particularly evident when there is much less attention paid to who will use the guidelines/information/checklists or whatever – and why they might (or more likely might not) be inclined to do so. Explanations for these trends require examination of the accountability systems, both internal and external, and the gendered incentives that operate within the organizations themselves.

We will explore the development of gender policy within FAO and Intermediate Technology. We focus on Intermediate Technology's Headquarters in England, on the assumption that it affects all the organization's appropriate technology work in Africa, Asia, and South/Central America, as we will show in Chapters 5 and 7. Although appropriate technology appears to be more people-centred than 'mainstream' technology transfer, it has been claimed that it is written about and promoted by men, who adhere to the same old androcentric values that dictate that 'men have the technical skills and make the technical decisions' (J. Smith 1983: 66). While there may be some truth in this, it will become clear that values within Intermediate Technology are far from evenly shared throughout the organization.

FAO as a whole has been scrutinized in the past regarding the success or failure of its gender mainstreaming (Rogers 1980; Carloni 1997) with fairly negative outcomes (Carloni implies that it is not as bad as the World Bank, but could do much better). The gender policy of the organization as a whole has its own particular manifestations and interpretations when it comes to the fisheries department. It is on these that we focus here. Despite the fact that critical links between gender and fish-farming do not leap to mind, the activities of the fisheries department with respect to these throw considerable light on the wider incorporation of issues of gender.

There are important differences between the two organizations – FAO and Intermediate Technology – that affect debates about gender. Attempts to institutionalize gender sensitivity in multilateral organizations, such as FAO, should be seen within the context of how international bureaucracies work more generally. In particular, the coming together of a number of nationalities within FAO raises many questions about gender. For example, which national stereotypical view of masculine and feminine predominates? To what extent do national culture or identity provide a uniting ideology beyond differences in gender? Woodward (1996) argues that in the European Union, where a number of nationalities also meet, there may be a tendency to grab at the few things that unite, including assumed beliefs about gender. There is some evidence for this in FAO too. Most British NGOs, conversely, tend to be relatively nationally and culturally homogeneous within their British-based headquarters. For example, between 1988 and 1993 about 95 per cent of the Intermediate Technology HQ staff were white, middle-class Britons. They saw themselves as sharing a mission, the promotion of environmentally and socially benign technology for the 'poor', which had pre-eminence over gender concerns.

## A job for the girls?

Gender analysis is usually treated as something done for women by women. There are default assumptions that the key players in technical areas are male while 'cultural' domains are women-dominated: the fish-farmer is apparently a man, business is for men, but cooks are always female. It was the predominantly female social scientists within Intermediate Technology, the perceived custodians of morality, who raised gender as a topic for discussion from the late 1980s onwards. It was a female social scientist who first expressed doubt in 1988 that Intermediate Technology had an adequate policy on women and made various suggestions for analysing women's roles in projects, impact on women, and the way that women were portrayed in publications and materials. The hesitancy expressed in the last sentence of her memo reveals how thorny a subject it was: 'it may be the case that we are already doing so well that there is no need for any further action but we need to find this out.' A senior male social scientist replied:

> during the last drafting of the Strategy Paper there was a debate on whether any specific statement on the important role of women in development (and in production) and on Intermediate Technology's commitment to women's issues should be included. The majority of those consulted (yes, there were women involved) felt that singling out women in our policy paper would smack of tokenism, and that we should let our actions speak of our commitment on this matter ... I suggest the most practical way to proceed is to work on ITDG's methods of evaluating on-going projects to ensure that there is commitment throughout Operations Division to analyzing the impact of our work on women (internal memo 1988).

Women were seen as one theme within the area of expertise of female social scientists and one area of their responsibility, along with market research, participatory planning, or evaluating impact. The male technician staff, meanwhile, turned to social scientists for advice on ensuring women's participation or considering the potential impact of particular activities on women.

A remarkably similar process took place in FAO. As in Intermediate Technology, women have tended to be treated as an category 'out there'. For example, the tasks of the Core Group on Women and Fisheries were to review projects to check for inclusion of women, to organize and promote workshops, and to 'sensitize counterpart experts and decision makers in recipient countries on gender issues' (Sen et al. 1991: 59). The implication is arguably that sensitization on gender issues in headquarters had already been achieved, and that there was no need to scrutinize internal gender relations. This is intuitively unlikely and there is evidence against it. In 1987 the Core Group, with financial assistance from NORAD, helped to organize FAO's first conference on Women in Aquaculture (FAO 1987). All of the presentations to the conference were made by women. The opening address to the conference was made by the then head of the Aquaculture Development and Coordination Programme (a man). One paragraph warrants quoting in full:

> I have been criticized for the organization of this workshop on two counts. First, I have been criticized (and only by women, no less) for not inviting men as principal participants. But I have no good reason to do so. Frankly, even in this small workshop of thirty carefully selected participants, there is probably not one question I can ask about aquaculture which cannot be answered by one of you. Thus, if during the next three days you need to know the typical labour force of a shrimp hatchery, or the organization for a credit programme in Africa, or the requirements of a project development document for UNDP, someone here among you will have the answer (FAO 1987: 6).

This statement reflects a view that is often only implicit: that 'women' can be dealt with separately and the process of technical planning can go on as before. It also clearly misunderstands why it is that men should have been present. Male gender identities are not questioned. Participants at the conference were predominantly academics and representatives of women's departments in international organizations. Some of them approached issues of gender from a feminist perspective. The conference document thus illustrates how very different interpretations and perspectives on gender can be incorporated and coexist within the overall policy-making process. The process of incorporation accompanying persistent marginalization is key in the slip from gender analysis to projects for women. Ferguson (1990) argues that the kind of guide to action produced by academic analyses is of no use to development agencies (in his case the World Bank), because they do not provide a charter for the sort of intervention that the agency is set up to do. The picture becomes more complicated when, as in the example above, the 'unhelpful analyses' are included within the mainstream. Rather than being rejected as useless, they are adopted and ignored.

## Meetings and guidelines

Accepting the need to pay attention to gender is one thing. Putting it into practice is another. A number of generally accepted mechanisms prevail: the establishment of working groups, the collection of information, and the creation of checklists and guidelines. These often bypass the conflict that accompanies attempts to address gender inequalities. This process, as illustrated within FAO's ALCOM project and Intermediate Technology, is described below.

In ALCOM's initial preparatory phase, 'women and youth' were identified as a separate target area. No specific budget was allocated 'as ALCOM has always stressed the need for a multi-disciplinary approach' (Sen et al. 1991: 77). The aim of this target area was, through literature and studies, to identify options and activities to be included in project activities. In November 1990, ALCOM hosted an international meeting at Victoria Falls to discuss gender issues in fisheries and aquaculture development. Following this workshop, and in response to its recommendation for more disaggregated information, the Japan International Cooperation Agency (JICA) agreed to fund a sub-project within the ALCOM programme, 'Enhancement of the Role of Women in Fisheries and Aquaculture Development'. The aim of the sub-project was the incorporation of gender issues in projects for inland fisheries and aquaculture development in southern Africa. Intended outputs were the production of gender-specific data, guidelines and checklists for collecting gender-specific socio-economic information, and the formulation of pilot projects.

A focus on data collection can avoid contentious issues. The discovery that more data were needed was the main outcome and finding of ALCOM's sub-project. According to the project final report, the principal conclusion of studies carried out in Tanzania, Zimbabwe, and Zambia (which were unrelated to project activities) was that: 'there is a severe gap in some gender related information, particularly on the division of labour between sexes, access and control over productive resources and responsibility for decision making' (FAO 1993: 3).

Guidelines for filling the information gap were therefore needed. These were drafted by FAO personnel and consultants and began from the premise that there has been little change in sectoral planning regarding gender issues because there is insufficient information on such issues. Furthermore, planners are not certain how or where to obtain such information. Given this apparent lack of information, the guidelines are surprisingly full of sweeping generalizations about both men and women. While lamenting the lack of information, the guidelines do not address other reasons causing planners and host governments to ignore gender issues, particularly those arising from their own motivation. They do not consider why and under what conditions issues of gender may be relevant.

While the guidelines and the meetings failed to confront the essentially political nature of gender relations, ALCOM's publicity machine produced plenty of evidence of the programme's gender sensitivity. Several editions of *ALCOM News* have contained articles on women and fish-farming. In January 1992, the front cover story was devoted to a photo-essay about women and fish-farming in Luapula Province, Zambia. It starts: 'Fish farming hasn't ushered in a blue revolution. It has in fact meant a dawn-to-midnight grind for some rural women. But it has given them another income alternative. It has stimulated an upbeat spirit in them. A new hope for tomorrow' (ALCOM 1992b: 9). The article provides a response to those who question the tangible benefits of fish-farming and express concern that it is so manifestly a technology taken up primarily by men. It also takes care of the pressure on programme management in Harare to respond to the two, not necessarily compatible, demands of producing fish and exhibiting gender sensitivity. In the meantime, gender issues remained largely absent from the rest of the programme's activities. At a staff meeting in Harare in 1991, gender issues had a place on the agenda as 'the women project'. This was relegated to 'any other business' in the list of priorities, but in the end not discussed because a socio-economist had not been appointed.

As with the studies, and with the recommendations produced by the Victoria Falls workshop, the vast amount of documentation, methodologies, and guidelines produced in the 'women project' fails to articulate the problem of women's position in a way that would be challenging or contentious. Despite the obvious fact that a fair amount of information about women in aquaculture has been produced, the issue of why it is not translated into practice has been bypassed. This reflects a more general tendency to depoliticize gender issues. In the background paper to the Victoria Falls meeting various policy approaches to gender issues over the previous twenty years are discussed. Approaches advocating equity and speaking in terms of subordination are contrasted with efficiency- and poverty-focused approaches. Equity approaches are dismissed: 'this approach [the "equity" approach] proved unpopular mainly because it sought to change the social relationship between men and women through a redistribution of power. Politically, therefore, the approach was not acceptable, nor was it easy to implement' (Sen et al. 1991: 63).

In Intermediate Technology as well, the early attempts to tackle gender were concerned with making a generalized discussion of gender more prominent and acceptable rather than with integrating an analysis of gender relations into the core of Intermediate Technology's work. Until 1990 there was no formal mechanism for assessing how projects involve and affect women and men differently. The situation changed when an alliance formed between a key female social scientist in the policy department and other women in the organization. A handful of male social scientists were involved in a peripheral way, but, more importantly, the female policy-worker had support from her male line-manager and the female Country Director in Sri Lanka (another one of Intermediate Technology's country offices). As a result of the gender 'experts', who effectively acted as catalysts for change, a gender working group was set up. It did not embody consensus, however. Many 'technical' staff, on hearing about the work of the gender working group, complained that its aims were inappropriate for Intermediate Technology. As examples: 'the justification for a gender policy refers more to African than Asian women', and 'Intermediate Technology should not impose its values on either project partners or beneficiaries', and 'in some instances project partners will not agree with our approach to gender, and it is not appropriate for Intermediate Technology to insist on policy changes'. Despite resistance, after some years, considerations of gender became a procedural requirement during both planning and monitoring. At the same time, very recently efforts have been made to ensure that responsibility for gender is held by managers rather than by social scientists.

While most project staff are fully prepared to explore the potential impact of activities on women, or to disaggregate 'beneficiaries' in terms of gender, some still argue that 'it is not our business'. The rationale given for considering gender hinges on arguments of efficiency, or enhancing the quality of projects, rather than addressing gender inequalities. One social scientist said recently: 'I never use the word empowerment in relation to women. We need to get people on board first by saying that a better approach to gender will improve the quality of our work.' While gender remains a methodological issue, many respond reasonably well even if they privately complain that it is not relevant to their work. Even so, a staff member reported in January 1997 that 95 per cent of plans do not develop gender-sensitive activities plans, and during the 1995–96 annual reviews it emerged that in just over half Intermediate Technology's projects needs were not identified in a gender-disaggregated way.

## The inevitability of it all?

What is behind this rather bleak picture of resistance and marginalization which seems far from 'transformational mainstreaming'? How can we interpret FAO's and Intermediate Technology's attempts at gender sensitivity? Positioning and background of individuals are clearly important. We are not suggesting that FAO, Intermediate Technology, or their associated projects are especially heinous or different from other development organizations and projects. Indeed, the efforts that have been made to incorporate gender are often extremely well-intentioned. Furthermore, processes observed in these cases arguably reflect tendencies found in many similar organizations. Kardam (1991) argues in a study of the World Bank, the UNDP, and the Ford Foundation that the integration of gender issues is constrained by both structural and individual choice factors. Similar findings emerge for SIDA (Himmelstrand 1997) and USAID (Jensen 1997).

A number of related influences, highlighted by the experiences of FAO and Intermediate Technology staff, are revevant to the apparent marginalization of gender issues. First, perceptions that the gender agenda is imposed from outside can be important. Some project staff within Intermediate Technology have complained that the only reason they are compelled to consider gender is to satisfy DFID and other donors. It is true that DFID's Joint Funding Scheme, the department that channels funds to UK NGOs, requires consideration of gender in all their applications. To some extent this has forced Intermediate Technology to incorporate gender into its procedures. The triennial reviews of Intermediate Technology, however, carried out by DFID as one of its main donors, scarcely mention women or gender. FAO has different external accountability pressures, reflecting the relative influence of different donors. This has resulted in a variety of activities. For example, in 1982, a major study of ten FAO field projects was undertaken. According to Carloni (1997) this 103-page document was never widely disseminated. The pressure for ALCOM's gender sensitivity may well be related to the fact that principal funders of the programme were SIDA and NORAD, both well known for their explicit concern with gender sensitivity.

Second, and obviously related, the lack of transformation can be explained by the different perspectives of different agents inside organizations. Policy regarding gender is interpreted in diverse ways by different people. This is influenced not only by their position within an organization, but by a wide range of other characteristics in other domains. Age, gender, ethnicity, personal history, all influence how people act on and interpret the policies they are required to implement (Long and van der Ploeg 1989). To understand why gender policies remain ineffectual, it is important to understand this kaleidoscope of influences.

Gender is often portrayed as a technical concept that, if only better understood, could be integrated into the planning process. However, an understanding of gender issues from a feminist perspective introduces questions of power, control of resources, and conflict, which are potentially challenging and certainly difficult to deal with. Staudt (1997) comments on male resistance to analyses of gender that threaten male privilege. If this is the case, the gendered hierarchies within development agencies are themselves plainly relevant.

In 1991 Intermediate Technology headquarters in the UK employed 102 staff. About 40 per cent of all 'professional' staff were women, which compares well for women against the World Bank's figure of 25 per cent in 1989 (ODA 1990). However, at Intermediate Technology, there were only seven UK-based women regularly travelling overseas for project work (about 21 per cent), and of a total of 17 managers, only two were women (about 12 per cent). There is an extreme shortage of women in Intermediate Technology at senior levels, partly due to the historical background of science and technology as a male-dominated domain. This shortage within the organization re-establishes a social order within which men are continually re-created as the dominant class. The gender make-up in the department responsible for international project work was more marked. The technical jobs were largely held by specialists from overwhelmingly male-dominated professions, and the majority of managers had a technical background. (See Table 3.1.)

The male technical specialists were mostly engineers. The 'technical' women, in contrast, had a background in food technology and textiles; one was a student, another was on a very short-term contract, and the third later moved to the fundraising department. Intermediate Technology had only one British female engineer, then working permanently in Kenya, but many pointed out that nothing could be done about the shortage since there were very few female engineers in Britain.

In FAO's Fisheries Department, there is a more diverse range of nationalities. However, this is cross-cut most obviously by differences in gender and position in the hierarchy. Unsurprisingly, most secretarial staff are Italian women. Among 'professional' grades, there is a much

**Table 3.1** Gender make-up, Operations Division, Intermediate Technology HQ, May 1991

| Job title/level of seniority | Specialization and gender | |
| --- | --- | --- |
| | Women | Men |
| Director | | 1 technical specialist |
| Sector managers | 1 marketing specialist | 2 technical specialists<br>1 economist |
| Programme managers | 1 social anthropologist<br>1 management expert | 9 technical specialists |
| Programme staff | 3 technical specialists<br>2 social anthropologists | 9 technical specialists<br>3 economists |
| Administrators | 5 | 0 |
| Secretaries | 9 | 0 |

greater range of nationalities, and many fewer women. The gender imbalance in the Fisheries Department is more pronounced than in the organization as a whole. Of 1,087 professional staff in Rome in December 1993, 219 (21 per cent) were women. On the other hand, women made up 1,311 of the 1,904 general service staff. Women in the professional grades tended to be clustered at the lower end of the salary scale. In the Fisheries Department, the proportion of women in professional grades was lower. There were 13 women as compared to 77 men (14.4 per cent). Of these, none was in the senior grades of directors of division or chief of service (13 posts). In the Inland Water Resources and Aquaculture Service, which has primary responsibility for aquaculture development, none of the ten professional staff was a woman (although all of the five general service staff were).

Femaleness is of course no guarantee for heightened gender awareness. There is not a necessary connection between being a woman and being a feminist. However, the evidence above about work on gender being something done by women for women indicates that male/female balances may be important. While a few men in Intermediate Technology and FAO were keen to be involved, many kept their distance because they claimed ignorance of the subject, argued that it was not relevant to their work, felt daunted by particular gender 'experts' who were seen as aggressive, or said that listening to criticism of men made them feel uncomfortable. Although entrenched sexism influenced some men, for others the feelings of being misunderstood, excluded, or alienated may point to a failure in addressing men as a gendered category within debates.

The gender imbalance in the Fisheries Department of FAO and Intermediate Technology does not of itself imply inability or unwillingness to take gender issues seriously. However, the people occupying senior positions are not neutral, value-free implementers of policy. They bring to their posts personal priorities, perspectives, and experiences. Influencing these, though not necessarily either visibly or consciously, is a view of the world in which sensitivity to gender may be low on the list of priorities. For example, the people working in the Fisheries Department as 'professionals' (as opposed to support staff) are considered to be 'technical specialists'. Most are employed on the basis of their technical knowledge in the expectation that their expertise will be useful in an advisory capacity. In the Fisheries Department they generally have a background in biology or fisheries management. Their main professional interest is, therefore, fish – how to make sure they grow, how to manage stocks of them, and how to negotiate competing claims for them. They may have strong motivations regarding the well-being of fish-consumers, but success criteria in their jobs generally relate to technical concerns.

To compound the tendency for segmentation along lines of technical specialization, each staff member has concerns connected with job security. FAO is an international agency answerable to its member countries and, as such, exposed to changes in the political climate. The appointment of a new director-general can result in significant changes in direction and focus. All staff members are therefore vulnerable to pronouncements from on high about the justification and form of their jobs. There is generally little that can be done about this, but one obvious strategy is consistently to raise the profile and importance of the area in which one has technical expertise – for example, fish production rather than gender sensitivity.

Although men control the senior positions within both Intermediate Technology and FAO's Fisheries Department, their dominance is not propelled by a calculated male strategy. Relations between men and women in the organizations amount to more than a functional system with people simply pursuing their own material interests. Rather, gender relations are patterned by both power inequalities and shared ideological schemes that inform agents about male and female stereotypes. Since women and men continually reconstruct the stereotypes as they work, often with women being unassertive and meek in relation to men, this particular set of gender power relations is hardly challenged.

By reconstructing a social order through gender divisions for work roles and behaviour, people define their social positions, their idea of themselves in relation to others (Bourdieu 1984: 480). The existing gender power relations rely on women being defined and redefined as vulnerable, understanding, emotional, and caring; men are technically knowledgeable, assertive, inventive, and consequently powerful. Women are sent on 'assertiveness' training courses and referred to as shy at meetings. One manager in Intermediate Technology was described as unable to resolve conflict with a project partner agency because she was a woman. When women make overseas trips an effort is made to protect them, while men are left to their own devices. Challenging these stereotypes, at home or abroad, and revealing them as mental and social, rather than natural, physical constructions, made people feel awkward or laugh because such a process was considered 'unnatural'.

For both men and women at all levels in any organizational structure there is also a need for simplification, which conspires against any full comprehension of the construction and operation of gender relations. On the one hand, there is a body of knowledge and argument pointing out the variety, complexity, and flexibility gender analysis should encompass. By their very nature, because gender relations are socially constructed, they are subject to change and influenced by other aspects of differentiation. On the other hand, development practitioners are unable and unwilling to deal with such complexities. They need a kind of conceptual shorthand – 'simple principles' and 'methodological tools'. In the course of such simplification, recognition of the potentially contentious and inherently political aspects of gender relations is usually the first to go.

According to many donors, the biggest barrier to addressing gender issues is a shortage of information, not what is done with it. As noted, one of the significant achievements of feminist scholars in the 1970s and 1980s was to illuminate the blindness of most development interventions to the different needs and interests of men and women. However, questions need to be asked about the context and the use of such information. There is clearly a difference between 'feminist knowledge', which is challenging, and 'data for development' (Goetz 1994), which is not. Merely collecting more information will not address the inequities it may reveal. The assumption that information will solve gender problems seriously misconstrues how projects work and assumes a commonality of interests of different actors that is unlikely to exist. As Bierschenk (1988) notes, it is more accurate to see development projects as arenas of negotiation for strategic groups.

In both Intermediate Technology and FAO 'women' becomes shorthand for 'gender analysis'. In the process, the political implications of a gendered analysis fade away. The influences at work in the process cannot be neatly read off as male resistance or organizational inadequacies. Among the stakeholder perspectives are those of men who believe that women should deal with things about women and that this is really not their concern. Such a view is reinforced by the fact that most feminist gender analysis focuses on women. As Sarah White has argued, regardless of discussions about the rightness of WID or WAD, GID or GAD, 'even if we use the term "gender", we almost always talk about it only in relation to women not men' (White 1994: 98). Although there are very good reasons for this, there is a tendency to further the idea that it is women who need to do the changing. While there is still a need, therefore, for men to be aware of women's interests, claims, and rights, it is equally crucial to make male gender identities themselves an issue. For example, if looking at who dominates in meetings, some women may be persuaded to speak out but some men might be encouraged to listen as well.

From the point of view of the organizations, the demands for simplification and categorization are strong. The more complex the information and analysis produced, the more difficult it is to act. And yet capturing men's and women's interests in simplistic, universal categories and systems is not useful. This is not an excuse for inaction. It is important to examine how the goals, objectives, and methods of an organization reflect particular gendered interests and how these affect their work. Challenging gender inequalities, within or outside organizations, is possible only with an understanding of power structures and relations in that particular context and a political will for change.

# CHAPTER 4

# Partnership

Donor treatment of recipients has long been under scrutiny. Many recent analyses of development have a common thread of criticism: that the local organizations with whom donors work are treated as passive recipients who are unable to manage their own affairs. They argue that the political and other organizational structures of developing countries are treated as being at a less evolved stage, which is presumed to be reflected in corruption, a lack of democracy, and occasionally childlike incompetence. For example, Manzo suggests that the metaphor of adult and child relationships underpinned many of the other dichotomies of colonial discourse (black/white, civilized/uncivilized) (1995: 236). Guardianship is a central principle whereby people apparently need to be looked after and even protected from their own foolishness. Such assumptions are an aspect of the evolutionary thinking we described in Chapter 2 and evident in the practices of aid.

In the 1980s and 1990s too, an important aspect of much aid is the fact that it comes with explicit conditions. These are symptomatic of donors' assumptions that they have a better understanding of a country's needs than its own government. Conditions relate to the nature of the political system, to the human rights record of a country, and to economic policy. An obvious example of economic conditionality is provided by structural adjustment loans. These have required a complex set of economic changes usually characterized by reduction of the public sector, fiscal reform, and elimination of subsidies. Structural adjustment has been extensively criticized in terms of both its rationale and its effects (for example Cornea et al. 1987; Elson 1995). Irrespective of its impact, structural adjustment continues to convey the idea that 'we know best'. The same is clearly true of the good government or 'governance' agenda that dominates much of the aid policy of both bilateral and multilateral agencies. The notion of 'governance' reflects both a concern for human rights and a belief that democratic pluralism is the most appropriate and just method of social and political organization. More acutely even than structural adjustment, the strengths and weaknesses of the good governance agenda are difficult to evaluate. On the one hand, the single-minded support for democratic pluralism can be seen as a form of cultural imperialism and an erosion of national sovereignty (Schmitz and Gillies 1992). On the other, few would refuse to draw some line with regard to human rights abuses. The problem is of course in deciding where to place the line. Meanwhile, what is important in this context is that good governance and aid conditionality imply a clear acknowledgement of unequal power – 'We have the money, you want it, so you had better behave as we think correct.'

Paradoxically, the emergence of the governance agenda has taken place alongside another shift in the language of development policy that suggests very different principles. It is no longer common for either NGOs or government donors to speak in terms of 'beneficiaries' or 'counterparts' when referring to the institutions, groups, and individuals who are the recipients of aid. Such terms imply unacceptable passivity. Rather, those on the receiving end of aid are portrayed as if they were on equal terms: they are partners – with implicitly the same objectives, and the same ability to articulate these as the donors. This interpretation of partnership has an apparently strong moral dimension.

At the same time, partnership has served a more instrumental purpose. The perceived failure of aid is often attributed to a lack of 'sustainability', an important aspect of which is construed as inadequate organizational or institutional capacity. Aid agencies have often been accused of failing to transfer skills or responsibilities to 'local' agencies, with the result that projects collapse when the funding ceases. One of the solutions proposed to cure this problem has been to improve partnerships. The partners of aid agencies are expected to achieve self-reliance through capacity-building. Most aid agencies aim, in theory at least, to become redundant within the partnership. For example, the Development Assistance Committee (DAC) of the OECD calls for partnership as a central aspect of its strategy for the twenty-first century and argues that:

> Acceptance of the partnership model, with greater clarity of the roles of partners, is one of the most positive changes we are proposing in the framework for development co-operation. In a partnership, development co-operation does not try to do things for developing countries and their people, but with them. It must be seen as a collaborative effort to help them increase their capacities to do things for themselves. Paternalistic approaches have no place in this framework. In a true partnership, local actors should progressively take the lead, while external partners back their efforts to assume greater responsibility for their own development (OECD 1996: 13).

The World Bank was described by its president in 1994 as a 'global partnership in which more than 175 countries have joined together for a common purpose' (World Bank 1994). The Bank pledged itself to work increasingly in partnership with NGOs too, apparently to take advantage of their closer links with 'the poor' and better meet their objective of fighting poverty. It has even encouraged NGOs to lobby against it, claiming that it has decided to consult local NGOs about projects because 'the most successful examples of Bank–NGO collaboration are those in which NGOs have worked as partners' (World Bank 1994: 20). Arguably, employing, funding, and consulting with NGOs could of course result in a much diminished critique of the World Bank by its NGO partners.

Partnership is also a popular, if not obligatory, strategy for NGOs. As Fowler argues:

> The ultimate legitimacy of development NGOs, south and Northern [*sic*], can only be derived from what they achieve in their relationship with the intended beneficiaries of their existence and efforts – the poor. Southern NGOs can obtain this legitimacy directly in the Third World, most Northern NGOs that are not operational can only obtain this via their partnerships (1992: 21).

Given the good governance agenda, and aid conditionality, the portrayal of partnership as a process of cooperation between equals is inherently problematic. Is the idea of partnership therefore merely empty rhetoric, a form of 'political correctness' without substance? What does the rhetoric tell us about the relative power of givers and receivers? In this chapter we explore both the emergence of 'partnership' and some of the realities lying behind the relationship between the 'partners'. In the main, we are concerned with institutional 'partners', whether these are government bodies or locally organized groupings.

## The evolution of 'partnership'

In this section we explore what is said about partnership, by both supporters and critics of the idea. Partnership within the development industry is now used to describe a wide range of ideal relationships between development agencies and/or community groups. There is a multiplicity of types of formal and informal organization. Government aid agencies channel their funds, usually raised through taxation, either bilaterally (directly from government to government) or multilaterally (through international agencies such as the United Nations and the World Bank). NGOs are run on a commercial, charitable, or voluntary basis, and either earn money through employment or receive money from private donations, government grants, and/or business sponsorship, or rely on voluntary labour. If they donate money it is usually sent to other NGOs, or directly to beneficiaries, and sometimes, though less often since the mid-1980s, to national governments. Recipients of aid might be a government ministry, a large, formal charity with hundreds of branches, a business, a religious association with a network across a particular area, or an informal meeting of a few individuals within one village, and so on. The countries within which both governments and NGOs operate plainly contain very different histories of the relationship between the state and voluntary sector, political structures and systems of patronage. The language of partnership has encompassed the whole spectrum, without much differentiation between types of partner, their history, and their context.

Partnership as an idea also refers to a diverse range of activities from giving grants, technical assistance or equipment, sharing information, managing projects jointly, and joining forces to lobby decision-makers. Christian Aid describes its recipients of funds as partners, stating in its 'Guidelines for project applicants' that it 'works on the principle of partnership. As such we undertake no projects ourselves but work directly through local NGOs and community groups' (Christian Aid 1987: 1). Charity Projects (now known as Comic Relief), which does not give funds directly to agencies abroad, relies on 'good working relationships and strong partnerships with other UK registered charities' (Charity Projects undated). On the other hand, in a slightly different use of the word, NLCB will fund only applicants who have 'close partnership with national, local or community organizations' (1996), and DFID's Joint Funding Scheme suggests that all applicants should name their local partners and consider whether local organizational capacity will be strengthened (ODA undated). NGOs who undertake development project themselves, including Action Aid, ACORD, CARE, and Intermediate Technology, often refer to their 'beneficiaries' or community-based organizations (CBOs) as their partners. Intermediate Technology refers to all the more formal African, Asian and South American NGOs it works with, or gives advice and/or funds to, as partners: they range from governments to registered women's groups. Partnership is so broad that it is not surprising that a recent review of Intermediate Technology's work revealed that:

> in order to maximise use of limited resources and enhance the prospects of sustainability, Intermediate Technology works with partners in its projects. The organisation as a whole does not define criteria for the selection of

partners. Occasionally unsuitable partners have been selected, which has led to subsequent implementation difficulties (EPA 1992: 21).

Given this plethora of uses, it is not easy to pinpoint what is meant by partnership. Indeed it is arguable that, as with other loosely used terms such as empowerment and participation, part of the attractiveness of the term lies in its slipperiness. As Stirrat and Henkel have argued, partnership is an ambiguous concept: 'on the one hand, it can involve a denial of individual identity: we share everything ... For the donors the great advantage of this model of partnership is legitimation in that it allows them to claim a certain authenticity' (1997: 75). In some ways, therefore, the language of partnership helps with the problems of legitimacy and accountability that plague all development donors.

Despite the differences in interpretation, it is revealing that both NGOs and bilateral donors engage in the language of partnership. This shared discourse is at least in part attributable to the fact that most NGOs rely on financial support from governments. This dependence has increased as governments have increasingly seen NGOs as essential components of civil society. Indeed, Hulme and Edwards (1997) argue that the high dependency of NGOs (both Southern and Northern) on official donor funds undermines their relationship with those they ultimately intend to help. For example, since over half Intermediate Technology's funding has come from DFID, DFID's advice is, not surprisingly, critically important in Intermediate Technology's policy formulation. DFID conducts a thorough review of Intermediate Technology's progress every three years, advises on policy and managerial matters on an *ad hoc* basis, and receives copies of all proposals for new projects. The objectives of the proposals are studied and questioned occasionally, and it is understood that continued funding to Intermediate Technology relies upon improving policy according to DFID's requirements. In Intermediate Technology's case the main donor by no means explicitly attaches conditions to the donations it offers. On the other hand, when DFID asks (even informally) why Intermediate Technology does not have a policy statement on the environment, as a recipient of considerable financial support, it addresses the omission immediately. As DFID is presently reducing its funding to Intermediate Technology, some of the staff see the cut as an opportunity to embrace a more radical agenda.

Some do acknowledge that there are problems with this ideal of partnership in practice. Fowler points out that Southern NGOs are at a disadvantage because they know less about their Northern partners than vice versa, and he tries to redress this problem by imparting information about the latter. He suggests that the Southern NGOs will be in a better negotiating position if they know more about their prospective donors (Fowler 1992: 19). Inequality between them, even, can be redressed by better transparency:

> how much do the grass-roots contacts of the southern NGOs weigh against the technologies and information that a northern NGO can offer? The only way that these and other questions can be answered in order to make up the balance and provide a sense of equality in relationship, is when the 'product' of the joint efforts is mutually agreed (Fowler 1992: 20)

Better communication between partners might provide a sense of equality but it does not alter the structurally unequal relationship of donor and recipient. As in a relationship between landlord and tenant, at the centre of the donor–recipient relation is an 'exchange of deference and compliance by the client in return for the patron's provision of minimal social rights' (Scott 1977: 34). Compliance may be more appearance than reality and the donor needs the recipient as much as the other way round; even so, the exchange is inherently unequal and, at times, coercive.

It is rarely recognized by donors that their relationship with recipients cannot be a meeting of equals. For example, Intermediate Technology staff tend to assume that difficulties with partners should be blamed on particular organizations or differences in objectives, rather than understood as a political relationship. It was partly difficulties with partnership, and its interpretation of the causes, that led Intermediate Technology to create its own 'in-country offices' in Africa, Asia, and South America. The rationale was that the branch offices would be in a better position to carry out institutional feasibility studies, to ensure that the prospective partner shared Intermediate Technology's objectives and had the capacity to fulfil their role in the project. If no partner could be found, the branch office could always be the main implementation agency.

Attempts to redress the failure of intended partnership have also involved adjusting Intermediate Technology's objectives. In the 1980s it was assisting or helping partners, for example, by transferring skills from the UK to other countries; by the late 1980s and early 1990s it enabled or cooperated with partners so that they could realize their potential to, for instance, develop appropriate technology. Attempts to portray partners in a less passive way and to encourage their greater participation in planning became a familiar chant in Intermediate Technology and other British NGOs. As the struggle to find partners with matching objectives continued, Intermediate Technology and others increasingly worked directly with their intended 'beneficiaries', calling them community-based organizations (CBOs) or groups.

Thus many recommendations about partnership, by both practitioners and academics, have more to do with management of projects than with challenging power relations. Some do recognize that power imbalances should be addressed. Clark writes that:

> decisions over project funding should increasingly be transferred to Southern specialists. It is lamentable that, as the century draws to a close, there is a colonial residue which still believes that decisions concerning poverty alleviation in India can be better made in London or New York than on the spot, where the real expertise lies ... The North–South partnership must not be a jealous one ... Northern NGOs must be prepared to move to a more secondary place (1992: 193–4).

His implication is that this power transfer will be brought about by a voluntary shift on the part of Northern NGOs from project work to advocacy. He does not explain how they will move to a 'secondary place' if they continue to distribute or cut funds and their partners remain financially dependent on them. Even if differences in objectives are sometimes acknowledged, the possibility of conflictual interests between local and foreign agencies in aid transactions tends to be glossed over, or even ignored, in both development studies literature and policy discourse.

There are exceptions. For example, Perera (1997) highlights a conflict between donor and recipient organizations in Sri Lanka. He describes how the Sarvodaya Movement found that its donor 'partners' treated it 'as a subcontractor, not a partner' and forced policies upon it that directly undermined its own priorities and bottom-up, decentralized approach. Staff were intimidated by the 'laptop toting consultants who fly in and produce dozens of recommendations' (1997: 163), while senior management coped with a plethora of commands about business development, centralized management, and monitoring. To illustrate how unequal the partnership and how inconsistent donors can be, Perera points out:

> while espousing participation, devolution, stakeholder analysis and so on, donors sought to impose hastily prepared plans produced by visiting consultants ... The temptation for donors (who are ordinary humans after all) to throw their weight about is almost impossible to resist (1997: 167).

According to Perera, to please the donors the production of professional reports and properly audited statements is of paramount importance.

He adds 'everything should be shown on paper ... the quality of work in the field matters less to the donors. Basically, they do not have much of an idea what goes on there anyway' (1997: 167). The obsession with scientific method, layout of reports, and classification arguably reveals a quest for symbols of professionalism as much as a rational process to ensure accountability.

Another rare articulation of the asymmetries within partnerships was voiced at a conference held in 1987, where the role of NGOs was discussed from a 'Southern' and a 'Northern' perspective. Kajese (from Zimbabwe) asked donors to accept that responsibility for development in the south lies ultimately with Southern countries and met with considerable resistance. Smith (from the USA) argued that allowing indigenous NGOs to make decisions regarding resource allocation, accountability procedures, and project performance evaluation was premature (1987: 87–9). The indigenous organizations are not fit, he argued, because they tend to be corrupt, lack management capability, do not reach the poorest sectors, and exclude grassroots participants (especially women) from decision-making. Smith also claims that to satisfy the donors' demands for greater 'accountability', we apparently need more than the current humanistic, informal, qualitative evaluations popular among indigenous NGOs; we need 'empirical verification of effectiveness' and 'careful and systematic evaluation', which presumably makes greater use of quantitative methods.

Kajese's and Smith's comments echo what we have heard repeatedly during fieldwork. The recipient's perspective is characterized by an exasperation with the arrogance of donors who, they often argue, feel it is their duty to develop the backward South, impose their decisions through a promise of aid, and give little respect to national experts. Donor agency representations often contain derogatory claims about the inadequacy of their African or Asian partners: 'they are not ready to take charge yet', 'they always take project funds', 'they couldn't organize a picnic let alone a development project', 'they could not manage without us', and 'they're so lazy because they don't really care', are all comments we have heard. Another recurring complaint about 'local' partners is that they recruit staff according to patronage rather than merit, an ironic criticism in view of the fact that in many NGO 'partnerships', recruitment and contracts to expatriate consultants are made through *ad hoc* personal contact or even kinship relations. The extent to which such criticisms of partners in the South prevail is difficult to judge and our examples may be particularly crude. Even so, the aid industry continues to rest on an assumption of inadequacy on the part of the institutional recipients in 'poorer' countries.

The ideal of partnership may be laudable in some ways. But it emerges in a context where, whatever is said, there are structural inequalities. An obvious aspect of this arises when donors decide to cut expenditure on aid: such cuts are out of the control of the recipients. Indeed, some would argue that the rhetoric of partnership arises partly as a justification or rationale for these cuts (Baylies 1995). OECD acknowledged in its 1996 *Development Cooperation* report that: 'It is a troubling irony that this strong and deepening consensus on the best uses of development assistance coincides with continuing stagnation or decline in the resources that can be made available' (OECD 1997: 93). In 1995 total overseas development assistance from Development Assistance Committee (DAC) members fell to just 0.27 per cent of their combined GNP – the lowest figure since comparable statistics began in 1950. In addition, there is evidence that patterns of donor activity are still far from the equal partnership espoused in the 'strong and deepening consensus'. It is this that we explore in the following case studies.

While our first two cases show that conflicting objectives can leave practices almost unchanged, the second two, about Intermediate Technology, illustrate that donors do not control recipients in a straight-forward manner. There is an obvious power imbalance between the giver and the receiver of money, especially if the funds always go in the same direction. The power inequalities, however, do not determine the behaviour of those involved, as these case studies demonstrate. Rather the impact of the practices of each group are conditioned by their place in power structures.

## Tales of partnership in practice

*ALCOM and its partners* The general principles underlying ALCOM's work included: 'people's participation, nutritional improvement, a greater focus on women in rural development, sustainability' (ALCOM unpublished: 3). All of these broad ideas were integrated into the programme's rhetoric about its intended attainments. Equally import-ant, and closely connected, were ideas about the process through which these were to be reached. This was to be 'bottom-up' – learning from the intended beneficiaries. Critically, initial objectives were left open-ended. They were tied neither to the provision of infrastructure nor to quantifiable outputs. At the same time, the member governments who were hosting the programme were also construed as its owners. There was to be, according to Rome, a partnership in which the ALCOM programme, Rome, and the host governments had mutually compatible objectives. This all presents a problem. In the case of a project such as

ALCOM, there is an obvious tension between the need to be flexible and open to change and the very idea of having objectives whose achievement can be assessed – and hence which are not supposed to change. Equally, however the picture is painted, ALCOM was potentially bringing resources and therefore should have been producing results.

In Harare, ALCOM's institutional relationships were complex. It was formed as an interregional project, executed by FAO. The pilot projects took place in SADC countries but there were no personnel or financial inputs from SADC to ALCOM. In each individual country, the programme worked directly with relevant departments or ministries, but responsibility for results and inputs rested with ALCOM. There were no SADC counterparts in Harare. However, SADC ostensibly had influence over the annual workplan. Furthermore, the programme was funded through several donors. Apparently there was very little contact between the donors themselves, between the donors and FAO, or the donors and the recipient countries. SIDA, the principal donor, had an office in Harare that had no working relationship and little contact with the programme.

The relationship with partner governments is presented in ALCOM's literature as straightforward and transparent. It in fact comprises a number of actual and potential conflicts of interests. Aquaculture in the SADC region has been treated by governments as a separate sub-sector, but at the same time has received little budgetary support compared to agriculture or fisheries despite its generally high priority in official documentation. In some cases, other priorities (such as the effects of war in Angola and Mozambique) have meant that aquaculture is not even nominally important. ALCOM's assumption that host governments' main shortfall was in information and techniques for aquaculture development was naive. It ignored the political and economic realities of resource shortages and competing demands, as well as decision-makers' own strategic needs. Given straitened economic circumstances, persuading governments to devote resources to aquaculture requires more than rhetoric. Tangible inputs are also important. However, ALCOM was not set up to provide such inputs, and there were no procedures for ensuring that any other organization would. Furthermore, ALCOM's own funding crises did not make for continuity in either design or approach.

An evaluation at the end of ALCOM's preparatory phase in 1989 had expressed a concern that host governments were becoming disenchanted with a failure in the programme to 'come up with the goods'. Given ALCOM's rather loosely defined objectives, such a criticism is arguably not justified. It is not clear what coming up with the goods might consist of other than production of the required reports and holding 'consultations'. For example, nothing as concrete as fish-production figures or the number of ponds dug was ever specified. According to the interim evaluation:

> The donor, FAO, and the project must convince the recipients that this is indeed not a normal development project, which may provide resources and other benefits in the near future, but a research programme whose tasks/objectives are chiefly to carry out research and experimental pilot activities (SIDA 1989: 4).

As time went on, the divergence between host and ALCOM perceptions of its own role became increasingly marked. The question of target groups became focal. ALCOM's partners in the SADC region expressed worries that the identification of target groups was essentially externally determined. The SADC members argued that they had a sustained increase in fish production as a first priority. This was, they maintained, more likely to result from working directly with farmers with higher levels of resource endowment than from ALCOM's focus on the poorest. ALCOM's orientation was seen as short-sighted. The Programme Manager explained that 'the main aim of ALCOM was to assist members in overcoming the constraints to the development of fish-farming in their countries, particularly through identifying and trying new practical approaches' (ALCOM 1989a: 4). This explanation was inadequate for representatives of countries who perceived their needs to a large extent in terms of resource shortfalls. In most member countries, extension services were under-funded and infrastructure for the development of aquaculture was limited. From the point of view of SADC delegates to the meeting:

> It was strongly emphasised ... that ALCOM programme should not [only] embark on pilot projects without taking into account implementation after the pilot phase. This results in pilot projects being doomed to failure if the national governments cannot afford to finance them (ALCOM 1989b: 5).

In other words, host governments were unwilling or unable to extend pilot project activities after ALCOM's departure. The success of the projects was largely tied up in their continuation in a more widespread form, but this was not something the partners could ensure.

Officially, the activities of projects such as ALCOM follow the request of host governments. Here this was not the case. ALCOM was devised in Rome and the host governments accepted what was already devised. The priorities of hosts are none the less important. For ALCOM, co-ordinating the priorities of not one but nine host governments, there were numerous imperatives to respond to competing demands. The steering committee meetings thus became fora for requests. To an extent this resulted in a proliferation of activities that were not necessarily within ALCOM's original remit: mariculture, seaweed collection and culture, national fish marketing, intensification, and commercialization. Another response was to reduce the possibility for intervention. By the sixth steering committee meeting in February 1993, any idea of host collaborators creating the agenda had almost completely disappeared. Rather than report discussion or debate, the document simply presented ALCOM's new plan of action, and listed those present at the meeting.

Among its objectives, the institutionalization of ALCOM's activities is nowhere explicitly mentioned. This presents a policy paradox. Because ALCOM was not owned by any one government, the responsibility for producing results was also not the responsibility of any one government. Commitment from host governments could therefore not be taken for granted. Equally, counterpart staff within countries could not be expected to see a future for themselves after the pilot projects had finished, given the lack of commitment of tangible resources.

*The Big Fish*  A key element was crucial for the success of ALCOM's Luapula pilot project: the cooperation of the local Department of Fisheries (DoF). However, from the inception of the project, that cooperation was assumed rather than the basis for it being explored. The pilot project was conceived and developed in Harare. Discussion between the various collaborators took place in Mansa, but from unequal positions; although the language of cooperation permeates all planning documentation, this disguises both real and incipient conflict.

First, there was conflict over objectives. The main DoF objective in Luapula was 'maximisation of fish production through rational exploitation of fish stocking' (DoF 1990). The objective said nothing about small-holder food security or rural income increase – ALCOM's main objectives. Luapula province is the principal fish-producer of Zambia. During the 1980s, Luapula fisheries were responsible for about 40 per cent of all fish marketed in the country, but the natural fisheries have suffered from both competition from Zaire and a decline in production. Legislation is in force to contain over-fishing and the use of small-mesh nets. DoF's main role in relation to natural fisheries was therefore one of policing the waters, checking on and restraining the use of illegal gear, and ensuring that people did not go fishing during the closed season. Given the enormous area covered by the natural fisheries, and their relative importance in the provincial economy, the Provincial Fisheries Development Officer (PFDO) held this role to be very important. Arguments used to support aquaculture development stress that, despite the overall provincial importance of fisheries, away from the lakeshores and the Luapula valley people have only restricted access to fish. However, so far as DoF was concerned, it could make as much sense to concentrate on improving marketing facilities and management of existing fish stocks as to promote fish-farming. Furthermore the department was constrained by shortages of cash, by non-availability of fuel, and by low morale among staff, who were seldom paid their allowances on time.

There were also differences in perceptions about how objectives should be reached. Two major points of conflict emerged: whether or not the government should be trying to supply fingerlings (fish seed), and the question of which farmers should receive assistance. DoF maintained that the supply and distribution of fingerlings to farmers were essential. The two government fish-farms were constructed partly for this purpose. By the late 1980s, both fish-farms were in a state of disrepair (ALCOM 1989b). So far as DoF in Mansa was concerned, the rehabilitation of the fish-farms should have been a priority. ALCOM, on the other hand, strongly believed that farmer–farmer supply was a much more sensible approach and that the rehabilitation of the fish-farms was necessary, but principally to facilitate their function as research centres.

Furthermore, ideas about suitable target groups for development did not converge. ALCOM's focus was on the fish-farming activities of small-scale, mainly self-provisioning farmers. Richer, semi commercial or more intensive fish-farmers, particularly those with an urban base, were not such appropriate subjects for development assistance. DoF's stated target group was all fish-farmers in Luapula, without specification of size or nature of the operation. However, behind this policy statement was a belief that assistance and extension advice should be given to 'knowledgeable and progressive people' – who, it was argued, could then create a firm economic foundation for fish-farming. PFDO expressed frustration that ALCOM was not interested in giving loans to the few richer, semi-urban fish-farmers in the province.

Crehan and von Oppong (1988) describe a development project in northwestern Zambia. They quote an angry politician: 'You promote small-scale farmers, small-scale equipment, small-scale industries … small! small! small! You have grown big and you want to keep us small! Worse than the colonialists!' (Crehan and von Oppong 1988: 126). Parallels can be drawn with the feelings expressed by PFDO. From his point of view, the project entered with potential clout (which was not translated into tangible gifts), but with too many preconceived ideas.

From the point of view of the PFDO, donor assistance was a potentially useful way of enabling the smoother running of the department. Donor assistance also carried with it the danger that staff time would be used, and policy directions changed away from predetermined lines. DoF had received financial support from various donors including Finland (FINNIDA), Sweden (SIDA), Dutch volunteers (SNV) and the Worldwide Fund for Nature (WWF). Activities included the rehabilitation of the government fish-farms, assistance to extension, assistance to a fish-stock assessment survey in Lakes Mweru and Bangweulu, and the conservation of the wetlands natural resources. ALCOM, however, was in an unclear role as a donor. The pilot project entered as a donor-financed operation, with stated objectives concerned with fish production. At the same time, the project provided only a vehicle for its own use and staff time over which DoF had no control. Simultaneously, DoF was to allocate its staff to ALCOM, for activities the PFDO thought were of dubious benefit.

There were personal considerations too, compounding professional resentment. These centred on the repeated reminders of the PFDO's own disempowered state in relation to ALCOM, and notably, its representatives in Luapula. He had held his post for many years. Among the nine PFDOs in the country, he believed his position to be relatively important, because of the significance of fisheries overall. He was a native of Luapula and felt he had a good understanding of the problems of the province. In Mansa, he was widely known as 'the Big Fish'. He had also, during his time as PFDO, seen both his personal standard of living and the resources of the department severely eroded. In the early 1970s, he had his own car and DoF had a new vehicle and a functioning fish-farm. By 1992, the car had gone, his salary, like other government salaries, was worth little, the departmental offices were crumbling, and its vehicle was scarcely roadworthy.

While he had had years of experience, creating an understandable belief that he should be accorded respect and status, he was forced to live in poor housing, with no transport or visible evidence of his position. The ALCOM workers were half his age, white, and newly arrived in Zambia. However, they were paid international salaries, which enabled them to live in comfortable housing and have personal vehicles in addition to the project vehicle. One ALCOM worker responded to the rather shabby office he was given (next to that of the PFDO) by repainting it, complete with royal blue woodwork and FAO logos.

These symbols of difference – in power, in resources, and in choices – were obviously present among the many other expatriates in Mansa. What made them more galling to the PFDO was that they were not something to be put up with for obvious benefit. He often complained there was no reason for the ALCOM project. However, straightforward obstruction was not an option for him. His room for manoeuvre was curtailed by the hierarchy within which he was situated and, to an extent, he had to play the game – maintaining an illusion of collaboration. He therefore took his place at the head of the table at the seminars for fish-scouts and was formally grateful to ALCOM in his written reports. But he also did not go out of his way to assist the project activities: the majority of his time was spent in work connected with lake and river fisheries. At programme headquarters in Harare, people complained about the local bureaucracy: 'That X – he's a disaster. The whole department in Mansa does nothing. How can we be expected to get anything done ourselves?' However, these complaints, like the complaints of the PFDO himself, did not enter the public presentation of the project, in which shared objectives were paramount.

*Intermediate Technology: patron or partner?* The first example from Intermediate Technology concerns its relationships with project partners in Sri Lanka. The first was with Sarvodaya, a Sri Lankan community-based organization. Sarvodaya had been the leading stove agency in the country, until the government also embarked on a national programme to promote the Sarvodaya rural stove. Although Sarvodaya had had some success disseminating small numbers of stoves through their extension workers in Kandy District, they could not compete with the extensive government network and resources when the new government programme began. Intermediate Technology saw the potential for using Sarvodaya's Kandy District Headquarters as a production centre, where new production and marketing techniques could be tested. It decided to provide funds for setting up adequate facilities to develop production, which should eventually become commercially viable. Intermediate Technology paid the salaries for three members of staff (Rs. 3,780 a month), purchased a motorbike, and covered the expenses of the workshop. As a consequence the three members of staff were no longer given wages by Sarvodaya Head Office. Since the coordinator was paid slightly more by Intermediate Technology than the District Coordinator in the Kandy Office, resentment from other sections of Sarvodaya was inevitable.

In 1989, an Intermediate Technology staff member visited the project and decided that the funds were no longer giving Sarvodaya any incentive to establish a commercially viable stove-making enterprise. Funds were withdrawn but, according to project staff, the wages were not reinstated from Sarvodaya Head Office. The Sarvodaya Stove Project tried unsuccessfully to secure funds to cover their salaries from other parts of Sarvodaya, but managed to obtain some finance from the Tea Estate Development Boards for installing chimney stoves in tea planta- tion 'line houses' in Nuwara Eliya District. Meanwhile, stove production increased at a sufficient rate to cover most of the expenses of the workshop, including the employment of a stove-making potter. Accord- ing to Sarvodaya staff, Intermediate Technology's project was in their interests in the short term, but damaged their relationship with Head Office, which had jeopardized their long-term interests. Thus, once they found that support from donors, and even their own Head Office, evaporated, this Sarvodaya branch moved away from community work into a commercial stove enterprise for its own survival.

From 1987 Intermediate Technology's attention in Sri Lanka was mainly directed towards working with the Sri Lankan government on an urban stove programme. DFID agreed to give a proportion of the funds through Intermediate Technology, while the Ministry of Power and Energy of the Sri Lankan government put up the remainder. Part of DFID's funds covered the cost of technical assistance by Intermediate Technology's consultant advisers – the production engineer, marketing specialist, and socio-economist. In addition, an American consultant ceramicist trained the potters, and a Sri Lankan social anthropologist was employed part-time by Intermediate Technology to carry out various monitoring surveys. There was substantial input from the ex- patriate advisers, as reflected in the project expenditure. During the project DFID gave just over £100,000 while the CEB (Ceylon Electricity Board, a part of the Ministry of Power and Energy) contributed about £4,000 (excluding the value of supervisory services provided by senior staff) (Aitken et al. 1989: 32). Intermediate Technology's expenditure, as a percentage of the total, was as follows: 74 per cent was spent on 'external support' (project management in the UK) and 19 per cent on 'direct support' (technical assistance in Sri Lanka) – that is, a total of 316 days of Intermediate Technology/consultants' time. The remaining 7 per cent was spent by CEB (on salaries, publicity, transport, and miscellaneous in Sri Lanka).

From an economic point of view you might expect that Intermediate Technology had complete control over this project, but the CEB staff did not express the relationship in these terms. First, the enormous amount of money spent on expatriate salaries gives the misleading impression that their inputs were critical all the time. In fact, their fee was relatively high, the number of days spent on the project was relatively small, and their presence was sporadic, with the result that the CEB would be in complete control during much of the course of the project. Second, the CEB was not displeased by the considerable expatriate involvement since, even if its training and management skills were certainly not lacking, it was already overstretched with its rural programme. Since the Intermediate Technology funds did not cover CEB salaries, it had every reason for not wanting to take on too many additional responsibilities. In particular, in view of the way the project was designed, with an emphasis on generating demand and establishing a new market for stoves, the marketing advice from Intermediate Technology was perceived as especially useful. Third, the CEB is part of an enormous state structure with its own planning system, store of knowledge, and connections with other government departments. Although Intermediate Technology was under the impression that the CEB had been 'influenced' into accepting that subsidies were inefficient and unsustainable, the ministry later approved an extension to the subsidized rural stoves programme, as a strategy for attaining higher dissemination rates and having greater environmental impact. Ultimately, the ministry was in control of the programme, not Intermediate Technology.

In general, the relationship between staff in Intermediate Technology and the CEB has always appeared to be amicable, and Intermediate Technology had no means of enforcing suggestions. As part of the ministry, with the personal backing of the president for its fuel conservation programme, and money from the Dutch government, the CEB was in a strong position. During the urban stoves programme the CEB could take up Intermediate Technology's suggestions when they fitted in with its own objectives or ignore them if other matters were more pressing. For example, the CEB chose to continue to subsidize rural stoves even though Intermediate Technology argued strongly against them. On the other hand, as far as Sarvodaya was concerned negotiating with Intermediate Technology was more complicated. As we have seen, the financial arrangements made by Intermediate Technology rendered the Sarvodaya Stove Project dependent on Intermediate Technology for its survival.

The second example relates to Intermediate Technology's relationships with project partners in Kenya. While relationships in Sri Lanka have been characterized by a relatively high degree of agreement, the opposite might be said about relations with the first energy project partner organization in Kenya. Although Intermediate Technology was primarily concerned to improve income-earning opportunities for women potters, stoves were still firmly perceived as part of the energy sector the time, and so that KENGO (Kenya Environment and Energy Organizations) – the main energy NGO in the country – was chosen as a partner. In 1986, Intermediate Technology entered into a formal agreement with KENGO as the implementing agency of a stove project in Western Kenya. At the time, it was anticipated that interests might conflict:

> objectives can vary depending upon the viewpoint of a particular organisation. Thus, while DFID, KENGO and Intermediate Technology would all agree on the general objectives of the stoves programme, namely to: (1) help alleviate the growing shortages and increasing monetarisation of fuelwood being experienced by households and to (2) help create employment for low income groups, through the production and sale of stoves, it is likely that the emphasis may vary. For example, Intermediate Technology's prime interest is to help the rural poor, whereas KENGO is more interested in maximising fuelwood savings. ODA may be more interested in maximising the number of stoves in use, while stoves producers are likely to want to maximise sales and profits. Conflicts inevitably arise (Burne 1985: 2–3).

Sure enough, this foundation of different interests and objectives signalled the beginning of many disagreements over policy, objectives, and, more usually, resources or equipment. Differing objectives were expected but Intermediate Technology had not considered how conflicting interests would be resolved when they arose. Intermediate Technology felt that KENGO was not putting sufficient staff input into the project, and so it established an Intermediate Technology Project Officer in Kisumu; KENGO felt that Intermediate Technology was behaving as if it was in charge, thereby allowing KENGO no autonomy or independence. As far KENGO was concerned, there were other activities to which it gave greater priority than training women's potter groups. It concentrated on afforestation, rather than stoves, once it had become widely known that the latter could not substantially reduce the rate of deforestation. Partly for this reason it invested fewer resources in the stove project than had been planned, and so Intermediate Technology, rather than adjusting the project or institutional arrangements, implemented most of the plans itself.

Most project activities continued virtually without KENGO, with one of the pottery groups being Intermediate Technology's nominal project partner in Western Kenya. Then, in early 1989, the Ministry of Agriculture (MoA) instructed their Home Economists (HE) to include the dissemination of stoves as part of their work. The MoA was already collaborating with GTZ, and asked Intermediate Technology to work with the HEs in both Siaya and Vihiga Districts. Installation training began in January 1989, and has continued for some years as part of an informal partnership. Intermediate Technology has not donated funds to the MoA, or entered into a formal agreement with the ministry, but considers it to be a project partner in practice. They chose new producer groups together, and Intermediate Technology consults the MoA about plans and objectives. There is an understanding that Intermediate Technology is responsible for training producers, while the ministry ensures that stoves are sold and installed. Effectively there is a complementary, fixed division of labour with disagreements rarely arising. Once again, it appears that Intermediate Technology was able to effect a more long-lasting partnership with a government department than with an NGO. In both Sri Lanka and Kenya, the financial transactions with governments were minimal or even non-existent. Intermediate Technology's leverage, and therefore its partners' economic dependence, was greatly reduced.

## Exposing conflicts

So, as we found in debates about gender, the talk of partnership often fails to address potential conflict and inequalities. Unlike gender, political relations between organizations in different countries are seldom even discussed. In particular, there is silence about the fact that the identities of international aid and development practitioners and planners are often intimately bound up with nationality and race. Since the whole edifice is founded upon the giving or lending of aid by one group of countries to another, nationality is, at the least implicitly, relevant. Those countries that once colonized Africa, Asia, the Caribbean, and South/Central America, and now give aid, are mostly dominated by white people (although majority black countries have plainly colonized other black countries). The former colonized countries, which now receive aid, tend to be populated mainly by black people (although Eastern European countries are an obvious exception).

In the majority of cases, at the least, nationality and race both play a part in aid as they did in colonialism. As if to add weight to the argument that there are significant continuities, independence from colonialism has not diminished the number of Europeans 'assisting' the former colonies. In 1989 the total number of expatriate staff employed by international development organizations was around 150,000 (World Bank 1989: 181). In the perpetuation of the links between past and present even the people involved are often related; Stirrat argues that 'one of the striking features of development personnel is how frequently they are the children of colonial civil servants, military personnel, missionaries and so on' (1997: 2). It should also be borne in mind that Europeans and Americans, including those working in international development agencies, belong to societies where racism persists. Its form has altered since colonialism – for example, the perception of biologically inferior races has been largely replaced with a cultural racism (where certain groups are excluded or vilified on the grounds of their 'beliefs', 'customs', or 'values'). Racism is also plainly constructed and expressed differently according to the country concerned, especially within Europe. Wieviorka (1994) points out that the shape of national-ism, the political system, and industrial decline have given rise to very different forms of racism in Germany, France, Italy, and Britain, for example.

Yet can we simply say that since predominantly white countries appear to control the welfare and government of predominantly black countries, the aid industry is simply racist? While various racisms are important to power struggles within the development social order, not all political relations can be reduced to or essentialized by this one principle. A black British man working for the United Nations in New York is likely to forge different positions of power for himself compared to a black Tanzanian woman community worker. Numerous structures of power are at work, created partly by people's identity (gender, age, class, nationality, as well as race) and partly by their institutional position within development 'partnerships' (junior/senior, donor/recipient, governmental/NGO).

Even membership of the most powerful donor agency does not, however, bestow power upon the individuals within it at all times. For a start, donor–recipient categories overlap: almost all donors are also recipients. Even European governments depend on funds from their public. If you take a superficial glance at the relationships between Intermediate Technology or FAO and its partners, as represented in the case studies above, you might be tempted to suppose that at least in some cases the donors were trying to control project planning while poverty-trapped recipients were forced to accede to their decisions. As Mauss pointed out: 'to give is to show one's superiority, to show that one is something more and higher ... To accept without returning or repaying more is to face subordination, to become a client and sub-servient' (1970: 72). But the idea of donors grasping at power, as if it is something that can be acquired, measured, and taken away, rests upon faulty reasoning. It involves observing the present, describing those observations as a result of past actions, and then claiming that various agents planned to achieve those effects for their own interests. There is no objective reason for assuming that because something happens, someone necessarily intended it. The donors may appear to be in control, but they do not objectively determine the course events take during projects as they might wish. In fact, it is well known that events in so-called 'planned' development rarely occur as planned.

Furthermore, people within recipient agencies obviously construct their own interpretations of what is going on. The Sri Lankan ministry continued to subsidize stoves, despite Intermediate Technology's claims that it had convinced it to commercialize all its programmes. In Kenya, KENGO declined to invest its own resources in training women potters because it was obvious that Intermediate Technology could manage on its own. ALCOM's partners also had their own priorities, which they pursued as best they could. For both national and local-level partners this was manifest in a reluctance to invest resources with uncertain benefit. Even so, the rationale behind these apparent 'strategies' is not necessarily an attempt to resist the powerful position of the donor in order to acquire power for themselves. Rather, staff within recipient agencies are responding to their own interpretation and material realities within the limits of their economically dependent position. Whether they depend upon them financially or not, they defy the control of the donors by giving the appearance of obeying the rules of aid exchange without actually putting them into practice. Meanwhile, their constructs are inaudible and invisible to donors, who can afford to ignore them because they are in a stronger economic and political position.

The recipients' room for manoeuvre, however, should not be over-stated. The 'expertise' of the Intermediate Technology staff is classified into such narrow technology departments that freedom of choice is minimal for the recipients. Furthermore, the technical specialists advising donors also have an enormous influence over resource allocation. This means that their advice is extremely difficult to ignore. The situation is different in some respects among the larger donors, but equally partial. Many donors insist on engaging 'internationally reputable consultants to ensure impartiality and lend authoritative legitimacy to their pro-posals' (Nindi 1990: 52). Since the donors choose their own consultants, and then decide whether or not to finance their own experts' proposals, it is hardly a surprise to find that most development projects reflect donors' rather than partners' or recipients' preferences.

Donors are sometimes portrayed as strategically wielding the control they have over recipients for their own ends in a coordinated way to uphold the present capitalist system. These arguments are characteristic of much of the simpler 'anti-development' literature. Such conspiracies are unlikely, as we discuss in Chapter 9. Also, often donor interventions are neither strategic nor for their own ends because frequently, in practice, abuse of power is overshadowed in importance by a lack of coordination between donors. The International Monetary Fund (IMF) limits the staff and supporting services that recipient countries can allocate to development projects, as part of the structural adjustment programmes that are conditional to aid, and yet donors very often demand that staff salaries are paid by the recipient government (Nindi 1990: 44). The proliferation of projects can be so substantial that some governments are forced to employ large numbers of expatriates and divert much of their resources to managing the various activities. As examples, in 1980 Zambia had 614 donor-financed projects to administer, while in 1981 the small country of Malawi was managing 188 projects supported by 50 different donors, which distracted them from determining their own policies and kept them fully occupied 'simply trying to please their donors' (Nindi 1990: 44–5).

In this chapter we have described aspects of the relationships between recipients and donors. The transfer of aid from a relatively rich, capitalist, ex-colonialist power (such as Britain) to a relatively poor, ex-colonized nation (such as Zambia, Kenya, or Sri Lanka) is plainly not an equal exchange. It defies Gregory's neat scheme dividing exchange into two possibilities: (1) gift exchange of inalienable objects between interdependent givers and receivers; and (2) commodity exchange of alienable objects between people who are reciprocally independent (Gregory 1982: 100). Development aid involves the exchange of alienable objects (such as money or equipment) in return for the acceptance of 'technical assistance' (which in turn 'gives' money and employment to donor/ adviser agencies), between interdependent givers and receivers. That is to say, in return for gifts or loans, recipient agencies accede to the rhetorical assertions of donor agencies, giving the false impression that the latter are the 'experts', powerful and in control.

Our comments on the way power structures the relationship between the donors and recipients, and how it conditions not their behaviour but the impact they have on each other, may not sound new to some. Aid recipients are obviously only too aware of such processes. We are left, then, with a puzzle. Why is power in partnership so rarely debated? In contrast to gender relations, an analysis of relations between aid givers and receivers is rare, even in academic literature. Despite a swelling orthodoxy advocating understanding different stakeholders, participation, capacity-building, and partnership, the political processes surrounding these objectives are rarely analysed. In a similar fashion to the debates around gender, partnership is converted into a technical issue to improve management rather than redress (or even address) inequalities. Could the reason be connected to the fact that those eligible for aid fear that their donors will find such questioning uncomfortable?

# CHAPTER 5

# Technology and Expertise

Technician: 'Have you been on a trip?'

Social scientist: 'I've just come back from Sri Lanka. I heard about an interesting new food-processing technology while I was there, a new way of preserving fruit.'

Technician: 'Really, where did you hear about it?'

Social scientist: 'In a small village near Nuwara Eliya, an elderly woman showed me.'

Technician: 'Oh, I see, you're not talking about technology, you're talking about some old biddy mucking around.'

In this chapter we consider the validity of prevailing assumptions about technology and expertise against people's technological practices. We argued in Chapter 2 that there has been a tendency to fetishize technology in much development intervention. 'Underdeveloped' has been seen as synonymous with poorly developed technology or with lack of access to modern technology. At the same time, technical change is treated as value-free and neutral, with scant consideration of the social context in which it takes place. Male/female differences are perceived by many technologists as being associated with the private 'cultural' domain and outside the remit of gender-neutral technology development. However, the assumption that technology can be introduced or developed without affecting social relations is clearly problematic. Since technology change always has social, economic, and political consequences, it cannot be neutral. Evidence from the range of technological revolutions (for example, the Industrial Revolution, the Green Revolution, and the globalization of information networks) has shown precisely how much the path and effects of technical change have been influenced by class, gender, and nationality. While the benefits of technological innovation are recognized, examples of technology being associated with increased inequality and a breakdown in social relations now form standard reading on most undergraduate courses on development (as Gardner and Lewis (1996) point out).

But what is the 'technology' that is apparently central to notions of development? We suggested in Chapter 2 that technology can be seen as the organization of tools and techniques for the performance of tasks. This is fine as a definition, but it is also extremely broad. It is easy to use 'technology' in so many different ways to refer to so many different processes that meaningful discussion recedes. This in itself is revealing and central to the argument we make in this chapter: technology is neither neutral nor value-free but a product of who defines it and how. This is most obvious when it comes to differences in nationality and in gender. On the one hand, we find that indigenous technology is denigrated by being portrayed as less than technical. In addition, technology itself is often defined as something associated principally with men. It is as if, by definition, when women organize tools and techniques for the performance of tasks, neither the process nor the result is technological. Although Intermediate Technology has broadened its policy definition of technology in recognition of women's innovations, in practice 'real' technology tends to be defined rather narrowly as hardware produced in 'modern' environments. On the other hand, there is an increasing movement within development agencies that eulogizes indigenous knowledge. The division between indigenous and Western or scientific knowledge is, however, based on ideas about people rather than on objective differences in knowledge or expertise.

A belief in the neutrality of technology is soon lost when one looks at the value-laden nature of attributions of expertise. An 'expert' is not an equal. He or she is by definition better than non-experts in at least one respect, that is in having greater expertise. The prior definition of certain forms of knowledge as 'expertise' according to who has the knowledge, rather than because of the nature of what is known, effect-ively excludes a wide range of people from the central discourse. In Chapter 4 we indicated that what is said about 'partnership' often obscures unequal capacities to define the terms of the partnership. The fact that technical expertise in development is still associated with expatriate advisers and with men is another aspect of this inequality. However, such processes are by no means mechanical impositions from the outside. They involve negotiation over meanings. Nevertheless, attributions of expertise have very concrete effects when it comes to the practices of development.

Given the diverse nature of technology and technological change, we need to limit the parameters of our discussion. We are concerned with the kind of technological change induced and promulgated by development institutions, but only in a fairly circumscribed way. Most obviously, our focus is rural rather than urban. But also we do not discuss in any depth technological change in agriculture, the sector that has attracted the most attention in studies of rural development. This has been the subject of extensive study, ranging from early (and now largely discredited) accounts of the determinants of agricultural innovation and transfer of technology to assessments of the effects of various forms of agricultural change. A limited number of studies have also looked specifically at the gendered effects of technological change in agriculture (for example, Ahmed 1985). Our principal focus is on one relatively narrow area of technology development that is, in contrast, rarely written about: improved cookstoves.

The history of cooking stoves highlights a number of issues about technology particularly effectively. First, it is more obviously closely tied to a gender division of labour than others. Farmers may be either men or women, but in most countries where technological intervention takes place with regard to cooking, it is almost always women who are the cooks. Despite this gender division, and women's obvious problems of overwork, agencies have promoted new cooking technology principally to conserve energy rather than to reduce domestic labour. Second, although there is some romantic rhetoric to the contrary, cooks themselves are seldom seen as technologically competent or the holders of technological expertise. For this reason, the technological innovation that does take place in kitchens is dismissed or overlooked.

Cooks' innovations are not marginalized merely because they are women – this dismissal should be seen as part of a wider pattern of classifying experts. Building from some of the arguments in Chapter 4, we want to explore the role of expatriate advice in perpetuating particular kinds of ideas about the nature of expertise. Most importantly, behind ideas of partnership are other, perhaps more pervasive, ideas about who holds technical knowledge and how.

## Who are the experts?

The use of expatriate technical expertise is still a key aspect of most development intervention. According to Nindi, the use of expatriate experts consumes an estimated $7–8 billion of donor money a year (1990: 59). Clearly 'expatriate' does not necessarily specify nationality or race – an expatriate is simply not a national. In the UN system, which hires according to a quota system from all its member states, only 10 per cent of professionals work in their own country (Hancock 1989). However, there is a tendency, in the development world at least, for 'expatriate expert' to be equated with Euro-American (and more recently Japanese) people.

In the commercial sector, US multinationals and British companies working in 'developing countries' (for example, in the banking, petroleum, and engineering sectors) have replaced most of their expatriate employees with nationals (Brewster 1991: 11). Some development organizations, especially NGOs, have also tried to instigate this process. Concerns about building up the capacity of local NGOs are now central to policy-making within international development agencies, partly because this route is seen as more sustainable. They are also beginning to ask who is managing projects, and not just what are they trying to do, giving preference to projects that are in the hands of 'locals'. In many cases, however, the reduction in permanent expatriate staff has been accompanied by an increase in the use of consultants at key stages in the project development process. While local NGOs are increasingly given control over the management of the delivery of services, it is still common practice to employ expatriates to give them assistance and advice or to evaluate them.

Rationales given for the use of expatriates can be extremely dismissive of experts elsewhere. For example, one Finnish informant (who described himself as an 'inventor') at a conference about appropriate technology said: 'There is a place for us because we must stop people in developing countries reinventing the wheel.' Another did not even see the necessity for visiting developing countries: 'Surely one can learn what one needs to know from books in preparation for creative design work for those countries?' At another conference a British technical trainer argued that technicians from developing countries are knowledgeable about the countryside but struggle with technical matters, and explained their failings as follows:

> In my own experience with technicians from the UK and from developing countries the former always seem to have a greater background on which to draw (although they are likely to be less motivated in so doing!). My initial reaction when confronted by such discrepancies was to explain it away by a straightforward lack of knowledge ... It is only recently that I have seen an extra dimension to the problem ... Their experiences in childhood are very reminiscent of experiences described by people born in the early part of the century. They have grown up and spent their formative years in a predominantly agricultural and rural environment. Their knowledge of technical matters and systems is much more recent and much less comprehensive (Snape 1990: unpaginated) .

It is extremely unlikely that these technicians all came from a rural environment. It is also very interesting that the author opposes agricultural/rural environment with technology, and quite bizarre that 'their' experiences remind him of people born over half a century ago.

These examples are, however, extreme. For some years, it has been more typical within Euro-American development agencies to find that policy documents and project proposals reiterate the claim that their work will make use of 'local' experts. 'South to South' exchanges, whereby experts from one aid-receiving country will give advice to another, are becoming popular with both UK-based and South-based NGOs/governments. In 1998, when asked by one of us whether nationality made a difference to the usefulness of expatriates, two Ugandan occupational therapists expressed a preference for recruiting other African (rather than British or American) therapists as advisers. They explained that British/American occupational therapists had a tendency to bring preconceived ideas about assessing clients' needs that were not always relevant to Uganda. In contrast, specialists from Zimbabwe, Kenya, or South Africa, where occupational therapy is well established, would have a better understanding of the African context, they suggested.

Some practices even reverse assumptions about expertise: very occasionally specialists from South/Central America, Asia, and Africa have been funded to give advice to NGOs in Britain. As examples, the Baring Foundation offers British NGOs funds for employing consultants from those continents to advise on how to strengthen the British voluntary sector; and Private Agencies Collaborating Together in Washington and Community Networks International in London have both brought people from South Africa to give advice about housing and the democratization of NGOs, respectively. These instances, although they are not the only ones, are exceptional, and expatriates from Europe and America are still widely used as experts in the development industry.

Rationalizations for sending Euro-American expatriates to advise aid-receiving states and NGOs often involve a mixture of arguments but tend to centre on either their neutrality and objectivity or their specialist knowledge. Increasingly the role of the expatriate is not to advise about service delivery, but to give advice on developing the recipient organization itself. This 'capacity-building' encompasses activities ranging from skills development (for example, learning to write proposals, report to donors, accounting, and auditing) to creating alliances or networks with others. Even if the 'local' organization 'identifies its own problems and assesses its own needs' (in the words of a British NGO manager running a capacity-building programme in Africa), various assumptions about knowledge prevail. The 'local' organizations are deficient, while the British NGO has knowledge worth transferring. 'Local' consultants, donor agency staff have told us, can be tricky, unpredictable, or 'lousy at report writing'. An assessment is rarely made, however, of the value of the British NGO staffs' collective character, skills, or knowledge.

Why is the knowledge of Euro-Americans assumed to be superior? Arguably technical knowledge is not measured and valued according to its utility for users when put into practice; the value of knowledge is predetermined by the source of knowledge, that is, the identity of the innovator. More accurately, the identities of both the innovator and the evaluator are relevant – the process of evaluating development technology expresses the unequal power relationship between the two. Although it is not a conscious strategy, experts effectively reinforce themselves as such by the use of language and the creation of techniques and tools that have a particular exclusionary mystique attached to them. For example, in Intermediate Technology there are many words and phrases (some of which also exist elsewhere) that have a specific meaning within the organization: comms, OVR (overseas visit report), inputs, appropriate, HUM (Home Unit Manager), stovies, third floor, to name but a few. FAO has also developed a code of acronyms: for example, BTOs (back to office reports), TCPs (technical cooperation projects) and APOs (Associate Professional Officers). Of course, the use of abbreviations and coded language is not the sole province of development organizations. A cursory glance inside the university system and most larger businesses will reveal the same process. Labelling is necessary for imbuing a sense of belonging in members of a group; learning the labels is an essential initiation process for new members. Any 'community' does it, albeit with fewer bureaucratic terms. Certain codes, labels, or languages gain hegemony in certain contexts and some people are inevitably excluded from belonging, as we have seen in the case of the definition of expertise. A Sri Lankan development practitioner, writing about fellow Sri Lankan colleagues, sheds light on the cumulative effect of this hegemony:

> they believe that the authority of knowledge belongs to the Europeans and Americans. They are not ready to accept the fact that Western science is not the only source of knowledge. They completely forget the innovative capabilities of their own and of other people in developing countries. This, I believe, is not because of their fault but rather due to Western domination, which expresses itself from two ways – money and so-called knowledge. The people who are working in North-based organizations give interpretations by themselves, that knowledge is derived from Western science. The people in South-based organizations follow this for funds and other opportunities (anonymous pers. comm. 1991).

Experts legitimize their role by claiming more up-to-date expertise, whether it is in the field of 'hard' technology or science or 'soft' social science. Since those in positions of power are, by definition, the very people who create and define the 'up-to-date' expertise, their access to the latest information, skills, and techniques makes it a self-fulfilling prophecy. This is especially marked when it comes to the various techniques associated with development expertise: logical framework analysis, the project cycle, environmental impact assessment, practical and strategic needs analysis, cost-benefit analysis, and participatory rural appraisal (PRA).

The extent to which PRA can be classified as a tool of expatriate expertise is of course contestable. There have been many 'local' initiatives, especially in India, in which nationals have actively and explicitly rejected expatriate and outside attempts to define their reality and have denied the Western origins of the approach. Robert Chambers (1996) argues that Rapid Rural Appraisal (RRA) and PRA originated in the South, specifically at the University of Khon Kaen in Thailand. On the other hand, it is also true that not only is Robert Chambers seen by many as the principal architect of PRA, but that it is still often expatriates who are held to be expert in its use. This may be partly because, as Pankhurst (pers. comm. 1998) has suggested, many PRA techniques do not require speech and are, therefore, particularly useful to outsiders who do not speak the local language.

If you take a closer look at some of the other techniques, there are clear problems. For example, logical framework analysis and the idea of the project cycle rely on a segmented view of causality. It is assumed that if an agency makes inputs (equipment, time, and money), it should be able to predict the outputs (results of project activities), the effects (achievements), and the impact (meeting long-term goals) by taking account of the 'externalities'. The concept of project 'externalities' or 'environment' involves those factors over which the project has no control (such as the weather, the actions of other agencies, illness of staff), implying that a project has control over some factors. The view of development as akin to a scientific experiment, where all the possible variables can be identified, is extremely misleading. It is impossible to isolate social, economic, ecological, political, or ideological variables from each other, and predict how any will change in the future, because understanding social life is a matter of interpreting relationships and not recording behavioural elements or 'variables'. A number of academic commentators may have argued against linear and oversimplified views of development intervention, but these have not generally influenced the continuing practices of development organizations.

If the expertise promoted by donors is problematic, why does it continue? Is it the result of the experts pursuing their interests? The director of a Kenyan NGO related examples of how expatriate advisers continually assert their perceived superiority over the 'locals' by means of various strategies. They do so, according to him, to secure further employment. These strategies may include putting them down by quoting recent foreign publications (which can be difficult to obtain); contradicting them; capturing as much speaking time in meetings as they can; referring to their own work in other countries, providing a contrast to the locals' apparently meagre national experience; and using high technology (such as computers). The director portrayed this process as a deliberate power strategy. There are certainly pressures on consultants to prove their worth, irrespective of whether they are angling for further employment or not. Short-term expatriate consultants often have very little time to demonstrate their technical 'know-how'. Models, methods, and matrices are not only visible and tangible evidence of the consultant's presence, but they have an apparently technical, and therefore professional, appearance. They are symbolic of the consultant's performance as a professional, rather than intrinsically superior techniques for planning or evaluation. This pressure may be less intense on longer-term consultants, but they too are forced to present their expertise in a positive light (for example, in an attractive report) to justify their presence and fee.

The actions of particular consultants still does not explain why international development agencies employ them so widely. Agency staff are making decisions in response to their own situation and are limited by their own assumptions. All too often, international agency staff, or individuals contracted to do their work, do not know anyone in the country concerned who can carry out a particular task. The reasons for this are multifarious: the spatial distance between the recruiting agency and the country in which they are working is usually large; people rely on very limited social networks created by personal contact. On many occasions, we have been asked by donor agencies, NGOs, or consultancy firms to carry out a piece of work because they know us, or know someone who has recommended us, on the pretext that 'there is no local person who has the necessary expertise'. Furthermore, the conditions that are often attached to grants/loans (for example, work must be new and innovative but targets have to be set) means that preparatory assessment is difficult to fund and proposals are written with little information about local experts. Despite the exorbitant cost of Euro-American consultants and staff, they are sometimes used simply because they are known, tried, and tested. Those in international agencies assume that the known consultant will 'speak their language', understand their priorities, and have good communication skills.

International agencies do not merely employ Euro-American consultants; they pay more careful attention to what they say than their African and Asian 'counterparts'. We will describe this process in some detail in relation to a particular field of technology development, improved cooking stoves.

## The impact of experts: the case for and against stove programmes

The abandonment of improved cooking-stoves by some organizations, and their popularity with others, illustrate how the perception of technology, its value and the use to which it is put depend on your perspective. Although electrification has long been generally considered desirable within both international agencies (including donors) and recipient governments in Africa, Asia, and South/Central America, progress has been extremely slow. During the 1980s it was an environmental concern that made a critical impact on energy policy: the 'woodfuel crisis'. European and American energy experts made a series of related assumptions about the environment and woodfuel use: that deforestation was caused in large part by the cutting of wood for domestic fuel use; that population growth was exacerbating the problem; that 'traditional' stoves were energy-inefficient; and that fuelwood shortages were resulting in increased time spent on wood collection, the burning of inferior fuels, and a reduction in quality of diet (see Chapter 1 for details).

By the late 1980s these stove programmes were largely dismissed as failures for two reasons: they were apparently rejected by many users, and they were not reducing the rate of deforestation. The problems besetting stove programmes led to their widespread abandonment. By the middle of the 1990s UN agencies (except for FAO), the World Bank and bilateral donors (except for the Dutch government and GTZ) had deleted stove programmes from their agendas. Many international NGOs, inevitably, have followed suit. What is interesting to us are the processes influencing this. In 1983 two British writers, Foley and Moss, had concluded not only that most improved stoves were making very small reductions in fuelwood consumption, but that some were even increasing the amount of fuel burnt. They also pointed out that the policy premises were flawed: woodfuel consumers were the victims but not the root cause of deforestation (Foley and Moss 1983: 19–21). Since people cut trees primarily to clear land for cultivation or livestock, rather than to burn wood in their stoves, deforestation is ultimately a land and not a fuel issue (Foley et al. 1984: 11).

Foley et al. were only trying to conjure a more informed picture of the relationship between biomass use and deforestation. But the result of their work when applied by agencies was the replacement of one pessimistic generalization about energy problems (fuelwood use causes deforestation) with another (improved stoves are a failure). Furthermore, years before Foley wrote about domestic fuelwood consumption, 'local' researchers had been pointing out that cooks do not cut green trees. For example, when Indian researchers asked residents of Gujarat, India, about felling trees one of them said: 'Who will cut the green trees? Don't they give us our livelihood? It is outsiders who cut them' (Nagabrahmam and Sambrani 1980: 14). It was, however, European and American experts following this line of argument who were referred to when justifying a change in donor policy. During interviews with staff in USAID, the Energy Sector Management Assistance Program (ESMAP) (World Bank/UNDP), and DFID, it was Foley, Eckholm (an American energy expert) or their own Euro-American consultants who were cited when rationalizing the funding cuts to stove programmes. Indian researchers, such as Nagabrahmam, were not mentioned because they were not known and, in any case, would not carry the same weight or authority. It was the Euro-American expatriates' advice that acted as a catalyst and an excuse for giving up the tricky business of working with overworked cooks to improve their kitchen technology.

There were certainly many other reasons given for the policy shift – for example, a commission reviewing ESMAP advised that NGOs can more easily implement household energy projects, and since ESMAP gives aid to government agencies only, it was suggested that funding for this sector should be substantially decreased (ESMAP 1990: 31–2). Individual donor agencies act for different reasons and, although they influence each other, do not act *en masse*. In fact, DFID's first White Paper signals a possible reversal in negativity towards stoves. The summary cites stoves as a successful application of science: 'new wood-burning stoves which cut the amount of fuel wood needed for cooking by half have been developed costing as little as £2. This in turn reduces deforestation and air pollution and the cost can be recovered in just a few days' (DFID 1997: 11).

The struggle against deforestation has been magically revived as an aim, air pollution is added in line with new environmental priorities, and the time for recovering cost has been astoundingly underestimated. In most cases it can take around two months, rather than days, to recover the initial outlay. Most significantly, the priorities of users (principally their workload) are not mentioned – in fact the cooks themselves are invisible in this example.

To put this more strongly, the decision by international donors to reduce support for stoves programmes can be seen as an expression of the low value attached to improvements in the domestic domain. French warned in the 1980s that 'when stoves are viewed in this way – in relation to the alternative ways of helping women – both women and governments are almost certain to assign them a very low priority' (as quoted by Foley et al. 1984: 85). A senior manager in a NGO specializing in reproductive health points out that parallels can be found in debates about population. Since population has been presented as an issue of women's choice and health, or even empowerment, rather than a matter of controlling fertility for the sake of the environment, funding from most donors has been significantly reduced.

A consideration of the impact of improved stoves on the women who use them inevitably begs questions about changes in their work-load. While the link between agricultural technology and women's labour has been widely discussed (e.g. Whitehead 1985), household technology and work are rarely considered together. According to cooks in Sri Lanka and Kenya, some of the problems associated with cooking have been alleviated by improved stoves. They report that the cooking (or supervision) time has been shortened, the discomfort of smoke emissions has been reduced, and the process has become safer, cleaner, and more convenient. New stoves in Sri Lanka have improved the quality of working conditions for women and their workload has been reduced by approximately an hour a day, which frees up some time in an arduous day.

Stove programmes have done nothing, however, to challenge women's total responsibility for household work. Furthermore, even though the stoves can free up time, this can bring its own complications; some women in western Kenya reported that they are careful to conceal the time saved otherwise their husbands will demand that they work longer hours for them on their farms. In Sri Lanka, some women potters using rural stoves claim that they spend less time cooking and so invest more time in their husband's businesses. None of this is, of course, the fault of the stoves. In fact the decline in popularity of stoves in official aid agencies should be lamented. There is a convincing case for arguing that improvements to household technology should be prioritized in some contexts, to alleviate women's immediate problem of overwork or as an entry point to supporting women's longer-term strategies for bringing about a more equal share of household work. But to recognize that they have a place in certain contexts is not necessarily considered useful. A manager in UNIFEM, for example, revealed during an interview in 1990 that it would fund stove programmes in Asia only if it could be proved that time saved by improved stoves was used by all women in a particular place in productive, rather than reproductive, work. The universalized assumption was that women will (or should) be empowered by gaining access to income; since stove programmes could not guarantee this, UNIFEM and other women's organizations avoided them.

Despite the reduction of donor support, new forms of cookstoves have been developed in many African and Asian countries. Some energy experts in Africa and Asia (and in some NGOs in Europe and America) welcome stove programmes; two African energy analysts, Ogunlade Davidson and Stephen Karekezi, argue that an environmentally sound strategy for Africa should focus on more efficient use of energy rather than growth of supply (1993). On these grounds, they add, the promotion of wood- and charcoal-burning stoves should be a component of energy plans in Sub-Saharan Africa (1993: 19, 21). Karekezi establishes that unlike wood-burning stoves, more efficient charcoal-burning stoves do reduce the rate of deforestation, since they can decrease the amount of trees felled for charcoal-making (Bhagavan and Karekezi 1992). Davidson and Karekezi also recommend expanding the use of other renewable sources of energy, mobilizing local funding mechanisms, and making better use of local experts and institutions (1993: 17, 10). Such arguments challenge various assumptions that tend to be made by planners in donor agencies: that the model provided by the 'West' is the ultimate goal (for example, electrification and increased supply of oil), that funding is inevitably sought through international aid channels, and that local experts scarcely exist. To accept such fundamental challenges might lead some to question the need for both aid funding and expatriate expertise. The path of least resistance, and the one taken by most international agencies most of the time, is to ignore them.

The perceived need for expatriate expertise is partly fuelled by the assumption that technology transferred or adapted from Europe or America is superior to 'traditional' technology. But is this necessarily the case?

## Traditional technology: open fires and improved stoves

One of the fundamental assumptions about the need for improved or modern stoves is that they replace something that is inferior. But this is not necessarily an easy or valid judgement to make. In the first place it is not appropriate to draw a simple line from three-stone fires to microwaves, and describe one end as 'primitive' and the other as 'civil-ized'. Foley et al. have claimed that 'properly designed stoves, adapted to their environment, and meeting the needs of the users have been a mark of progress and rising quality of life through human history since the beginnings of settled habitation' (1984: 15). On the other hand, they also point out that, although technologically simple, wood-burning cooking-fires have many advantages over 'improved' stoves. Consider-able diversity of cooking-fires is illustrated with examples from three continents and they conclude that they cost no money; offer a social or ritual focus; are more flexible because they can be easily moved; produce heat which can be easily controlled; can burn any size or type of fuel; can support any size or type of pot; can provide lighting and heating; and release smoke, which preserves food, dries fuel or clothes, deters insects, and lengthens the life of thatch (Foley et al. 1984: 18–21).

When cooks have found open fires unsatisfactory in other respects, cooks or artisans have developed mud, ceramic, or metal designs that also vary according to climate, fuel availability, household structure, types of food, economic position, and so on (Foley et al. 1984: 22). In some cases the improvements are so small that it is difficult to know when an open fire becomes a stove. For example, making a 'traditional' *chula* (stove) in Bangladesh involves no more than digging a tunnel in the ground with a pot-hole cut in the roof at the end, making a fire beneath the hole, and feeding it with wood from the open end of the tunnel. Foley et al. also describe more complicated constructions, with chimneys, fire-doors, dampers, or other means of controlling the flow of air through the fire, from all over the world. Revealingly, however, all these versions of cooking technology are categorized by them as 'traditional' or 'unimproved' stoves. The implication is that 'traditional' technology is part of an old, established, inefficient, static technological set-up. Yet their own account of so-called 'traditional' models indicates that older systems are neither fixed nor inferior. Even the declared 'thermal inefficiency' of open fires has been taken out of context, since the heat that escapes between the stones, and that is not directed at the cooking-pot, is far from wasted in cooler climes where warmth in the house is greatly valued. The 'traditional' ceramic stoves are considered by users to be efficient in other respects (for example, they are portable and retain more heat), and so should not be described as unimproved or inefficient in any absolute sense.

If so-called 'traditional' stoves are not necessarily inefficient, what are they? Traditional is apparently supposed to mean no more than 'already in existence', or 'well-established', or 'prior to modern'. Even so, when you consider that the *Megan Chula* from India is described as an 'improved' stove, even though it was designed more than forty years ago and has been superseded by many other wood-burning chimney-stoves, you begin to realize that other assumptions enter into the classification. It appears that the label of tradition is more closely connected to ideas about 'expert' people than it is to temporal considerations. If the technology has been designed by seeming non-experts (such as potters or cooks), then the stove is often described as 'traditional' irrespective of when it was created. For example, when a potter showed his brand-new design for a sawdust-burning stove to a British engineer, the latter asked: 'Do you make any other traditional stoves?' In contrast, when formally educated engineers or scientists develop technology, then the stoves are automatically described as improved or modern. Electric stoves are undoubtedly seen as modern within Europe, even though they have been in use for almost a century. Earlier models are described as old-fashioned but never as traditional. Implicit in the phrase 'traditional stoves' is an evolutionist assumption that as a society becomes more advanced, its people move up the energy ladder from traditional biomass stoves to expert-designed specialized, electric models.

Stove users' views tend to be seen as backward and as distorted by exotic traditional beliefs, in contrast to the apparently sophisticated, detached technical expertise of the engineers and even social scientists. It appears that technical knowledge is not measured and valued by so-called experts according to utility for users when put into practice; its value is predetermined by its source and the social context from which it emerges. In effect, it is the inventor who is valued rather than the invention, and the evaluator will rank the inventor according to the power relationship between them. Cooks, despite their daily practice of cooking, apparently have less technical knowledge in their so-called cultural 'perceptions' than designers in laboratories do in their scientific 'findings'. The implication is that while users perceive (through the trammels of cultural tradition) but do not know, the technical experts find and do know in an objective, scientific sense. Technicians 'know' because there is a perception of 'Western' science as the only path to objective knowledge in the sense of truth. But what makes science true? It works? And yet, watching a cook at the stove alerts an observer to the complex technical skill involved in manipulating fire, stones, air, earth, and wood, which also works.

E. F. Schumacher, Intermediate Technology's founder, once asserted that the poor are so lacking in education that they are only capable of understanding practical matters (Schumacher 1973: 165). Constructing principles, which is beyond the reach of the ordinary people, is the job of the clear-thinking, educated experts who then have the responsibility of sharing their knowledge. He pays tribute to Mao Tse-Tung for his explanation of the process of acquiring knowledge. He proposes going to practical people to learn from them, synthesizing their experiences into theories, and then returning to the practical people to put the theories into practice to solve problems (Schumacher 1973: 211). He appears to be showing respect to the practical people by giving value to their experience but then undermines their knowledge by assuming that it contains no theory.

In Chapter 2 we explored some of the conceptual problems with such an assumption, which continues to be hugely influential. The practice of technical experimentation, in development or otherwise, confirms that the dichotomy between practically and theoretically oriented people is flawed. When a Sri Lankan potter or an engineer try out a new clay composition, they are both working according to a set of assumptions about how mud and sand react to heat. The sets of assumptions do not have to be identical to be workable. Many Sri Lankan potters assume that physical or chemical reactions are not the whole story, since demons can cause clay to crack in the kiln. The relevant point is that demons are no more practical, impractical, true, or false than physical laws. Whether the clay 'expert' is reacting to physical or spiritual knowledge, the practical decisions are made on the basis of theoretical schemata. Finally, Schumacher mistakenly implies that expertise is associated with abstract principles that are then trans-mitted linguistically. Bloch points out that it is 'only when they do not think about what they are doing in words' that people become truly experts (1991: 187). Thus Sri Lankan potters are experts not because they explicitly expound upon the principles behind transforming clay into ceramic, but as a result of developing a cognitive mechanism through practical experience. This enables them to work efficiently and skilfully without the encroachment and distraction of language.

Bloch illustrates the importance of practice over language in the use of expertise with the example of a Malagasy farmer choosing a bit of forest for 'good swidden' (1991: 187). When the farmer decides on a good plot he whizzes through an incredible processing feat in minutes: he recalls the complex yet flexible mental model of what good swidden is like, takes in the image of forest before him (the vegetation, the slope, the surrounding countryside, the hydrology, the soil, and so on), and then compares the two. This could not be achieved through a simple comparison, with the mental processes running down a single line of analysis, but must involve what Bloch calls 'multiple parallel processing'. Similarly, it is only through the 'complex yet familiar task' of cooking that the cook can compare a new stove against an old one, taking in information about what kind and size of wood it needs, how well air is drawn, how much heat and light is provided, how many sparks fly about, how much smoke is released into the room, whether the heat can be easily controlled, and so on. Such familiarity builds up over years, which, not surprisingly, makes them the most experienced experts at cooking with wood.

## Women cook, men innovate?

In theory, women as both development agency staff and 'beneficiaries' are excluded from technical development, which is primarily a male business. In practice, women are just as technical in their own areas of expertise, as the development of stoves demonstrates. In rural areas of Africa, Asia, and South/Central America technical improvements to stoves were probably carried out by female cooks, until potters became involved in designing ceramic wood-burning stoves, and metal-workers began making aluminium or tin charcoal-burning stoves. Since Indian technologists started working on new biomass stove designs in the late 1940s, technical stove development has moved into the domain of almost exclusively male engineers and technicians, a mixture of nationals and expatriates. Cooks have not usually been involved in the development of improved stoves, except to test their 'acceptability' after a bout of technical work is complete. Producers are usually consulted only to see if the manufacturing processes are technically and financially feasible. Thus both the users and producers have been displaced from the centre of the technical innovation process. Goody points out that in Europe the kitchen was the birthplace of many technical operations and apparatus but that 'when these processes left the kitchen for specialist control they generally shifted from the hands of women to those of men' (1982: 193). This is also true within stove development in Africa, Asia, and South/Central America.

The perception of technology as 'man-made' filters into development interventions through the assumptions people make about gender, work, expertise, and technology. In the example of stove development, Intermediate Technology's stated policy is to build on existing technical knowledge and innovation. In practice this has usually involved giving instructions to cooks or stove-makers, generally via their project partners, whilst the 'real' design work takes place in urban-based laboratories and workshops. Even when new designs are rejected, rather than questioning their own knowledge designers account for the failure of their model by complaining that users have not been properly trained in how to use the stove. In practice, it is not training or good sense that are lacking. The stove-user has a different perspective on her own work and, for example, may not have the time to chop the fuelwood into small pieces, which is often necessary for new improved stoves. Or she may not want the chimney that is attached to some new stoves when the mosquitoes are particularly abundant and can be kept at bay by smoke from an open fire.

In both the Gambia and Zimbabwe, fuel-consumption studies have shown that women using fuel-conservation strategies with a three-stone fire have saved more wood than those using particular apparently fuel-efficient stoves (Howorth 1992: 24; Bennett 1990: 20). For example, some Zimbabwean cooks build walls around the open fire, lower the grate on which the pot sits, extinguish the fire as soon as the cooking is finished, and arrange the sticks so that the most efficient performance is attained. In wood-burning stove use, the user is a more influential variable on fuel consumption than the equipment. In any case, if stoves are promoted for the benefits to cooks, rather than to designers, then the technical skills and views of the former should surely be central to the process.

Evidence of women's technical innovation can easily be found, of course, outside the kitchen. Recent research has also publicized women's success as technical innovators in other areas (Appleton 1995). Women in Uganda have been developing new ways of preserving fish in response to an increase in scarcity (Wekiya 1995: 186). Mpande and Mpofu relate that in Zimbabwe 'while the attempts by expatriates and development agencies to promote drought-tolerant crops have not yielded any signi ficant results, Tonga women have managed to identify, collect and process forty-seven indigenous plants whose leaves are used for relish, and over 100 tree species with a variety of edible parts' (1995: 189). The innovation can be found in the ways in which these plants and tree products are processed for both consumption and sale. In India silk-reelers have made numerous improvements to their equipment and production process (Shekar 1995: 218–22) and in Peru women have designed effective oil-lamps to cope with the lack of electricity in some areas (Yturregui 1995: 130). Although women's 'indigenous knowledge' is often portrayed as traditional and, by implication, static (for example, Mishra 1994: 3–5; Quiroz 1994: 12–15; Ulluwishewa 1994: 17–19), the examples of women's innovations do demonstrate that in practice even recent technology is not all made by men. Clearly what is at issue is the question of who defines what is technical.

The fact that women's knowledge is often deemed to be cultural rather than the result of innovation and expertise is partly the product of social relations. At every level, in households, national government departments, and donor agencies, men control key resources and decision-making processes while women's work and expertise tend to be undervalued. The expertise of women cooks is often invisible or silenced because, following Chambers's criterion for low status in development projects, their work is often not part of the market economy, and is considered messy, tradition-bound, and dirty (1986: 143). On the other hand, it is not through a calculated strategy for power, status, or economic strength that men conceive of technical matters as the male domain. Gender relations are patterned by the practice of working within or against shared ideological schemata that inform all agents about male and female stereotypes. Within Intermediate Technology the existing power relations are nurtured by attributes constructed through gender (as examples, women being defined and redefined as vulnerable, passive, and good communicators, and men as technically knowledgeable, assertive, and inventive; see Chapter 3 for details). Although other associations would work, these are particularly effective for rationalizing the association between technology invention and manufacture and maleness. Since women and men continually reconstruct the stereotypes as they work, with women in Intermediate Technology often being relatively unassertive and compliant in relation to men, there is less room to challenge these particular sets of gender power relations.

The perceived dichotomy between technical men and non-technical women is often reaffirmed by social relations within development agencies. Many agencies consist of men as the technical experts and women as their clerical servants. As we noted in Chapter 3, in both FAO and Intermediate Technology there is a clear division of labour (and hierarchical status) between the technical and the support staff. The (predominantly female) social scientists, who deal with social issues, are treated as if they are in the arena of soft rather than hard science and so fall somewhere in between the two. Since professionalism is tied up with hard science and technology, the pressure to establish themselves as experts can be fierce.

Two of the most important activities that re-create social relations in development agencies are travel and attending meetings. Men make overseas trips and hold meetings, where the 'real' work takes place, and women arrange the travel and take minutes. When men meet, the most common greetings are: 'Where have you come back from?' or 'When is your next trip?' (depending upon how tanned the traveller looks). As an anomalous female social scientist with Intermediate Technology, with diluted expertise, when a trip or important meeting approached, you were often asked a version of the following: 'What are you up to now, women again, is it?' The temptation to deny any gender content, or make it more technical by referring to training, assessment or tools of analysis, was strong.

It is, therefore, people's way of explaining their experience of technology that marginalizes women from the account. It is social history that informs people rather than their desire to repress. If engineers see themselves as the technologists of British society, and only one in three hundred engineers are women (Pacey 1983: 80), then it is hardly surprising that many British development agency staff jump to the conclusion that technology is a male business. Pacey describes a Warwick University course in engineering as a course taught by men for men; graduates from other universities echo his observation. Universities do not adopt such practices in order to keep women out of engineering courses, and their approach would undoubtedly change if half the course members were female. The fact remains, however, that until either the definition of technology widens, or more women enrol in engineering, technology will be interpreted as man-made.

## Conclusion

The excellence of expatriate expertise may be continually reinvented, but this takes place simultaneously with calls for reductions in expatriate input. Even so, development tales told by expatriate experts about their success with the 'locals' affirm the authors' place in the wider social order of the development industry. Their body of superior knowledge relies on constant reiteration and renewal of technical language, methods and orthodoxies. This process is silent so that the experts appear neutral in theory, while in practice they reinvent and legitimize their expertise. The situation seems to have changed very little since Adams wrote:

> it's not knowledge or skill alone that's wanted of the expert; there would be less costly, more efficient ways of acquiring them. What matters is the halo of impartial prestige his skills lend him, allowing him to neutralize conflict-laden encounters – between governments, between a government and its governed – and disguise political issues, for a time, as technical ones. An expert helps disguise the government of men as the administration of things, thus making it possible for men to be governed as if they were things. The full title is 'development expert' ... that which creates and sustains the function of expert is the idea of 'development' as one and indivisible' (1979: 474).

This partly explains why technology is so useful. It disguises political processes but has other valued attributes as well. Technology is observable, tangible, and measurable; it is far easier to see, touch, and measure the physical performance of a road than changes in community networks. Priorities have shifted, on the other hand, since Adams wrote about development. Organizational, institutional, or human resource development has become, if not as important as technology, then at least an obligatory component of any up-to-date programme. Meanwhile, experts still try to produce measurable evidence of their contribution, most vigorously by introducing methods for greater accountability. As accountability gains in importance, the attention paid to the complexity of what happens from day to day, and public acknowledgement of failure, seem to diminish.

Although problems have been identified with the transfer and/or adaptation of technology and knowledge, the response is commonly to alter strategy rather than question the goal. For example, a 'techno-fix' approach whereby modern technology is merely transferred from one place to another and then marketed is recognized as inadequate. For many years social scientists (and others) have been employed to ensure that technology meets needs, is culturally acceptable, and can be maintained. Also strategic questions have been raised about what kind of technology is needed in different circumstances. The appropriate technology (AT) movement (including Intermediate Technology), and the more recent debates about indigenous knowledge, have challenged the superiority of the 'West' and its often environmentally and socially destructive technology. And yet AT proponents do not scrutinize the positive transformative potential of technology and knowledge. A look at the practices of development shows that their transfer is still treated as the most important means for alleviating or even reducing poverty. There is a strange side-stepping in many development organizations of the issue of how technology or knowledge actually do this.

To justify the central place of technology specific examples are given to show how specific groups increase access to, or save, resources (principally time and money). Particular groups of people certainly accumulate wealth as a direct result of using technology (for example, tractors) or producing it (for example, stoves). But the links between technological change, on the one hand, and overall levels of national poverty, on the other, are far from clear. While making small groups of individuals richer through technology can be relatively straightforward, Intermediate Technology staff have often faced economic and political obstacles when trying to bring about change at national or even community levels.

Some of Intermediate Technology's most successful projects have involved surmounting such obstacles. In Kerala, South India, its improvements to fishing technology would have achieved little on their own in the face of the low prices paid by wholesale fish-sellers. Strengthening a fishing cooperative led to negotiation for better terms (especially prices and debt repayments) and a more profitable industry for all small-scale fish-workers. In Kenya, attempts to disseminate low-cost housing were halted until Intermediate Technology and others successfully campaigned for a relaxation of the government's building regulations. In Nepal, Intermediate Technology's development of micro-hydro schemes was threatened by the proposal of a large-scale hydro scheme, the Arun dam, which would have wasted funds and produced more electricity than people in Nepal could afford. Partly as a result of pressure from NGOs, the scheme was scrapped, so that micro-hydro for local consumption was once again a viable option. In all these cases technology has had extremely positive results, but only when accompanied by economic and/or political change. Technological change outside development projects can clearly benefit people too. As a result of the market rather than aid, increasing numbers of pastoralists in Kenya find mobile phones extremely useful; they could even be empowering in some contexts. But examples do not prove a rule – they do not prove that technology on its own can reduce overall poverty levels.

The link between technology and poverty is further complicated by the lack of agreement about what 'poverty' means. As we will see in the next chapter, fish-farmers in Luapula, Zambia, do not apply new technological knowledge and dig ponds to raise their income. They do so, for example, to fill seasonal gaps in their diet, to create an asset that may generate income later, or to lay claim to a particular piece of land. Do these constitute poverty reduction? They may do for some if a reasonably broad definition of poverty reduction is drawn (for example, including fulfilment of basic needs, building up of assets, better control of resources), but their poverty would remain unaffected if it is taken to mean level of income. The assumed causal link between technology and poverty reduction is often beyond this kind of scrutiny because it is deemed automatic. The generalized link is a convenient device for avoiding the definition of either in specific cases.

The faith in technology is partly perpetuated by those anthropologists and social scientists who maintain that problems in technology projects have been merely the result of poor communication: the cultural brokers discussed in Chapter 1. For example, David Seddon (1993) discusses the role of anthropologists in the preparation of International Fund for Agricultural Development (IFAD) projects in Niger and Mali. He stresses that for IFAD, 'the participative approach' is essential, but describes a case where the need for a project is assumed in advance, and where a mission (consisting predominantly of expatriates) took only three weeks to establish the parameters of the project. Seddon argues that the particular value of the IFAD project was its predisposition to employ people with an anthropological background. However, 'participation' meant little more than consultation within a predetermined paradigm. There was no questioning of the paradigm itself or the power relations embedded within it. The experts distinguish themselves from the 'others' who become the objects to be understood and possibly changed for the better. In the next chapter we look at what why the 'other' people get involved in development projects, contrasting the assumptions made by the experts with the practices of those they hope to help.

# CHAPTER 6

# Money and Motivation: 'My Wife Helps Me with Everything'

Why do farmers choose to dig fish-ponds or to look after them? Why do cooks adopt 'improved' stoves? Questions such as these as are often posed by the promoters of new technologies. In this chapter we explore their ideas about motivation and look at what is behind the assumption that people are driven by material gain. We have described some of the explanations that developers resort to when accounting for actions by beneficiaries or, more specifically, why the intended 'beneficiaries' of their intervention choose to adopt a technology or not (see Chapter 2). We have focused on the predominance of ideas of economic rationality and argued that these are largely rooted in a modernization paradigm that has withstood the deconstructions of positivism embodied in much post-modernist thinking. Within aid organizations there is a concern to understand why people do things, and at the same time there is a pressure to assume a uniformity and predictability in human behaviour that may not exist. It is presupposed that the decision to adopt a new technology, such as fish-farming or improved stoves, involves a calculated decision-making process, an informed weighing of costs, benefits, and risks, with a completed outcome.

We will review explanations of behaviour by looking at what beneficiaries actually do. In particular, we will question three assumptions that underlie many discussions of motivation, particularly that of farmers. First, it is assumed that the interests and motivations of all members of rural households are equal. There is a tendency for developers to drift from talk of 'farmer motivation' to 'household motivation', without critical examination of whether the needs, interests, and priorities of all household members can be equated with those of the (male) household head. As we indicated in Chapter 2, there is now an extensive literature documenting both the conceptual and empirical flaws behind such assumptions, yet they continue with remarkable persistence. In this chapter, we look at how such assumptions are expressed or played out in practice, and offer new evidence to show that both motivation and interests within households diverge.

Second, simple material gain is assumed to be a primary aspect of motivation. But the reasons people do things cannot always be neatly reduced to material interest. We argue that for the promoters of fish culture it may be obvious that this is what digging a fish-pond is about; for the people doing it, on the other hand, there may be different associations. Similarly, as was clear from Chapter 5, improved cooking-stoves may attract their adopters for reasons other than their supposed fuel efficiency and, therefore, money savings. The nature and importance of these associations or reasons, as compared to those of the performance attributes of the technology itself, will depend on context. For example, individual adopters (or non-adopters) will be greatly influenced by their perception of the constraints they face.

Finally, and relatedly, the assumption that the decision-making process of individual actors should be viewed as an informed weighing of costs, benefits, and risks – with a completed outcome – is queried. Where constraints and benefits are obvious, and likely gains equally clear, this may be the case. There are, however, many occasions when action is less the result of such a calculation and more part of a continuing process of response and adaptation to new information.

We examine these three assumptions about farmers' economic motivation with particular reference to our case study of digging fish-ponds in Luapula Province, Zambia. Digging fish-ponds does not make people rich and yet people continue to get involved. This puzzle offers an especially convincing challenge to the idea that people are uniformly driven by opportunities for wealth creation alone. The case study draws on ethnographic material derived from fieldwork concentrated in two areas of Luapula: the Monga area near Mansa, the provincial capital, and the Chibote area in Kawambwa district. Each area comprises a central village (Monga and Chibote) and a number of outlying villages. In each of these areas, the ALCOM project had been active in promoting fish-farming, with reportedly limited success.

In 1992, ALCOM had produced an issue of *ALCOM News* devoted to women and fish-farming in Luapula Province, Zambia. A number of messages were conveyed: that fish-farming has introduced important changes in people's lives, that the promoters of the technology are keen to encourage women, and that men and women work together in harmony – '"my wife helps me with everything" says Stanislaus proudly' (ALCOM 1992b: 8). Behind this optimistic picture the promoters of fish-farming were concerned both with uneven adoption and with poor pond management. A number of questions recurred. Why do people dig ponds if they do not know how to manage them, and do not have, or do not realize they do not have, the required resources? Why do they devote time to constructing fish-ponds if the significance of the fish they produce is so small?

Problematic assumptions about motivation are far from unique to fish-farming. They illustrate more general tendencies among developers to rely on simple, universal explanations of behaviour. The tendencies can also be found within stove projects, for example. Household and individual interests are often conflated by stove project staff; cooking technology has non-material significance that often eludes the developers; it is assumed that 'beneficiaries' weigh up costs, benefits, and risks before making decisions. Such simplifications – which, we argue, are common throughout development agencies – are essential to account for project failures. They can also be converted into predictions of action that can greatly facilitate the process of producing impressive plans.

Before we enlarge on specific examples of these tendencies, we should acknowledge that people's actions are plainly constrained by both ability and capacity. Motivation can be fully understood only within the context of what is possible. In the case of fish-farming, access to land, labour, and a limited amount of cash are important before a farmer even considers whether or not to get involved. Obviously ability and inclination are closely linked: not only do you have to want to do something, you also need to believe that it is possible and appropriate. When people make decisions, a complex and self-reinforcing combination of both material and psychological factors plays a part.

In Luapula, there is perceived abundance of the resources required to start fish-farming. Population density is low (around ten people per square kilometre), and despite localized shortages, there is generally thought to be plenty of land. Most ponds are constructed by men using their own labour during periods of slack agricultural activity. Furthermore, there are few alternative economic opportunities, and people like eating fish. For the many potential adopters who have access to land and labour, the question 'why not dig?' might seem more appropriate than 'why dig?'. On the other hand, there are seasonally determined shortages and stresses that are felt strongly by vulnerable groups, such as older women without family to support them, the sick, and those with few assets. Such vulnerable groups are, therefore, seldom adopters of fish-farming. Indeed, most fish-farmers, although not from a recognizable 'elite', have certain characteristics in common. Adopters are more likely to be men, slightly better off, slightly better educated, and much more likely to be active participants in social and political activity than others in the community (Wijkstrom and Wahlstrom 1992;

Harrison et al. 1994). These facts are closely connected with one another and to some extent causally associated.

In Luapula, few women own ponds in their own right. This is due partly to constraints in access to land and labour, but also because in the past fish-farming has been promoted as a technology for men by men (see also Mbozi 1991; Woodford Berger 1987). The assumption that fish-farmers are men is compounded by the attitudes of both men and women in rural communities and by extensionists. The effect is that women are less likely to seek advice or to attempt to become pond-owners in their own right.

Ability and capacity also constrain potential stove-producers, but limits on their decisions take rather different forms. While labour and capital are equally vital to a potential stove-maker, pottery or metalwork skills, production facilities, and access to markets are also prerequisites to stove production. In Sri Lanka, pottery skills and production facilities are available to all living in potter households, irrespective of gender and age, although men control the use of equipment. Markets, labour, and capital are usually accessible only to men. Gaining access to marketing and credit, which tends to require regular contact with male non-relatives, is deemed inappropriate for women in potter households. In the government's national stove programme both project staff and male potters assumed that it was men who should control the household's involvement in the project. Although married couples shared labour inputs into stove production, it was nearly always men who sold the stoves and received payment from the government.

The belief that a particular new technology is a feasible option is partly the product of the associations that are made between the technology and ideas about appropriate behaviour. Fish-farming, for example, is seen as something that comes from outside, but that can be learned through contact with promoters. In this respect it is similar to other 'new' crops that are seen to be dependent on outside assistance and advice, such as hybrid maize and European vegetables. A recognizable group of farmers in rural Luapula identify themselves as part of 'development' through their associations with external institutions, a point pursued in detail in Chapter 7. They tend to grow 'new' crops – and to be fish-farmers. Thus willingness to adopt the technology and belief that it is a feasible option will be mutually reinforcing, as these farmers are more experienced in ensuring that they are visible to the agents of extension. In western Kenya too, those women potters who were persuaded to take part in the stove-making project had usually been involved in 'development' projects before, some of which were initiated by foreigners. Like some farmers in Luapula, they saw involvement in the project as developmental in itself, irrespective of whether they personally gained any income from it.

## Household motivation

The fact that few women in Luapula own fish-ponds in their own right does not mean that they do not take part in fish-farming. In some cases, women and children play an important role in pond management, as we illustrate below. The phenomenon is also common in other parts of Sub-Saharan Africa. The now widespread recognition of women's contribution to agricultural labour in the continent has been replicated in some ways when it comes to the farming of fish. As with agriculture, this is less frequently translated into action when it comes to organizing extension support. Equally importantly, female participation in pond management is used to equate farmer motivations with household motivations, as if they were one and the same thing, implying mutual and compatible interests within the household. In practice, there is more to motivation than this.

There are a number of problems with developers assuming that individual and household motivation are in harmony. First, although at any point in time it may be possible to identify a 'household' according to agreed definitions such as co-residence or joint economic management, this entity is unlikely to be fixed. In Luapula, the most common household form is that of two adults and their dependent children, with an average household size of four children. However, unstable marriages and frequent temporary migration result in a continual shifting of the reality behind this broad description. Thus the household of one man (given that households are identified by the male adult, if present) is likely to comprise different individuals from one period of time to the next. Marriage and divorce are, after the first marriage, fairly straightforward procedures in Luapula. Today's nuclear household may not be identical to tomorrow's. This is also plainly true outside Luapula, although the reasons for fluctuation may vary. In Sri Lanka, for example, divorce may be less common but household membership is also dynamic due to reproductive life-cycles. For example, brothers may live together with their parents after marriage but tend to split into separate households when the numbers of people become too large. In Luo households in western Kenya polygamy is reasonably common and household composition is consequently very different from Luapula or Sri Lanka. The endless variation and fluctuation should make us wary of generalized definitions of household across countries or localities and even within them.

Second, treating the household as a unit of joint utility is not warranted. Relations within households reflect individuals' priorities, cooperation, conflict, and negotiation. Household members may talk about these in different ways according to the place, but patterns clearly emerge. In Sri Lanka much of the stove manufacturing work is carried out by the female relatives of the main producer; one even claimed that she was happy to do so as her interests, her husband's interests, and her family's interests were identical. In contrast, women stove-makers in western Kenya often portrayed their own and their husband's interests in stark contrast; one woman said: 'A living husband is as good as a dead husband, except to do occasional ploughing if he has a bull. But they do make sure you don't get beaten up, that is unless they beat you themselves.' Given that, for example, unequal access to resources on the basis of gender exists in both places, how can we make sense of these different representations of household interests? The woman in Sri Lanka is talking about her/her husband's/her household's interests in opposition to non-household members, such as her neighbours or the government officials involved in the project. Her statement is true on one level, but on another level – when examining her interests in relation to other household members – structural inequalities emerge.

In Luapula, there will be many occasions when a decision, such as the decision to dig a fish-pond or to harvest it, is the agreed result of perceived mutual interests. But it would be wrong to assume that this is the norm. The transitory nature of many marriages in Luapula influences many men and women to adopt separate economic strat-egies, or at least ensure possibilities for independence in the event of changes in marital status. On the other hand, Christianity's emphasis on the nuclear family unit, combined with the existence of such units, militate against this. The result is an identifiable sexual division of labour according to certain tasks, and a flexible and varied control over the products of labour according to the nature and apparent stability of the marriage tie.

Households with the greatest annual income from their fish-farming were those in which the wives were taking a much less active part in pond management. In such households, women were also taking more independent strategies with regard to the production of other crops, and were farming maize or groundnuts independently. The separation of activities and budgets was partially a function of a greater cash orientation of production generally. Thus, even where pond location might suggest female participation in feeding and pond maintenance, this generally did not occur in practice.

In the following discussion, rather than assuming that farmer motivation for digging ponds is the same as that of other members of the family, we focus on the motivations of individual fish-farmers, usually men. The extent to which their motivations and interests co-incide with those of other members of their household needs to be empirically established and not assumed. The importance of different motivations for men and for women will be similarly varied.

## Why farm fish?

Material gain seems a reasonable explanation for adoption of a technology. This can of course mean many things. In the case of fish-farming these might include the acquisition of cash or goods, better diet, and increased access to land. For many development practitioners, the acquisition of cash is seen as the most important proxy for material gain. This in itself is doubtful: the meanings of money depend on the social context within which it is exchanged. Importantly, even if people do value material gain, this is not necessarily part of a recognizable calculation made in advance of action. In addition, a number of other factors may also be important, not all of which can be neatly read from behaviour. Where ALCOM and others assessing motivations for fish-farming have tried to understand these more nebulous factors, they have been lumped into the residual category 'status'. This category often has pejorative overtones. Attempts to disaggregate what is meant by 'status' are, however, rare despite the fact that it is plainly complicated and has diverse meanings.

In a survey conducted by ALCOM in 1988 (Wijkstrom 1991), it is argued that most small-scale fish-farmers view fish-farming as an 'economic' activity:

> Farmers want to earn an income from fish ponds. They see the ponds as a source of cash, and try to maximize their cash balance by keeping down their spending on pond culture. Thus raising tilapia in ponds, like crop-growing or livestock raising, is an economic activity; three out of every four farmers treat it as a commercial activity (1991: vi) ... Income is earned as tilapia is consumed or sold. Other purposes for engaging in fish culture are entirely subsidiary in nature and can be forgotten by the public planner and international aid official (1991: 4).

The survey reports that 76 per cent of practising farmers sell a part of the tilapia produced. Such a straightforward interpretation of farmers' reports simplifies reality. In contrast to the survey findings, fieldwork in the area revealed that very little cultured fish is in fact sold or exchanged

(Harrison et al. 1994). The fact that fish-farming is not, for most fish-farmers, an important income generator does not of course repudiate the suggestion that cash income is an important motivation. Indeed, many fish-farmers do report that cash income is an incentive for pond-digging. A few also speak specifically of 'profit and 'business'. For example, one farmer declared: 'With only one pond I cannot see a profit. That first pond is for consumption, but later I will dig more and then I may begin to see profit. One day the ponds will be for business and then I will keep one for the house which will not be for business.'

There are different ways of interpreting such claims. Opportunities for gaining cash income are relatively rare, so it seems reasonable that this should be an incentive. Perhaps. But Chapter 2 pointed to caution in such a simple assessment of motivation, for a number of reasons. First, making an informed assessment of inputs and outcomes when deciding whether to dig a fish-pond may be unusual. For one thing, as discussed above, the valuation of resources used is based on assumptions of abundance (for some adopters of fish-farming, if not for everybody). For another, expectations of outputs are usually vague. The farmer quoted above had harvested only one basket (about 10kg) from his single pond, but had no idea what he might get from the ponds he intended to build. He thought he would sell fish, but said that he was not certain to whom, especially as most people in his village fished in the river. Another farmer had constructed one pond two years previously from which he had never taken any fish. He was divorced and living alone but regularly visited by his children who, he said, often took fish from the pond without permission. He planned to build three further ponds 'for business'. Again, though, he had little idea of how many fish he might get out of the ponds and said he would be unable to control how many his children chose to take without asking.

Furthermore, those farmers who do have an idea of likely gains often have unrealistic expectations. For example, a farmer in one village had applied for a loan of 30,000 kwacha for buying fingerlings, maize bran and cement. He explained: 'The loan can be repaid at a rate of 8,000 kwacha a year. This will be no problem with five ponds, each one giving me 20 kilos which could be sold for 2,000 kwacha.' This calculation is not entirely convincing. While hand-sized fish sold at the time for approximately 100 kwacha/kg, without the facilities to transport fish to market the farmer would have to have sold from the pond-side. Village prices are much more strongly influenced by availability of cash and customers on any one day. Moreover, the estimated yield is unlikely. Problems of over-production of fingerlings meant that much of his harvest consisted of very small fish, which would fetch a lower price.

At the time of the discussion, he had gained a total income from his five ponds of 100 kwacha and most earlier harvests had been given away in the hope that later his friends would 'remember' him.

Critically, prices vary immensely according to context. As noted in Chapter 2, a view of economic decision-making that adheres to a strict opposition between 'economic' (implying money or a calculated substitute) and other exchanges is excessively narrow. This is particularly salient in the imperfectly commoditized economy of Luapula.

The role of farmed fish when exchanged is complex. It would be wrong to suggest that when the fish is exchanged for something else it becomes a 'commodity' with a price that is somehow independent of social context. Fish are sold, but the price varies according to the relationship of the seller to the buyer, or according to the circumstances of the transaction. For example, when a farmer sold 450 fingerlings for only 220 kwacha (as opposed to the common 5 kwacha per fingerling), he explained that he did not charge more because the fingerlings were going to be eaten, not farmed. Another farmer gave some fish to a group of men who had assisted him in digging. He insisted, however, that this did not constitute payment. He was relatively new to the area and did not have enough mature cassava. In addition, fish-farmers who harvest fish for relish (that is to provide an accompaniment to the staple food, *nshima*) often obtain significant amounts of fish from elsewhere as well. On several occasions people gave away large proportions of their meagre harvests. Clearly such exchanges cannot be neatly valued and allocated to the realm of commodity or gift. There is not a hard-and-fast boundary between the two because behind each of the exchanges are the personal histories and relationships of the people involved. Even though cash transactions may be involved, these are not simple and transparent.

The claims to have adopted fish-farming 'for business', as identified in ALCOM's survey and observed in fieldwork, were widespread. Arguably, however, they reflect a more general symbolic distinction, common in Luapula, based on whether people or activities are seen as more or less 'developed'. When individuals were asked to rank themselves and their neighbours according to well-being, most put 'farmers' at the top of their classifications, that is, those who grew maize for sale but were not necessarily rich. 'Farmers' were 'modern-minded', were visited by agricultural extensionists and used purchased inputs for agricultural production. Others, who grew cassava and groundnuts for subsistence only, were not labelled as 'farmers' at all, even if they were wealthy (for example, through owning assets or controlling land). Well-being was, therefore, associated with development rather than wealth. 'Farmers' would be more likely to be labelled 'progressive' by developers as well. For some, though not all, self-identification with such progressiveness is highly valued. Fish-farmers who spoke of 'business' were also proud to identify themselves as part of this progressive culture, a point to be pursued in the following chapters.

If people do not dig ponds for cash, why do they dig them? Among all farmers (without the emphasis above), the most commonly stated reason for adopting fish-farming was that of household food consumption. Fish is a highly favoured food, but its availability is unpredictable and unreliable. It may be seen as a source of food for general household consumption, but its role in household diets is relatively minor. Pond production accounts for a much smaller proportion of household fish consumption than that from other sources. In addition, fish-farmers who harvest most frequently for relish are often already obtaining significant amounts of fish from elsewhere. The nutritional impact on such households is felt less strongly than that on households that are, though less successful in fish-farming, without access to other sources of fish. The fish-farming households with fewest alternative sources of fish are those headed by women. This is both because they are less likely to fish in the river (no women were found to own fishing-nets and, although some women fish with baskets, this is relatively rare), and because they tend to have a lower disposable income with which to buy fish. For this reason, the few fish gained from the pond are likely to be of greater significance to a lower-income female pond-owner than to a male farmer.

For people with the least access to fish, the marginal benefits of adopting fish-farming are greater. Having poor access to fish often coincides with other factors influencing vulnerability, such as fewer income-generating opportunities, lower availability of labour, and a perception of exclusion from or irrelevance of external assistance. For the most productive fish-farmers who are in more regular contact with extension, the fish they eat from their ponds form a smaller proportion of overall consumption than those bought or caught in rivers.

Given the apparently minor role that cultured fish play in household diets, alternative explanations for the role of pond fish as food need to be sought. Fish is popular, but its availability is highly seasonal. Fish is always among the first three favourite relish ingredients, along with chicken and meat. However, people eat very little of these foods. Over the year, regularity of consumption of different foods varies according to their availability (from the market or gathered) and the economic status of the household. Fish-farming thus has a potential to fill seasonal relish gaps. For example, although there are enormous variations, the wet season from November to March is considered to be difficult for staple food consumption (cassava takes longer to dry), and the dry season from April to October is worse for relish as leaves dry out and less wild food is available.

For many, the attraction of a fish-pond for relish is parallel to that of owning livestock. The majority of people may go for several months without eating any meat at all but the slaughtering of animals is both an important sign of respect (*umuchinshi*) to visitors and a key part of major social events such as funerals. Thus neither meat nor fish will increase overall food consumption, but it is useful to have both on hand at all times for when they are needed. Reliance on marketed fish and on rivers is unsatisfactory: fish may be available to buy when there is no cash, or fish may be required to show respect to a visitor when it is inconvenient to go to the river. When these factors are combined with the attraction of being able to eat fish when cassava leaves have become too monotonous, the potential of fish as a source of food is clearly appealing.

Fish-ponds may also have a significance to farmers as a form of asset contributing to security that is greater than their immediate usefulness as a source of fish for food or cash. In communities where possession of material assets is limited, such security, whether real or imagined, can be very important. This significance takes two forms: the fish in the pond may be important to meet contingencies, and the pond itself may be regarded as an asset. Several farmers, when asked about their refusal (after as long as four years) to drain their ponds, had justifications along the lines of: 'I don't want to lose the fish – I am saving them for an emergency.' That emergency might take many forms: an unexpected visitor or a funeral, or slightly more predictable 'special events', such as the need to buy school uniforms for children. In one case, a fish-farmer drained a pond to raise the money to pay his fine in an adultery case. In another, the pond was harvested after three years to celebrate the return of an estranged wife.

The fish-pond itself also serves as an asset. In Luapula the phenomenon of people digging more and more ponds before seeing any benefit from the first one was common. For many, the fact of current lack of income is less important than potential, possibly many years in the future. A young farmer in one village had nine ponds, but complained that because he had no livestock or vegetable garden, he was unable to feed the fish properly. Nevertheless, he explained that it was better to dig now while he was strong: 'The food for the fish will come later, but it may not be so easy to dig a pond later.' The constraints he faced are relevant; he had few assets but his own labour and there were limited options for him to diversify. For example, vegetables or maize production required cash he did not have, while the digging of ponds is fitted around other activities and does not require cash inputs. He obtained fingerlings from a neighbour in return for some labouring.

Such views of fish-farming as involving the creation of an asset to be used far in the future, or left to children, are closely associated with people's perceptions of their own security of tenure. In the Central African Republic, a reported impediment to aquaculture development is the impermanence of villages: because people shift every few years, they may be less inclined to dig ponds (Moehl 1989). This is not so important in Luapula, where over the last twenty years there has been a reduction in the amount people travel in search of fresh bush to clear. The tendency to move less frequently is associated with changes in inheritance practices in Luapula. There is more reason to leave something permanent and tangible for children.

One aspect of the permanence of fish-ponds and the security of tenure currently associated with them is their role in claiming land that then may be used for other purposes. As particular types of land increase in value, control over them becomes more important. In particular, rules of access for *dambos* (which are low-lying wetlands) are less clear than they are for bush land. Given this lack of clarity, farmers recognize the potential of a more permanent structure such as a fish-pond (as opposed to, for example, a vegetable garden) in claiming land. In one village, a number of farmers said that they were unable to dig fish-ponds, because all the best land had been taken. Meanwhile, one farmer had started the construction of eight ponds without finishing any of them. When asked about this, he explained that they served as a means of securing an area of potentially fertile land near the river. He hoped that the ponds would one day produce fish, but was happy that they would also give him control of land that would later be used for a vegetable garden. In another village, a farmer started the construction of five ponds over two years, digging all of them initially to a depth of only a few inches. In this case, control of water to irrigate vegetables was an important consideration. Where ponds are used to claim land, the production of fish may be only an incidental benefit.

In summary, although it is true that some farmers want to earn an income from their ponds, the decision to adopt fish-farming does not arise unambiguously from this. To the extent that fish culture supplies fish that might otherwise have been purchased, and/or provides additional income, and as far as more nebulous motives such as increased security can be given a value, aquaculture could be said to have economic rationales for small-scale farmers. Such rationales cannot, however, be neatly correlated with the acquisition or saving of cash income. For one thing, knowledge and prediction of cash income and expenditure are often minimal. Furthermore, the meanings attached to transactions vary according to context. Finally, local use of the language of 'profit' and 'business' illustrates the incorporation of certain individuals into a particular discourse, as much as they derive from Western economic meanings of the term. Simplistically this could be viewed as 'status'. But there are clearly many ways of gaining status, giving generously, for example, being one that is not necessarily neatly compatible with the status gained from profit in business.

## Why make or use new stoves?

Just as involvement in fish-farming is not the result of a purely economic assessment of gains, benefits, and risks, those agreeing or refusing to make stoves within a development project are influenced and constrained by a complex set of social, political, and economic circumstances. Although it was assumed by project staff in Sri Lanka that income generation would be the benefit that would attract potters to take part in the programme, their decisions involved far more than predictions of profit. The Ministry of Power and Energy extension workers approached rural-based potters in the early 1980s and asked them to start stove manufacture. The government offered to teach them how to make the new ceramic stoves and promised to buy a fixed amount each month. Twenty potters were also offered a grant of Rs. 10,000 to upgrade their equipment (about £300 at the time). Most agreed to join the programme, partly because obstructing local government officials may have been seen as politically risky. Meanwhile, despite the material enticements, some remained sceptical.

A minority of potters were reluctant to join the government's programme for a complicated mixture of reasons, and not all of these can be easily reduced to material interest. They were influenced by one, or more, of the following. First, some younger members of potter households were searching for alternative employment in order to escape the caste identification of working as a potter. This reduced the level of family labour that potential stove-makers thought may be available to produce stoves in addition to their usual products. Second, having to respond to the government's orders would compromise their highly valued position of independence and freedom from outside interference. For some, an important source of their pride as potters was their self-employment. To be employed, in contrast, was demeaning. Third, many potter households live in villages or neighbourhoods entirely populated by other potter households. They were aware that if they developed a special relationship with the government it might cause social tensions between households. (Conversely, setting themselves socially above other households may have been an incentive for others.) While the prospect of generating more income from stove production was enticing for many, other values clearly influenced potential stove-makers.

For those who did agree to take part in the government's programme, many of their fears were realized. Many potters did become frustrated by their dependence on government officers, some of whom behaved with upsetting arrogance. Also, family labour often became insufficient for the high levels of stove production demanded by the government. As a consequence, potters resorted to employing waged labourers, a departure from the typical social organization of potter 'communities', which was previously characterized by relative political egalitarianism and economic equality (Kirk 1984: 17). This relative equality was transformed when a relatively small number of stove-makers became hugely wealthy. Considerable tensions also emerged within potter 'communities' not only as a result of stove-making potters accruing enormous incomes, but due to the steady stream of visitors to the potter workshops. Neighbours who were not involved in the programme, in both potter and other caste households, reported resentment at being 'neglected'. Their hostility then caused some stove-making potters to abandon the manufacture of stoves.

Material gain changes relationships, but the money itself may not be of central importance. In a village in Matale, Sri Lanka, one stove-making couple belonged to the only potter caste. They claimed that the present generation of villagers were more concerned about caste than their parents were. According to the husband, their stove-making enterprise had a far greater significance than simply the money it generated. Equally, or more, important was the apparent respect now given to him by higher-caste *Goyigama* neighbours. He pointed out that while some financial security allowed him to disengage from labouring, it was the visitors and association with progress, rather than his increase in income alone, that challenged the social order.

The Sri Lankan stove-producers were hesitant about working as government employees and were, therefore, not merely making financial calculations. Producers in western Kenya reported non-material motives for their actions too. The people chosen as 'beneficiaries' were women farmers organized into women's groups, who also had some pottery skills. Early evaluations of this 'income-generation' programme reveal that some of the women's groups who were first approached refused to make stoves because they thought trading in crops would be less trouble (Crewe 1989). They had more experience at trading, had better-established contacts, and could transport agricultural produce more easily than heavy, breakable ceramic stoves. New stoves were a new product that would require considerable training in both manufacture and promotion. They were not interested in this, particularly since the previous experience of foreign development agencies in the area was mostly negative.

On the other hand, over time a few groups of potters in Kenya invested huge amounts of time into the Intermediate Technology-run stove programme despite relatively low financial gain for at least the first five years. When asked why they had committed so much time, some replied 'because we want to progress', or 'it is a way for us to gain confidence', or 'because we trust you'. The confidence was gained not by the generation of income alone, although it eventually played its part, but because Intermediate Technology employed other members of the village and taught these employees new skills, and became well known in the sub-location. Local politicians visited them and pledged their support. Despite the inconvenience caused by their numerous visitors, many of whom came as part of the project and were given a drink if not something to eat, the employees valued these visits. The presence of visitors, especially white ones, in a compound was symbolic of participation in 'development'; to refuse them, or their project, would have meant turning away from progress.

Deciding whether or not to produce stoves involves complicated responses to non-material values. The use of stoves also concerns more than a question of money. Stove project-planners have tended to assume that wood-burning stoves that consume less fuelwood will be popular with cooks because either they can reduce the expenditure on fuelwood, a benefit that is more likely to affect urban households as they purchase most of their fuel, or they can save time spent collecting fuelwood, which tends to benefit rural households since they gather free fuel supplies but can spend the time saved on income-earning activities. Such a focus on material motivation, and more specifically the significance of cash income, should be treated with caution. Non-material factors plainly influence whether and how much cooks prefer one stove to another, such as how much heat it generates or whether the wood has to be chopped smaller (see Chapter 5). Although some people report that saving money on fuel is an important advantage, a large number of Sri Lankan cooks express a preference for new stoves over the three-stone fire for other reasons: because they are cleaner and safer, more comfortable to use, or cook faster, which frees up time for other household work. Some keep a wood-burning stove, but rarely use it, alongside an electric or kerosene stove in case their source of so-called modern fuel becomes unavailable or their new equipment breaks. Others make the purchase because stoves are being promoted by their women's group as 'modern', and owning one signals modernity and moving up in the world.

Time is critically important to the majority of women. It is plainly not a commodity with a purely material exchange value, however. Time freed up by a stove project cannot be spent earning money unless income-earning opportunities are also available and prioritized by women. Even if opportunities can be made, women do not always have control over their time. As we saw in Chapter 5, women using new stoves in Kenya said that they conceal from their husbands the fact that they spend less time cooking and collecting fuel, as otherwise they would insist that the wives spend more time labouring on their land. They may not engage in new income-earning activities even if they were made available, because it could make their husbands suspicious. But a time-saving technology can be valued by women even where other more remunerative work is not accessible or possible. More time for, as examples, resting, making social contacts, or even agitating for changes in government policy, are more important than an increase in income to women in some contexts, particularly if they cannot be sure that they would retain control over any extra money in any case.

Some economists working on stove programmes have suggested that the 'payback period' is an important factor for potential users when deciding whether to buy a new stove (see p. 37). They imply that the prospective customer calculates the cost, the monetary savings, and the length of time it will take to recoup the investment. Some have claimed that potential purchasers will not buy stoves that have a payback period of longer than three months. Such generalizations about decision-making are unconvincing: meanings, values, and priorities are obviously very different between and within places. We have shown that non-monetary costs or benefits can influence decisions about whether to buy and use a particular stove. Rather than merely calculating the return on their money, some cooks buy them, for example, because they 'believe in development'.

## Conclusion

Attempts by the promoters of fish-farming to understand why farmers adopt aquaculture have focused on fish-farming as the key variable. Similarly, stove-promoters assume that decisions made about whether to make or use stoves centre around stoves and fuel. This underrates the significance of the wider social context within which farmers, potters, and cooks make decisions. For the promoters of fish-farming, fish-farming is the central and most important thing on which to focus. For the farmers themselves, it is often a rather unimportant aspect of their lives. Stove-users may care about the performance of their stoves, but they are far from central to their lives. While stove-promoters treat cooking as if it were their main occupation, in the realm of work the users are usually more interested in, for example, food-processing, farming, and business. Farmers do not necessarily farm fish for cash: they dig ponds to secure their land, to vary their diet, or to associate themselves with progress. Some potters avoid stove production to retain their highly valued independence, while some stove-users keep buying new stoves because they are symbolic of development. Importantly, too, probing these motivations is problematic because they are seldom the product of a simple calculation.

Plainly, we are not the first to question the value of isolating economics from its social setting or the primacy of materialist motivation. Since Mauss wrote *The Gift* in 1924 and proposed a holistic approach to exchange where religious, legal, moral, and economic phenomena are taken into account, substantivist economists have rejected reductionist materialism (Dalton 1961; Sahlins 1976; Polanyi 1977). More recently there have been attempts to find indicators of poverty and wealth that are a better reflection of the complexity of people's lives than simple income-based statistics (for example Chambers 1988; Kabeer 1997; Sen 1995; UNDP 1995). This work draws attention to the importance of factors such as vulnerability and security, political freedom, a sense of autonomy, and an ability to make choices. Of course all of these things are closely tied to material conditions, but not necessarily determined by them.

Such academic and applied work appears, however, to have had a minimal impact when it comes to the practical realities of development planning in which a specialized (usually technical) focus carries far greater weight than any attempt at holism. In Chapter 2 we suggested that developers' assumptions about economics and motivation are not flawed in all instances, but that they are too mechanistic, presenting an overly stylized and limiting view of why people do things, leaving little room for inconsistency, maverick behaviour, and non-materialist values. Developers make generalizations about why beneficiaries behave as they do because they need to simplify and categorize. Furthermore, if they hold that the acquisition of money and the goods it can buy is the main aim of the recipients of their aid, and that they are guided by an aspiration to adopt a Western lifestyle, then in their eyes the aims of modernization are validated.

If we were to reflect on our own reasons for doing things, or those of our friends and family, the evidence of complex motivations guiding fish-farmers, stove-users, and potters is not surprising: people are less predictable than development planners are under pressure to think they are. If we were to consider the actions of the 'developers' themselves, we would find that within a so-called Western market economy, materialist explanations of behaviour are insufficient once again. Conversely, privileging ideologies, morals, or values above materialist explanations is also problematic. Hancock (1989) bounces from one to the other. He argues that highly paid consultants in multilateral agencies work in development for the money and/or career prospects; low-paid voluntary sector workers, in contrast, tend to give altruistic or humanitarian reasons for working in the 'Third World'. It is undoubtedly clear that staff within voluntary agencies, such as Intermediate Technology, are 'well-motivated'. They are often hardworking, and conscientious, and say that they are committed to the idea of changing poor people's lives for the better. But this could equally be said about those working in multilateral agencies. Many, in fact, claim very similar motives for choosing international development as a career. In either case, what people say about their motivation should not be taken at face value. People may be explaining their behaviour with a *post hoc* rationalization; there is no logical reason for assuming that their explanation points to a paramount cause.

If people's own explanations of their actions cannot be easily translated into reflections on causality, can we deduce the motivations from the actions themselves? We have seen from the case studies on fish-farming and stoves that people's readiness to get involved in development can be partly informed by material expectations, but that these combine with non-material influences. Similarly, those working in development agencies are pushed and pulled by a combination of limits and opportunities – economic, social, moral, and political. On the one hand there can be a perceived pressure on consultants to say what they think the employers want to hear because it increases the chances of further employment. On the other hand, consultants often refuse to appear cooperative, even when future employment by particular organizations is jeopardized as a result.

In other contexts, with other potential employers, the temptation to behave cooperatively may be far more tempting. The temptation consists, however, of various elements, including travelling in new places, working with new people, or learning new skills, as well as earning high fees or per diems. Individuals within Intermediate Technology (and undoubtedly other organizations) respond in different ways to such opportunities. Some refuse to carry out any consultancy on the grounds that it contravenes the aim of strengthening local innovation and expertise, and may involve working for an organization whose policy they do not agree with. At the other end of the scale, there are those who happily carry out contract work for other agencies, because it is an opportunity to exert influence. Plainly money alone does not drive the behaviour of those working in development, any more than it does that of fish-farmers, potters, or stove-users.

We would argue not only that materialism is insufficient for explaining why people take certain actions, but that to search for any functionalist motive that explains all behaviour is futile. People do not engage in a perpetual assessment of how to further their own employment prospects, gain more cash, expand their power base, or elevate their status. It is clear that sometimes people make choices that promote their social, economic, or political positions, but at other times the consequences of their behaviour work directly against their own perceived interests.

It could be countered that when people appear to act against their interests they are merely trying to appear altruistic in order to gain recognition, or they are making mistakes in their calculations, or the observer has misunderstood. But such assertions are part of an argument that greatly simplifies human motivation. Since we do not appear to be aware of calculating the potential profit of an action before taking it, the determining selfish drive must be largely unconscious. If the drive is unconscious, and its existence must be an *a priori* assumption, then such speculation about motivation can never easily be resolved. We do not deny that behaviour is structured but since individuals' histories are always part of the equation, predicting behaviour out of their particular contexts will always be uncertain.

Simple interests, then, do not drive behaviour. In the next chapter we will examine another set of ideas about what motivates the 'beneficiaries' of development.

# CHAPTER 7

# Cultural Barriers: the Triumph of Tradition over Modernity

'Cultural barriers' and gaps in local knowledge are often seen to impede the progress of development interventions. Gaps in knowledge, it is assumed, may be overcome with efforts such as extension, technical assistance, and training. 'Cultural barriers', often viewed as a triumph of tradition over modernity, are potentially more intransigent. As we argued in Chapter 2, 'cultural barriers' are characterized in FAO and Intermediate Technology as the antithesis of modern rationality, the possible explanation for apparent failures. They consist of breaks and inconsistencies in what would otherwise be perfectly rational behaviour. In FAO, the controlling forces of obligation, reciprocity, and levelling mechanisms are portrayed as obstacles to rationality. In Intermediate Technology, barriers range from male dominance to an undefined cultural conservatism of 'local' peoples.

While ideas about culture are vaguely articulated and rarely given specific characteristics within Intermediate Technology, assumptions in FAO about culture are expressed in some detail. In the case of the latter, barriers are thought to take a number of forms, but are often expressed as a conflict between values of individualism and those of communalism. This conflict is supposedly manifest in obligations to distribute the product of individual labour, and in so-called levelling mechanisms that control those who do not comply.

The developers' conception of 'cultural barriers' reviewed in Chapter 2 embodies the fairly simple view that social structure drives practice. Speculation about cultural 'barriers' and their articulation as conflict between individuals and communities also embodies oversimplified notions of their supposed constituents: obligation, reciprocity, and levelling mechanisms. These are treated as if they were one and the same thing, fulfilling the same function in their control of accumulation. Together it is implied that they make up the – almost tangible – entity of 'social structure' or 'local culture'. Although they are obviously related, there are differences in what these constituents mean and how they operate at the local level.

The main aim of this chapter is, therefore, to unpack the evidence for the conflict between individuals and communities, and the triumph of tradition over modernity, with particular reference to FAO working in Chibote and Monga. In so doing, we hope to question the credibility of the dichotomy itself. First, we develop an observation from the previous chapter: that people internalize, and selectively use, particular forms of the discourse of modernity. Second, we go on to look in more detail at the supposed conflict between individuals and communities, initially through a discussion about reciprocity, and then through an analysis of supposed levelling mechanisms, including witch-craft. One of the reasons stressed by ALCOM for its limited apparent success with fish-farming was the problem of 'cultural barriers'. It is for this reason that this project offers rich empirical examples of how assumptions about culture are played out in practice.

Finally, we will examine another assumption about culture that pervades development agencies. Culture is conceptualized as if it exists among the local people with whom development agencies aim to work. Since the whole process of development continues to rely on theories of modernization, and traditional culture and modernity are opposed, it stands to reason that 'they' have cultural barriers while 'Westerners' are guided by modern rationality. We will argue, however, that culture is a process that everyone is part of. Culture in the 'West' is often equated in popular discourse with creative work, such as fine art or the theatre. But it is plainly broader than that. We argue that culture is the creation (or re-creation) of ideologies, rules, and practices that allow people to make sense of the world in both different and shared ways. Evidence of such cultural forms within Intermediate Technology demonstrates that culture is something everyone does and has, and that it emerges within all development organizations as much as it does among the recipients of their aid.

## The reinvention of modernity

Ranger (1983) has argued that in colonial Africa, Europeans set out to codify and promulgate traditions, transforming flexible customs into hard prescription. Based on their own model of tradition marked by inflexibility, the assertion by many that African society was inflexible, tradition-bound, and living in a framework of hierarchical status was often intended as a compliment. 'Everyone sought to tidy up and make more comprehensible the infinitely complex situation which they held to be a result of the "untraditional" chaos of the nineteenth century' (1983: 249). Ranger suggests that the reality was far from the rigid tribal identities invented by Europeans, and that Africans moved in and out of different identities, defining themselves at different times according to tribe, clan, or chief. However, Africans themselves manipulated and invented traditions in different ways to suit their own purposes: Europeans believed Africans belonged to tribes, so Africans built tribes to belong to. This creation and manipulation of tradition worked in a way that hardened the vested interests at the time of its codification. Thus tradition was used by the young against the old, and by men against women.

In Luapula, the use and articulation of notions of tradition and modernity shift according to people's different perspectives. As seen in Chapter 6, among the many influences that may lead people to dig fish-ponds is their self-identification with 'modernity'. This modernity may involve many things, from owning a radio to speaking English. An important part of it is the use of introduced farming methods such as inorganic fertilizer, and a distance from 'traditional' practices, particularly those connected with magic and witchcraft. As a result of this, some people appear keen to distance themselves from other villagers whom they, like the developers, see as fettered by custom and tradition. Thus 'ignorance' is not simply a lack of knowledge – it implies that people have superstitious and false beliefs. This distancing is not simple and unilinear. The concepts of modernity and tradition are developed as hybrids, containing elements of beliefs and practices that are ostensibly rejected. The terms on which the distinction between 'traditional' and 'modern' is made vary. In particular, self-identification by some people with modernity does not necessarily preclude the incorporation of beliefs that might be construed by others, or even by themselves in a different context, as traditional (such as witchcraft or magic).

For example, a farmer who was one of the early adopters of fish-farming also had a vegetable garden, which had been developed with the help of the government Adaptive Research Planning Team. He had two ponds and was building a third, on which he intended to keep ducks. He said:

> The vegetable garden is like a grocery store; you can just keep on taking from it and it keeps you going. The fish-ponds are an investment. They are for my children, who are our African pension. These are very good things which you people have taught all of us – how to do modern farming and really be coming up. I want to have so many ponds that there is a canned fish industry in this place.

On the same day, he was asked if he could throw any light on local gossip about a man who had been banished from the area for using sorcery. The response was evasive: 'Oh no, I don't know about those kind of things. I am really a stranger here; I don't know what these people do, about their traditions. They do these things perhaps, but it is not for me.' Some months later, however, he attributed a bout of illness to the sorcery of a jealous neighbour.

Another farmer also associated himself strongly with 'modern' farming. He explained that those farmers who did not know how to grow maize with fertilizer were 'backward', that they were 'only subsistence'. On the other hand, he had no problems with combining inorganic fertilizer with *muti* (herbal medicines used for both plants and people) to use on his maize. He explained that this was good magic, and could work alongside the fertilizer.

While values of modernity may be invoked in particular circumstances for particular purposes, the same is true for tradition. For example, the Chief in Monga area, Chief Mabumba, attempted to use 'tradition' to legitimize his authority. He had become Chief in May 1992 following the suspected murder of the previous Chief Mabumba. During the dry season of 1992 he held a series of meetings in the area at which fines were imposed for non-attendance. The meetings served as a forum for the new Chief to stress the need to return to 'traditional values', including that of *mulasa* or tribute labour. Every able-bodied man and woman was expected to carry poles to Mabumba village to assist in the construction of a new school. In Monga village, the complaints about the Chief focused on the way in which he was using tradition to emphasize his power, but at the same time was being selective in what he was calling tradition.

It is clear from the above discussion that people's actions are not easily separable into a circumscribed social context of 'the village', which is unrelated to anything else. Development activities are not introduced into a vacuum, into communities that have been isolated from external influences. A memory of previous interventions, whether colonial or government- or donor-supported development projects, has a profound influence on the way in which local people respond to the latest one.

Pigg (1992) argues that in Nepal the concept of *bikas* or 'development' has been internalized and appropriated by local people, so that its meaning may differ but is not separate from that promulgated in international institutions: 'There are Nepalis who lay claim to development's vision of society. Nepalis do not perceive the ideology of development to be culturally foreign: they come to know it through specific social relationships' (Pigg 1992: 495).

In the process of interpreting the ideology of development, people learn to make certain associations and draw contrasts. Thus a number of material things are important: new breeds of goat, water-pumps, electricity. In addition, though, the use of many English words and phrases characterizes the discourse of development, and people are keen to adopt the polarity *bikas*/village in order to orient themselves in national society. What are at stake in the adoption of these terms are potential sources of wealth, power, and upward mobility: 'everyone wants a piece of the development pie' (Pigg 1992: 511).

Symbols of development and modernity may vary from place to place, but their importance is clear for many engaged in aid projects. In Kajiado District, Kenya, Intermediate Technology's housing programme staff asked a women's group whether they would like oval or rect-angular houses. One member replied: 'We may be Maasai but we are modern Maasai. Of course we want modern rectangular houses.'

Development and modernity can be linked to foreignness, but the association is not universal. In western Kenya, stove programme staff found that people associated new *Maendeleo* (development) stoves directly with foreigner-led development. In Sri Lanka, in contrast, de-velopment discourse in stove programmes is more obviously a hybrid of foreign influence, national ideologies, and individual interpretation. For example, new stoves were promoted by Sarvodaya as part of its Buddhist-inspired vision of self-sufficiency and community development. The government raised funds for stoves by arguing that they would generate income and bring environmental benefits. These aims were the product of both national priorities and an assessment of donor preferences. The stove-users, meanwhile, used the new stoves because they saw them as 'modern'. Users, or producers for that matter, did not neatly bracket modern with foreign. Most probably never realized that foreigners were involved with the programme, because the stoves were initially promoted by government extension officers and later sold through the market.

In Luapula too, certain farmers wish to be associated with develop-ment and progressiveness. This has deep historical roots. Moore and Vaughan (1994) note for neighbouring Northern Province that letters from aspiring 'progressive farmers' in the 1940s illustrate how a dis-course of development had become a shared discourse between colonial officials and certain groups of African men. They argue that 'it should not surprise us then, that when people respond to new development schemes and policies, they bring their history with them' (1994: 234).

In Luapula Province, from the days of colonial rule through to the 1990s, there has been a profusion of schemes and projects aiming to enhance the well-being of the population and to ensure sustainable development. One aspect of the legacy of development is the hope for and expectation of loans. The rationale for giving credit usually lies in its function of easing bottlenecks in an otherwise economically viable enterprise. In Luapula it is unlikely that fish-farming would be viable in this sense. Therefore, the potential ability of farmers to repay loans is very low. Nevertheless, requests for loans were rife. Loans have been equated with modernity, with being progressive. Farmers perceive that to take out a loan is part of being developed, and that loans themselves are of considerable benefit. At interest rates of 10 per cent, with inflation running at more than 150 per cent, loans must seem like a very attractive proposition. Of eight farmers in one village, each applying for loans of more than 150,000 kwacha from the Ministry of Youth and Sports, only one had an income of more than 6,000 kwacha from his fish-farming during the previous year, and none had any idea of likely yields the following year. The rationale from the ministry was that the money could be used to buy equipment such as shovels and wheelbarrows. The farmers themselves recognized that loans for fish-farming might be a cover for other activities. The money might be invested in other activities (seed and fertilizer for vegetables) which would then go some way towards earning money to repay the loan.

The 'development effect' is widespread. It is influential in decisions about the adoption of new technologies and subsequent behaviour. Not all farmers who adopted fish-farming did so in expectation of assistance, be it a loan or a gift. This expectation remains, however, one motivating factor in a stagnant economy where the government and donor activity have for many years represented an (albeit unreliable) source of funds. New projects do not enter into virgin territory as far as local people are concerned; there is a local memory of interventions through which people adapt both their behaviour and their language. But does this adaptation involve complete rejection of what is labelled 'tradition'? Not necessarily, as we aim to show in the next section.

## Individuals and communities in Luapula Province

A frequently posed dichotomy in studies of rural development contrasts the persistence of indigenous social relations and values against the penetration of market forces, characterized as 'modernity'. Luapula is no exception. In Luapula, the apparent conflict between individual and community orientation has been the subject of some speculation (Poewe 1978, 1981; Gatter 1990; J. Gould 1989). Such speculation is partially rooted in the problematic assumption that there is an inevitable trade-off (rather than complementarity) between doing things for one-self as opposed to for other people. Well-being is viewed in terms of accumulation over a relatively short period of time. The evidence from Chapter 6 supports alternative ways of viewing the dynamic between individual and community orientation. In particular, people may take actions, including those helping others, that cannot be neatly attributed to one or the other orientation.

Matriliny, and either its persistence or its decline in the face of forces such as the development of capitalism, has formed a central theme for a number of writers. Poewe's work on matrilineal ideology in the province (1978, 1981) has explored the theme in the context of fishing communities in the vicinity of Lake Mweru. She argues that the 'central structural contradiction inherent in matriliny' involves a conflict between the forces and relations of production, as she puts it, between productive individualism and distributive communalism (1981). The penetration of a market economy into the province during the twentieth century has led some people (most often men) to adopt alternative ideologies that support individual accumulation and limit distribution to the nuclear household. In particular, she argues that businessmen and progressive farmers have tended to join Protestant religious movements such as Seventh Day Adventists and Jehovah's Witnesses.

This theme is developed by one of the ALCOM studies in Luapula (de Kartzow et al. 1992). The discussion extrapolates from Poewe, although her analysis was based on fieldwork in what is now Nchelenge district, the one part of Luapula in which ALCOM did not operate because there were no fish-farmers. However, the ALCOM study is much more sweeping than that of Poewe. It states:

> In Luapula, the two ideological systems differ on the question of distribution of products. The traditional kinship system is based on distribution of resources, and mutual obligations to exchange goods and services. Equity is a practical policy, achieved through levelling mechanisms. The funda-mentalist Protestant ideology favours individualistic strategies for controlling and accumulating wealth and resources.
>
> Kinship obligations may hinder development for individual households. If a household is economically successful in agriculture, the extended family expects generosity. Accusation of witchcraft is frequently used against people who try to break with the expected norms (de Kartzow et al. 1992: 25).

It is certainly true that many of the external manifestations of matriliny, most obviously the practices of uxorilocal marriage and ex-tended brideservice (that is, where men contribute labour to their in-laws), are declining. With this, the economic role of the matrikin is less clear. However, the implications of this for social relations can be extrapolated only if kinship is viewed as a last vestige of older social relations rather than a variably important part of current ones. In the 1950s, Cunnison wrote about the importance of the matrilineage (the *cikota*) and clans (*mukowa*) as basic units of social organization: lineages are the focal point of individual interest as regards such valued institutions as succession to office, inheritance, and exogamy, but kinship extends out from them to clans and other lineages through bonds of perpetual kinship (Cunnison 1959: 242).

Cunnison maintained that for Luapulans, ethnic categories of 'tribe', such as Chishinga and Aushi, have less significance than clan affiliation, which is more important, and historically precedent to such notions as tribe. A clan is a grouping of lineages. Economically, it is an institution of distribution inasmuch as somebody from the same clan is classificatory kin and entitled to hospitality and respect. In present-day Luapula, clan identity and hospitality towards clan members is important. On the other hand, there is also a growing tendency for the primary unit of economic identification to be the more restricted conjugal family. There is tension between the demands of the wider family and the smaller productive and reproductive unit of the conjugal family.

The dichotomy between productive individualism and distributive communalism is, however, overdrawn in Poewe's work (and the ALCOM study that caricatures it). The idea that individualism is a new phenomenon eroding traditional structures is unconvincing. The tension between production, which is individualistic, and distributive needs is probably a continuity with the past. Gatter, in his research with the Adaptive Research Planning Team (ARPT) (1990: 193), distinguishes between 'productionism' and 'distributionism'. However, he argues that rather than seeing them as operating at some pre-conscious, ideological level and determining the subjectivities of those possessing them, productionism and distributionism should be seen as logics for the attainment of economic ends: 'logics which can be understood simultaneously by the same person and manipulated strategically' (1990: 305). Furthermore, there is little evidence to support the argument of the significance of the Protestant churches and their ideologies. Gatter's evidence suggests that there is no necessary connection between these and productive individualism.

The ALCOM study was based largely on questionnaires carried out in Chibote area, where more than 90 per cent of people profess themselves to be Catholic, and where only one adherent to fundamentalist Protestant ideologies was known to exist. The willingness to use Poewe's dichotomy is symptomatic of both the need for simplification and well-established beliefs about the nature of 'culture'. The ALCOM paper presents a simple picture of rural society that supports and confirms the possibility of manageability; there is less of a moving target. By supporting the notion that people's actions are essentially value-driven, the picture also gives less room for agency.

*Obligation and reciprocity* Developers, including the promoters of fish-farming, have tended to focus on distribution as a constraint following production. It is more accurate, in the case of Luapula at least, to see production as a necessary precursor of distribution whose form is not predetermined.

The production of most crops takes place principally within house-holds, households that generally closely resemble the model of the nuclear household with which developers tend to work. The household in this context has a meaning as a unit within which individuals co-operate with each other to meet at least minimal subsistence needs. The extent to which men and women actually work together and how this is organized are highly negotiated.

It is unusual for people from outside the unit to assist with productive labour unless they are paid, either in cash or in kind (for example with food, beer, cigarettes, or soap). The exception to this is the planting of millet. Millet-planting is frequently done on the basis of reciprocal labour, but this was the only crop or aspect of the production cycle for which this takes place. In addition, men still carry out brideservice for the parents of their wives. The duration of this, and the kind of labour undertaken, vary. In the past, a man was expected to cut *citemene* (selective burning and fallowing of plots of land) for three to four years for his parents-in-law. This no longer occurs. Instead, a young man will usually be given a portion of land to prepare, a task that can take anything from a few days to three months. On rare occasions, bride-service labour is replaced by cash payments.

The distribution of the product is not, however, so closely tied to the conjugal family. It is here that relations of reciprocity begin to have a more important role. These are frequently, though not necessarily, associated with kinship. Gatter (1990) notes that for Mabumba, matri-lineal ties have a less immediate tie than those of marriage: they are permanent and may always be resorted to, but in terms of meeting daily subsistence requirements they are subordinate during marriage. The term *ulupwa* is used interchangeably to refer to those of the immediate conjugal unit, and others to whom one has links of reciprocity and obligation. The specification of who those people are is flexible. When it comes to the exchange and distribution of small goods, especially food, *ulupwa* tend to be defined according to proximity. Those with whom such exchanges do take place may be the kin of husband or wife or both. When it comes to larger and more long-term needs, such as cash for school fees, principles of matrilineal kinship are much more likely to be resorted to. Thus one of the first people that a young man might be expected to make demands on for help with schooling would be an elder male to whom he is related through his mother's brother.

One of the most visible and important manifestations of distribution within the villages is the sharing of food. Children travel between houses, being fed and cared for by female relatives, usually the mothers and sisters of either their mother or their father. Adults also often provide each other with cooked food. This takes place either on a regular basis (elderly or sick relatives may be sent food, even when living in a separate house), or in a more apparently random fashion (providing food for an unexpected visitor, for example). This aspect of distribution is a fundamental part of social relations, but is not construed as sharing in the same way as the giving of uncooked food is. The feeding of extra people who are present when food is cooked is presented as a natural and unquestioned practice. So is the sharing of uncooked food, but it is slightly more rigidly regulated. People refer to others as selfish if they repeatedly refuse requests for items of food, whether some cassava flour (the most commonly exchanged item) or relish ingredients. On the other hand, people who make requests who have nothing with which to reciprocate and are not accepted as dependent (children, the old, the sick) are regarded as beggars and looked down upon. The ability and willingness to provide food for people is an important indicator of social standing and success. At the same time it constitutes an important investment in the future goodwill of others.

While ability and willingness to feed others and an allied assumption that everyone should take part in the productive effort are apparently fairly straightforward for the distribution of food, they are less so for other things that are only indirectly the results of farming work (either money itself or things that are mainly obtained with cash). Thus claims on neighbours and kin for money and consumption goods, such as soap, are less readily met. In the light of this, and because the economy in Monga and Chibote is only partially monetized, the ways that different crops are or are not part of this monetization need to be examined. It may not be correct simply to assume that all crops have equivalent meanings because they can all be consumed or exchanged.

Cassava, the main ingredient of *nshima* (the staple) is seen as the most important food. Without it no meal is complete. The disposal of cassava is generally under the control of women. As with all crops, such disposal can take place in three ways: the cassava can be consumed within the household, offered as gifts to kin or visitors, or sold and/or exchanged. In practice, though, cassava is seldom sold directly for cash; its main roles are meeting subsistence needs and acting as goods for exchange in networks of reciprocity. Maize, on the other hand, is grown explicitly for sale. It is also mainly under the control of men, except where women have been explicitly targeted for loans. Hybrid maize was introduced by the government. Farmers were expected to take on a loan for a package of seed and fertilizer, and to repay the loan by selling the maize. Although people eat maize cobs roasted as a snack and it is used as an ingredient in some local beer, it is almost never eaten as an ingredient of *nshima*. Eating *nshima* made from maize is seen as an urban practice and most people say the taste is bad and such food is 'not satisfying'. Maize is thus more closely tied to the money economy than other crops. For the latter, which are both possible foods for subsistence needs and also have a potential for sale and barter, their role in distribution is highly variable.

Fish-farming may have been introduced relatively recently but fish has been a valued part of diet for much longer. As discussed in Chapter 6, animal protein is relatively rare, and offering it is an important sign of respect. Animals are needed for contingencies, and among these contingencies are investments in social relations, for example providing meat for weddings and funerals. On these occasions, the meat could be a large animal such as a goat, cow, or pig (the latter, rarely). However, poorer people will make do with poultry. A widow in Chibote slaughtered six of her seven chickens for her son's wedding. Another widow in Chibote possessed about twenty chickens. Although she complained insistently about the monotony of her diet, having eaten only mushrooms for weeks on end, she refused to slaughter a chicken for variety: 'I could not just kill one. They might get all used up and then what would I do if I really needed one?'

Fish is both eaten more frequently and more regularly sold than other animal protein. It is not used for honouring visitors in quite the same way as other animal protein but is nevertheless considered a more prestigious relish than vegetable leaves, mushrooms, or caterpillars. Fish is also potentially valuable as a food with which to hire labour. The expectations of sharing connected with fish reflect its dual and shifting role both as something on which kin can make legitimate claims (as a foodstuff and valued relish) and as a source of cash.

'Obligation' has been characterized as a negative thing. An article in *Ceres*, the FAO magazine, argues that, from the producers' point of view, constraints can be classed into three categories: 'man-made', biological, and environmental: 'The first of these are imposed by the producers' peers in the name of tradition' (Wijkstrom and Jul Larsen 1986: 20). Social obligation is something to be avoided because it implies distribution, which prevents accumulation. It is also taken for granted that, given the choice, an individualistic farmer will avoid such obliga- tion if 'he' can. For the majority of fish-farmers in both Chibote and Monga, distribution is neither onerous nor to be avoided. Nor is it necessarily construed as obligation. These fish-farmers range from a woman in Chibote who gave most of one meagre harvest away, to a relatively successful fish-farmer in Monga area who keeps one pond 'for *ulupwa*' (family). For these people redistribution is important, although the conditions under which it occurs vary and are to some extent adapted to the growing influence of the monetized economy. It is not possible to assess the extent to which giving fish away should be construed as investment – probably scarcely at all, if this is seen as a strictly calculated act. On the other hand, in a relatively uncertain environment, building up stocks of goodwill makes sense over the long term.

There are, however, exceptions. The conditions under which people look for and find ways of avoiding reciprocity, or complain about the demands of kin, are very specific. Two situations can occur. On the one hand, there are people who have accumulated significant quantities of money, usually from migrant labour, and who choose to settle away from their village of origin for 'farming' – growing maize on a large scale. This move is sometimes explained as partly a strategy to avoid obligations to kin in the home village (Stromgaard 1985). Arguably, such separation may reflect the less risky nature of their situation. Only one fish-farmer (in Monga area) fitted into this category – and he was not yet producing fish from his ponds. On the other hand, there are the few, formally educated young men, who are keen to associate themselves with values that are entirely oriented around production for the market. A number of these expressed the need to avoid the demands of relatives as much as possible. For example, one farmer explained that he had moved from his own village in order to get away from the demands of relatives: 'How can I make a profit if they are always demanding?' Another reported: 'Our extended family system will hold me back – that is why I need to hide my business.'

*'Levelling mechanisms'* Despite of the existence of reciprocity, people do attempt to avoid obligation, and may be subject to social control. For example, the experiences of one farmer in Monga area during 1992 might be portrayed as an example of levelling mechanisms in practice.

He had excited considerable resentment and jealousy in the village. This resentment was partially based on the suspicion that he was controlling money, resources, and information that should have been available to everyone. When an opportunity arose to take him down a peg or two, many people in the village were positively gleeful about doing so. He was accused (justly) of adultery. This is a common enough occurrence, and fines are seldom of more than 20,000 kwacha. The fine eventually settled was of 100,000 kwacha – an impossibly large amount even for this relatively rich farmer. He had a benefactor from Mansa who was threatened with witchcraft and his two employees were chased away from the village. He drained his fish-ponds and stripped his vegetable garden in order to pay some of the fine. Once he had been sufficiently humbled and apparently taught a lesson, his erstwhile enemies rallied around to assist with the rest of the fine and to defend him against the husband of the woman he had 'stolen'.

However, the resentment did not derive solely from his diverse economic enterprises. Rather, the boastfulness and deviousness that were said to accompany them were unacceptable. Respect is manifest partly in participating appropriately in networks of reciprocity and in showing deference to elders. It is, however, more complex than this and encompasses notions of humility and honesty. According to others in the area, the farmer was guilty not only of attempting to avoid obligations of reciprocity, but of lying and manipulation. It is therefore important not to misread the reasons for his downfall. He was resented not because of accumulation as such, but because of his avoidance of codes of behaviour that continue to make sense to most in the village. The linkages to be made between accumulation alone and levelling mechanisms are tenuous at best. It is certainly hard to divine any systematic response to accumulation, beyond inevitable cases of individual jealousy.

Accusations of witchcraft and the fear of it may provide one key illustration of social control. Provoking fear of witchcraft may induce people to alter their behaviour, while accusations of witchcraft serve to drum up group hostility to the person concerned. The group may then feel justified in adopting punitive measures, such as banishing an individual from the village. Even this is not straightforward: some people are able to use rumours that they practise witchcraft to enhance their own social standing, especially if they are already economically or politically powerful. Rumours about the witchcraft practised by the headman in one village abounded. They served to inflate rather than reduce his standing. On the other hand, people were said to use witchcraft to induce the crops of others to enter their fields. Such accusations might be made to explain apparently abnormally high yields. They were not, however, common in either Chibote or Monga. Finally, people might be suspected of using witchcraft to bring direct harm to others or even to kill them.

In material terms, a fear of witchcraft can have disastrous effects. The cost of hiring a witch-finder (*shinganga*) to discover and accuse someone who is practising witchcraft can be exorbitant. A young farmer suffering from unexplained illness called in a *shinganga* to identify and exorcize the person who was bewitching him. The cost of the *shinganga* was 12,000 kwacha, which was half of the money he had just earned from a maize harvest.

At a rather obvious level, an association between witchcraft as a levelling mechanism and fish-farming is hard to establish given that people do not accumulate as a result of fish-farming. It is not yet a subject for either jealousy or social control. The low level at which fish-farming is currently practised, and its tendency to be a diversification rather than a primary activity, make it less likely to be subject to jealousy or demands for sharing. On the contrary, many fish-farmers are pitied by others within the village for wasting their time. The novelty of the activity may also be important: several people explained that it would be hard to tell if somebody was using sorcery because a fish-pond is not like a field: it is not so easy to count the fish. More importantly, water is generally regarded as a poor conductor of magic. A fish-farmer was banished from his village in Monga area following witchcraft accusations (none of which was related to his fish-ponds). Following this, the 'charms' or 'tools' with which he supposedly practised witchcraft were thrown in the fish-ponds in order to neutralize them.

More important still is the diversity and complexity of ways in which people interpret social deviation. It is not possible to make any simple and unilinear association between accumulation and levelling mechanisms. Given the continuing importance of distribution, and the status that may be attached to a willingness and ability to distribute, especially food, richer people are as likely to be accorded respect as to suffer social sanction. This is done more readily if their relative richness can be easily explained. Returned migrants, people who have held or hold salaried jobs, and well-educated people fall into this category.

Interpreting people's behaviour as the simple product of norms and beliefs is clearly inappropriate. The ways in which social obligation and social control work have to be contextualized. It may be true that, on occasion, people fail to harvest their ponds because they do not want to share out the proceeds. It may also be true that people suffer from witchcraft and the fear of it. These things can be empirically established.

But it may not be appropriate to impute determining power to them. What people do or do not do with their fish-ponds reflects what they mean to their owners: their importance in relation to other assets and activities, the reasons they were dug in the first place. Also, the dichotomy between individualistic or communistic behaviour, particularly regarding distribution, cannot be maintained. Although people may strategically associate themselves with one or the other, this does not take place in a unilinear way. Behaving in one's individual interest, even aiming to accumulate, is not necessarily incompatible with distribution. Distribution is not necessarily construed as obligation.

## Whose culture?

So far we have focused on case study material from Luapula Province to explore the problems in simple attributions of 'cultural barriers' to the objects of development. For developers, the notion of 'cultural barriers' simplifies complexity. It also serves to situate the 'failure' of their technology within rural communities. Failure is, however, far from simple. It means different things to different people, depending on where they locate themselves in relation to what success might be. For those adopting fish-farming as a way of identifying with 'development', whether or not they are failures is a moot point. Understandably, developers tend to focus on intended beneficiaries when accounting for failure because this is where they are attempting to induce change. But in so doing, villages are reified as the site of failure. The very idea of cultural 'barriers' presupposes some conception of the ideal state of affairs that these barriers impede, but that ideal state is also assumed to be within the village.

As far as development agency staff are concerned, whether working in Nairobi, Rome, or London, culture (like economic motivation) is something that locals have. But those staff would also acknowledge that there is a cultural side to their lives. We hope to go one step further. The cultural construction of identity and power relations within Intermediate Technology serves as an example of how organizations create their own distinct cultures.

If you pick one moment in the history of Intermediate Technology, people's identity shifts according to whom they are presenting themselves. For example, in 1990, officially to 'outsiders', Emma Crewe was the social scientist for the Fuel For Food (FFF) and Biomass Programme, within the Agro-Processing Sector, in the Operations Division, in the UK Head Office. Unofficially, to 'insiders' she was a stovie working on the third floor. When someone from outside the division, but within

Intermediate Technology, asked her who she was, she would give the official name of the programme and sector, and place the sector in the context of the others, perhaps explaining some of the differences between them and highlighting the strengths of her own programme. If a non-specialist from outside Intermediate Technology asked her what she did, she would explain the function of each division, and explain her role within Operations, but with no implied criticism of other programmes. When speaking to outsiders, protecting the reputation of the whole organization becomes paramount. Plainly, group identity is partly defined in each instance according to the identity of those present.

Patterns cannot be meaningfully divorced from their context and retain meaning. Once seen in context, it becomes apparent that the opposition of groups to which people belong is not a merely intellectual scheme, but a creative process linked to practice. To be more specific, the significance of the oppositions varies over time, according to changes in group interaction and perceptions about power within groups. Within Emma Crewe's small FFF Programme, members talked about the differences between 'our team' and the rest of Operations. For example, in relation to others in Operations, they prided themselves on always keeping each other informed about everything (although within the programme they complained about this behaviour to each other), holding weekly meetings, and staying in cheaper hotels than others when travelling abroad. Conversely, they did not identify with the Agro-Processing Sector, to which they belonged, or even refer to it except when a sector meeting was called. These meetings were perceived as an intrusion into the 'real' work.

The strength of the stove programme identity may be connected to the fact that, whereas Agro-Processing was perceived as relatively powerful in terms of securing more external funds than other sectors, funding for stoves in particular seemed to be in decline. On the other hand, the spatial arrangements that defined group interaction were probably just as relevant. In Agro-Processing, there were four offices – one for FFF, two for Food-Processing, and one for the Sector Manager and Administrator. The UK FFF team consisted of two Senior Technical Managers, three Project Officers (one engineer, one ceramicist, one social scientist), one editor, and two secretaries. For much of the time, this group sat together in the same room every day, chatting about work or other matters, overhearing each others' telephone conversations, calling *ad hoc* meetings, solving specific work-related problems, swapping jokes, complaining about the size of their in-trays, reacting to memos, making each other coffee, and, at least once a week, going out to lunch.

The project staff sometimes travelled together (usually in pairs), or at least overlapped for some time on project visits overseas. In contrast, interaction between the two programmes in the sector was virtually confined to approximately two hours a month for a meeting. The secretaries in FFF and Food-Processing did interact, but during breaks and after work rather than for the purposes of professional cooperation. It is hardly surprising, therefore, that programme team identity made far more of an impression than sector membership.

At the level of the divisions before 1992, a spatial distinction was drawn by Operations staff, who were all located on the third floor, to distinguish them from the 'paper-pushers' who worked on the ground floor. Sometimes Operations staff said that the 'ground floor' was not keeping people informed; at other times they were taking up too much of their time with memos and meetings. The people on the 'third floor' were doing the 'real' work, in the words of many Operations members, and the implication was that the more time you spent with the 'beneficiaries', and the closer you were to the technology, the more 'real' your work became. Those you identified most closely with were, by definition, also doing 'real' work.

In the late 1980s it was those who were processing information (press, information, publicity, development education, fundraising and so on) who were merely talking and writing about the 'real' work, according to many Operations staff. Operations complained that the journalistic style of Communications specialists contained too many generalizations and exaggerations; the latter retaliated by complaining that the technical style of Operations staff was impenetrable and boring. There were frequent disagreements over the accuracy of information relating to projects, for example, with Operations staff complaining that the Press Office would get technical details wrong. Operations was responsible for conveying and checking information sent to the press, but would still blame the 'communicators' for distorting the truth.

This changed, however, as communications gradually became an integral part of project work. From the beginning of the 1990s it was the 'policy people' who were perceived as being distant from Operations. It was thought that they were plotting to give too much control to the 'in-country' managers in other offices before the latter were 'ready' to take charge. Operations staff felt that they were not being consulted. According to some of the stereotypes voiced upstairs, the policy people were at best not interfering with Operations project work, or at worst building empires to satisfy their own career ambitions on the backs of the proper technical work. Some stressed the point that the 'ground floor' needed the 'third floor' more than vice versa, and the arrangement whereby Operations staff raised most of their own funds for the project work confirmed the point in their own eyes.

Despite the criticism between factions, there is no evidence to show that anyone was other than well-intentioned in practice. And the criticism itself was often relevant only to particular contexts. Even the most virulent critics of others within the organization would praise their opponents' work in other contexts. It was commonplace to hear the same Operations staff member complaining that another individual was grabbing power, and the next day defending the excellent publication they had recently produced. The comments about power-hungry individuals and what constitutes 'real work' appeared to be fluid, transitory interpretations that were often a response to the current perceived power relations between different departments. The reason that Operations staff talked critically about communicators during the late 1980s, and attacked policy-makers in the early 1990s, is linked to dramatic power shifts within the organization. Criticism through gossip was a way of making sense of micro-political change.

In the late 1980s the Communications Division expanded and secured a greater proportion of funds and staff appointments than it had before. The Operations Division expanded as well, but at a slower rate. Most of Operations staff remained cooperative with individual Communications staff in practice, but talked about the division as failing to recognize that technical project work was the essential key to Intermediate Technology's success. During the first half of 1990, the talk about other divisions shifted from discussing Communications to dissecting the behaviour of the Policy and Country Representation Unit (the Policy Unit for short). Initially, the planners/policy-makers and those supporting country representatives were seen as an unknown quantity. Their aims then became more explicit after a meeting held to discuss a new 'Management Information System' (MIS) for the whole organization.

During a discussion in Operations of the MIS proposal, one staff member asked how it was possible to create an information system without first devising a permanent international structure for Intermediate Technology. For many this was the first indication that a structural change was imminent, despite the fact that a planning document produced by the Policy Unit in 1989 clearly stated that the devolution of project management and financial control to the countries of representation would take place between 1990 and 1995. Many staff did not read the document (because it did not concern 'real' work), or found its unfamiliar, novel suggestions difficult to digest, or assumed that it would not affect their work for several years. The MIS meeting forced all staff to acknowledge that devolution would take place sooner rather than later. In 1992 financial and managerial control of project work was transferred to 'in-country' offices (see Chapter 6).

This devolution left Head Office in a state of deep-seated identity crisis. It became clear that since projects would be planned and managed 'in-country', and the national technical specialists outside the UK were also reasonably self-sufficient, the role of UK Project Officers was uncertain. Very abruptly, they might no longer be involved in the 'real' work. On the one hand they were impressed by the morality of devolution, and on the other they were losing a sense of professional identity. Consequently some Project Officers resigned. The others became preoccupied by the 'elephant process', a highly consultative planning process that aimed to design appropriate roles and strategies for the UK office.

Led by four middle- and junior-level staff, every single staff member was directly involved in commenting on documents, attending small group workshops and meetings of the whole office (around a hundred people), and writing down their own ideas for Intermediate Technology's future. The elephant symbolized the organization. While each department had a good view of one part (the trunk, the leg, and so on), the process was supposed to fuse all the different perspectives so that the plans reflected the will of the whole of Intermediate Technology. Although many felt frustrated at being bombarded with information, some of which they felt ill-qualified to comment on, the process itself certainly created some sense of 'group' identity and purpose within the UK.

One of the recommendations in the 'UK Strategy 1993–1998' that emerged from the elephant process was that the UK office should have equality with other country offices. Its Director would have equal status with the Directors of offices in Africa, Asia and South America. An International Secretariat, also based in Rugby and headed by Intermediate Technology's Chief Executive but with International Technology Programme Managers in the UK and Peru, would provide coordination and manage all the work, including the activities undertaken by the UK office. The latter would take advantage of its proximity to European-based donors and NGOs and focus on advocacy and development education, thereby promoting appropriate technology in the North. These aims have since been revised. Significantly for the culture and micro-politics of the organization, the UK office as a whole has been reinstated as the Head Office (as indicated in Intermediate Technology's 1997 Annual Report).

Since 1997, Intermediate Technology has also been advised that NGOs need business plans, the language of marketing, and a more 'professional' appearance. Convincing potential donors of professionalism is, apparently, more difficult if offices in Africa, Asia, and South America have parity with those in the UK. As 'professionalism' in Britain becomes increasingly bound up with ideas derived from marketing and public relations, NGOs such as Intermediate Technology appear to be following suit. Some Intermediate Technology staff now claim that their documentation 'will not be taken seriously unless it sounds up-to-date and modern'. It is clear that as control over Intermediate Technology's international work has returned to the UK, its 'modern' culture and philosophy are being redefined by British staff in Rugby.

In this example of identity construction and micro-politics within Intermediate Technology we have tried to demonstrate that people make cultures wherever they live, and both at home and at work. We have emphasized recent cultural formation; the dynamism of Intermediate Technology culture is, therefore, plain. It also has longer-standing cultural 'traditions', as does any organization, micro-society or wider society. Intermediate Technology, for example, has paid ritual homage to its founder, Schumacher, in most of its publications since it was founded. In the private domain it has also developed 'traditional' rituals for staff who were leaving, as most organizations do. This consists of a lunch in a local pub for all UK staff and an elaborate present-giving ceremony with speeches (preferably on the last day before leaving). In theory the ceremony is always a surprise, in practice it is inevitable and so those leaving know it will happen but pretend that they do not. Emma Crewe left the organization twice (once to go on a sabbatical) and transgressed the rules by going through two leaving ceremonies; this provoked many jokes about how she should return the first lot of presents. Clearly Intermediate Technology has both older and newer cultural forms, just as 'communities' contain both cultural continuity and change.

American anthropologists have pointed out that business, industrial, and governmental organizations have had their own culture since the 1920s (Schwartzman (1993) gives an overview of these studies). More recently, British anthropologists have been doing research within the private and public sectors – for example, Young's research with the police (1991) and Shore's study with the European Commission (1993). Anthropological studies of organizations confirm that people working in organizations, just as within wider societies, endlessly negotiate power hierarchies, interpretations of reality, and cultural rules that often operate independently of the organizations' rational goals. The effect and potential function of culture, therefore, do not determine what shape it takes. However, such findings have not found their way into development studies literature.

Development studies, or more specifically the study of 'human resource development', has been more influenced by management studies than by the anthropology of organizations. The former does not seem to have rejected functionalism. In fact, it has been argued that it has revived the functionalist paradigm in its examination of culture in organizations, partly by reworking Weber (Roper 1994: 15), borrowing from a mixture of psychology and economics and, more recently, simplifying anthropological ideas, most notably those of Geertz and Douglas. It has portrayed culture as, among other things, a 'form of mental programming' (for example, Hofstede 1991: 6) or 'relatively stable beliefs, attitudes and values' (for instance, A. Brown 1995: 7). The culture of an organization, it is assumed, either impedes or enhances its rational functioning.

Applied management specialists or change managers advise about how to create the right kind of culture for a particular organization so that it is more efficient in reaching its goals. But such advice is based on flawed assumptions about culture. In the example of identity construction and power shifts within Intermediate Technology we have tried to show that culture is closely connected with power relations, but is created or re-created at least partly independently of the organization's rational objectives. The adoption of marketing language by Intermediate Technology, for example, may be rationalized by referring to a rational aim – that is, that it might make fundraising easier. It appears, however, to have more to do with a resuscitated discourse of modernity that puts marketing at the centre of professionalism. Marketing is not, of course, modern in the sense of 'new'; the fact that it appears so is a cultural construction in itself. Culture may be a 'mental' process, but it consists of active, creative rather than passive programming. Creating 'attitudes' may be a part of cultural construction. However, they are far from stable, express what people know rather than what they believe (seen from their viewpoint), and can be understood only within a wider context of power relations.

## Conclusion

Rather than acting as 'barriers', cultures define appropriate behaviour. We have seen in Luapula that people develop practices that, for instance, dictate what is suitable food for eating, selling, or exchanging; what obligations one has with whom; and what punitive measures should be taken when people transgress cultural rules. We have argued that these cultural practices cannot be reduced to functional purposes, such as diminishing the wealth of particular people. Furthermore, although obeying or breaking particular cultural rules may thwart the aims of development project staff, to present rules as barriers puts development aims in too central a position. Development might, but equally unconvincingly, be portrayed as a barrier to the delicate cultural process of regulating people's behaviour within the context of social relations.

Although not all development agencies formulate detailed models about culture, such as FAO's traditional levelling mechanisms, obligation and reciprocity, most make some assumptions about local culture. 'Culture' is often used as a shorthand for categorizing what cannot be identified or explained. Into this category, for example, Intermediate Technology staff have also placed a wide range of 'beliefs' and practices, including the belief in witchcraft, the preference for cooking prepared in clay pots, fear of new technology, female subservience, and so on. The category 'culture' can very easily become a description for anything that appears to be different from what so-called 'modern' people do. It is partly because culture is a concept usually employed to explain differences between 'tradition' and 'modernity' that cultures within development agencies tend to go unnoticed.

In our examination of culture within Intermediate Technology, we placed the creation of multiple identities within a context of micro-politics. People do not define themselves in relation to others in isolation. The definition is predicated upon whom they are presenting themselves to, their perception of power relations between groups at that particular moment, and their idea of the purpose of the identity construction. When raising money from a donor Technical Project Officers may describe themselves (and think of themselves) as part of a heroic organization the whole of which is working for the poor; to another Technical Project Officer, they may complain that other departments are out of touch with the poor or tangential to 'real' development work.

Ideas about culture are themselves culturally constructed by both 'locals' and 'developers'. The opposition between tradition and modernity in the minds of 'developers' roughly corresponds to the classificatory division between locals and themselves. This statement is, however, very rough. Even the developers distinguish between different kinds of locals, such as 'traditional' or 'indigenous' people who have culture, and other developers, nationals in Africa, Asia, and South/Central America, who are associated with modernity. The so-called indigenous people themselves, meanwhile, create distinctions between people with traditional and modern outlooks among themselves. Clearly, not only does the traditional culture versus modern dichotomy collapse on further scrutiny, but the categories 'local' and 'developer' are problematic. In the next chapter we begin to look more closely at how 'local' people negotiate power in different ways; their actions are not only simplistically represented as 'resistance' by some commentators, but they seem to be mostly ignored by developers.

# CHAPTER 8

# Who Is in the Driving Seat?

In this chapter we reflect further on notions about the supposed 'recipients' of development aid. In Chapter 4 we argued that the idea that recipients are passive targets has become unfashionable. For this reason, categories such as 'targets' and 'recipients' have been replaced by notions of 'partnership' for capacity-building. We focused principally on the organizational 'partners' of development donors: governments and local NGOs or groups. This implies a dichotomy between organizations and individuals – the latter being the ultimate 'beneficiaries'. While we will show in this chapter that such a dichotomy oversimplifies reality, it is initially useful because it is apparently meaningful for many of those involved in development intervention.

There is a greater readiness to attribute 'failure' to problems within local organizations than to those they are meant to be serving, criticism of whom is much less acceptable. True, culture may be construed as a barrier to be overcome, but this is accompanied by an often romantic celebration of 'local' knowledge, or even wisdom, and by discussion of the 'resistance' that ensues when these are not taken into account. In both cases, 'local people' are reified. Work on 'resistance' has taken exception to writings that portray local people as passive, powerless, subjugated, and repressed. It has been argued that people resist in different ways and that the 'powerful' are not always in complete control. James Scott's work on 'everyday forms of peasant resistance' (1985) is an important example of this kind of critique. Although different words may be used by development agency staff (in our experience they are more likely to talk about lack of cooperation than about resistance as such), ideas about how locals' priorities may diverge from their own expectations, and should be respected, have gained currency. The popularity of calls for greater participation of local people in the development process is arguably another aspect of the celebration of the 'local'. As one administrator at FAO in Rome put it: 'We want to put local people in the driving seat.'

But who are the 'local' people exactly? And what makes local people local? This has been a recurring question in this book and is a central theme of this chapter. There is a need for caution in the use of simple statements about what or who is local because labelling particular groups of people may overlook the ways in which 'people may be "outsiders" and/or "insiders" according to their activity or purpose' (Cornwall et al. 1994: 101). As a result, simple notions of 'resistance' may present an overdetermined picture of what 'local' people do that still leaves developers at the centre of the analysis. We suggest that the 'misbehaviour' of projects (that is, people not doing what is expected of them) may be less the result of conscious resistance than of practices born out of the selective internalization or hybridization of a number of apparently conflicting ideologies. At the same time, a sharp division between those who resist and those who are resisted is not always tenable: relations of domination and subordination are not so fixed. An alternative is to suggest that while individuals are differently constrained by their structural positions, including their access to resources, each makes choices within these constraints, and the nature of the choices needs to be understood. Clearly structural considerations influence which voices gain ascendancy.

## Local people in the driving seat

In this chapter, we further explore the complexity of local 'resistance', and question whether this label is always appropriate. In Chapter 7, we argued that formulations of concepts of tradition and modernity are adapted and internalized by specific agents in particular ways – a process that has deep historical roots. This is often manifested in a desire to be associated with 'development' or 'progressiveness', and the appropriation of the symbolic as well as the material aspect of such association. Olivier de Sardan (1988) has argued that the symbolic as well as the material and economic benefits of projects are the subject of tension, manoeuvring, and competition. We suggest that this stretches beyond discrete intervention to the ethos generated by a legacy of 'development'.

In Chapter 7 we discussed local internalizations of a culture of modernity which was influenced at least in part by external intervention. The history of development intervention in Luapula, for example, clearly shows that people not only learn discourses of development but interpret and continually update them. An Intensive Rural Development Scheme of 1957–61 was a 'dismal failure' (J. Gould 1989: 147), but had lasting effects: 'it made legitimate both the expectation that the central government had a responsibility to assist in the development of the rural areas, and the complaint of neglect' (Baylies 1984: 168). From

1964, rural development in Luapula has been closely associated with foreign assistance. From the mid-1970s, LIMA (Learned Improved Methods of Agriculture) schemes, which had originated in Zambia as a response to the national concern for food security, were the principal medium of rural development and extension in Luapula. In 1992, a wide variety of donor-funded projects were operating in the province tackling a range of activities from nutrition to animal traction. FINNIDA, SIDA, IFAD, GTZ, FAO, UNICEF, World Vision, Water Wells Trust, and WWF were present, in addition to volunteers from Finland, the UK, Denmark, Norway, Belgium, Japan, Germany, and the Netherlands.

Such a diversity and quantity of assistance is not unusual. A glance at the numbers of donors active in other provinces in Zambia, and in other countries in Sub-Saharan Africa, shows a similar picture. As is the case in many parts of Africa and Asia, people in Luapula associate development intervention with the prospect of material and status improvement. Individuals have internalized the interpretations of 'development' by developers, but have also formulated their own. Such responses are not necessarily in line with the stated objectives of the developers. In particular, while developers speak in terms of self-reliance and imparting knowledge, local people recognize projects as a source of resources to be used to meet immediate needs. Sometimes local people accurately identify where the control of material assets lies and adapt their behaviour to get a share.

To some extent, the process of aquaculture adoption is an example of this response. Partially because of its proximity to Mansa, residents of Monga area have seen an enormous variety of different agencies, projects and development schemes. Government extension uses Monga area as a focus of its activities: the Adaptive Research Planning Team (ARPT) is based in Mabumba, only a few kilometres away, and a number of farmers in the Monga area are contact farmers for ARPT. FINNIDA has trained LIMA farmers in maize growing. UNICEF has funded a women's farming project, also promoting maize growing, and a new, ostensibly poverty-focused, vegetable-growing group was being assisted with maize and fertilizer. The ALCOM vehicle was regularly seen down at the fish-ponds.

In tandem with various interventions, people have learned to adapt their behaviour in anticipation of where they see potential benefit. Many villagers understand that outsiders have control over goods and services that would otherwise be inaccessible. Some become adept at manipulating those outsiders, especially through the adoption of particular aspects of language. At an obvious level, the legacy of development is felt through consistent (and indignant) requests for assistance, loans, fingerlings, and inputs. Farmers, understandably, feel themselves to be heavily dependent on the state and donors and are particularly disenchanted by threats that such inputs may no longer be forthcoming.

A subtle process often ensues where some farmers have learned to respond to what they perceive as the developers' wishes, thereby fulfilling their half of a bargain. For example, over several years the idea that it is important to be operating as a 'good community' in order to receive inputs has circulated widely. One farmer had a large vegetable garden, which was partially financed by a sponsor in Mansa. He took visitors from the Ministry of Youth and Sport to visit the garden, proudly explaining that 'this is our community vegetable garden'. He was fully aware that if the well-cultivated and prospering garden was seen as the result of active and harmonious community participation, then development assistance might flow. He was also in the special position of being contact farmer for ALCOM, UNICEF, IFAD, FINNIDA, and ARPT – and 'Chairman' of the women's club.

An extreme example of an individual internalizing and using notions of development is that of the 'dream' of Mr Kaoma. Mr Kaoma was widely acknowledged as the richest, most highly educated man in Kaseke village. He had worked as a college lecturer in Serenje, was the owner of a hammer mill in Mansa, and had been politically active under UNIP. His 'dream' involved the complete redevelopment of the land adjoining Kaseke village for all manner of enterprises which he had seen promoted elsewhere: cattle-ranching, fish-farming, a recreational boating-lake. In the plans he listed the necessary facilities for the market: cold-room, store-room for dried fish, a market master's office, cashier's office, security officer's office. The dam was to be 400 metres wide by 2 kilometres long by 10 metres deep. He was still in search of funding for the unlikely scheme in 1992. When questioned about the implications for the current residents of the village of the complete loss of their farmland he explained: 'But it is all right. It will be a community project.'

The subtlety with which farmers learn to adapt to new messages is illustrated by a conversation following a visit from a potential loan-dispenser to the Monga fish-farmers' club:

A: We must learn to show that we are a good community to get these loans.
B: No, that is not what is important now. They are interested in individual farmers now. We must each show that we have a good plan. Then we will get the loans.

Recurrent examples were also found of farmers adapting their behaviour and responses to questions from outsiders once their ponds had been dug. For example, a farmer was reluctant to harvest his pond until a DoF representative was there so that he could 'prove' how well he was doing. In Chibote, a farmer was embarrassed about researchers attending his pond harvest because the grass around the pond had not been slashed. A common response to poor harvests, problems of predation, and shortage of water was 'But I will dig another pond.'

Because of the significance of symbolic factors, such as the association of ponds with development, it is obviously neither easy nor straightforward to read people's motivation from such behaviour. It is important to acknowledge the symbolic meanings associated with objects or practices, but they should not be seen as the pre-eminent or final cause of action. For example, although large numbers of people buy stoves because they look 'modern', they then use them over time not because they have mistakenly internalized the developers' view that they are superior but because they find they have other advantages over their old stoves. In Sri Lanka the majority value the time that can be freed up by a stove that cooks faster; in Kenya the most commonly reported advantage of new stoves is lower fuel consumption. So when the technology is being used over time, the users are not being passively obedient, but are responding to their own complex assessments, priorities, and values.

Conversely, when stoves are bought or accepted but not used after a time, users are not necessarily resisting development. In less successful stove programmes, for example in Nepal and Bangladesh, it is very common to hear people claim that they use the new stove all the time but then to see it sitting cold and unused in a corner. This behaviour may be interpreted as ignorance and traditionalism by the technicians working for the stove project. In Chapter 5, however, we showed that people often have technical reasons for rejecting a new stove – for example, it requires very small pieces of wood that take too much time to cut, it cannot burn the locally available fuel, or it consumes more fuel than their old stove. So, while use of a new stove is not obedience, rejection is not necessarily resistance. To suggest that the stove-user is resisting development by refusing to use new technology elevates the 'developers' inappropriately. The people trying out the new technology over time are responding to their own priorities within the context of their own worldview; in this instance, the 'developers' are peripheral and unimportant.

Just as behaviour can be misinterpreted, what people say should not be taken at face value as a representation of reality. Social scientists employed by Intermediate Technology claimed that 'traditional culture' among a group of women potters socialized them into rigid obedience to figures of authority. They wrote:

> the assumption among the potters is that the teacher knows best and that their role is to accept the teaching. [One group] said 'we were taught and accepted what we were told.' There was a sense that anything that outsiders, particularly Mzungos [*sic*], want to teach them, must be worth it: some groups asked for training in 'anything else we could offer'. The most extreme case of this idea of obedience was a comment at [another group] that 'even if you give us an axe and tell us to cut off her head, we will' (confidential project report 1992).

This particular group of potters is not, however, 'obedient' in practice. For example, many individuals ignore technical advice given by project staff or refuse to establish new stove-making businesses. They may have expressed the view above to present themselves as cooperative – often an explicit criterion for involvement in development projects, as they are no doubt well aware from the long history of aid in the region. In this way, they can avert exclusion from future aid, knowing that when the project staffs' backs are turned they can selectively use or ignore their advice without incurring their wrath.

Thus the extent to which processes of appropriation should be seen as conscious manipulation or the internalization of external values is a moot point, depending on how intentionality and the capacity for agency are viewed. Internalization implies passive and responsive individuals. Conversely, to suggest that what is taking place is manipulation may overstate the amount of intention involved. The answer lies somewhere in between: in conjunction with their own ideas, people may appropriate ideas that they perceive to be the currency of powerful people, and through using them in certain contexts find they are more effective in their relationships with these powerful people. But new ideas do also become part of their own system of ideas and values. These processes themselves reflect prevailing social and political relationships.

One response to the growing awareness that practitioners' and beneficiaries' priorities diverge, or even that beneficiaries resist, is the suggestion that problems may be overcome through better 'participation'. Since at least the early 1980s the idea of participation has influenced both thinking and planning in development, and it continues to do so. For example, 'the Bank has begun a process of mainstreaming participatory approaches in its lending operations and its research and analytical work' (World Bank 1996: 1). As with the related concept of 'partnership', the reasons for this are both moral and instrumental. In part they are a response to apparent development failure. People in development agencies recognize that weaknesses in their projects could be partially attributed to a failure to understand or consult with the intended beneficiaries of their efforts.

The recognition of lack of consultation was prompted partly by critiques of development that stressed both the value of indigenous or local knowledge and the faults of culturally insensitive and 'top-down' interventions. These arguments are encapsulated within the literature on 'Putting the Last First' and 'Farmer First'. The literature is not homogeneous, but two central points recur: first, a need for 'reversals' in the attitudes and approaches of developers, and second, a need for better comprehension of the needs and priorities of those for whom they are ostensibly working. The idea of 'reversals' reflects the tendency of much thinking in participatory development to see the world in terms of opposites – rich and poor, Northern and Southern, urban and rural. For example Chambers (1994: 187) argues that 'outsider professionals' need to learn new roles, and this involves changes in concepts, values, methods, and behaviour. The second point has become the focus of donor and development agency calls for greater participation, particularly when it comes to data collection – hence the popularity of participatory rural appraisal (PRA). The problem is still articulated as one of communication: with better understanding of what people already know and consultation about their needs, the process of development can proceed more effectively. Furthermore, the failure of communication has its roots at the local level – the villagers or the farmers. For this reason, 'they' are 'invited to contribute and participate in development activities' (Oakley 1991: 18).

'Farmer First' approaches to rural development have been subject to a number of criticisms as increasingly more subtle analyses of power relations are sought. There is clearly a disjuncture between the well-argued moral and practical appropriateness of avoiding top-down, non-participatory intervention, and the problem that exists in giving meaningful content to that participation. The application of PRA can genuinely lead to a more integrated and participative approach to development. For example, Action Aid's Regenerated Frierian Literacy Through Empowering Community Techniques (REFLECT) Programme has developed the use of PRA methods so that communities identify their own priorities and make connections between literacy and developmental concerns. However, even with this unusually well thought out application of PRA, the moral notion of allowing people to define their needs is weakened by the fact that it is the same individual, or group, who is in the relatively powerful position of choosing to allow something.

The issues that people are supposed to articulate in PRA are defined in advance. Defining what are or are not appropriate as needs is necessarily value-laden and people in positions of power are more able to make the choices in such definitions. Under such circumstances, participation can act as little more than a tool for developers. As Gatter says: 'Though in the 1980s, institutions have become increasingly enamoured with the rhetoric of participation and bottom-up development, what often passes for allowing people to articulate their needs is really a case of teaching them to do it' (1990: 433).

Participatory approaches also tend to overlook questions of power and conflict within communities. They are ill-equipped to deal with the fact that no community, group, or household is homogeneous, or has mutually compatible interests. Differences occur with respect to age, gender, wealth, and ethnicity, and so on. While marginalized or minority groups (such as female, landless or lower-caste people) may be physically present during discussion, they are not necessarily given a chance to express their views to the same degree as others. An apparent consensus may in fact be just the expression of a dominant view. The suppression of conflicts of interests coming from any decision to listen to one voice rather than another is not easy to identify. Other participatory 'techniques', such as drawing or making maps, offer no better guarantees that inequalities are addressed.

Attempts to address the apparent naivety of the 'Farmer First' literature have recently been made (Scoones and Thompson 1994; Davies 1994; Mosse 1994). These have tried to incorporate a better understanding of the way in which knowledge is created and is the product of the interaction between unequally powerful actors. Positivistic assumptions about the world and our understanding of it are substituted with arguments that our own language and reasoning provide only partial views – 'a multiplicity of equally valid ones also exists' (Scoones and Thompson 1994: 24).

## Women working together

While greater participation has become *de rigueur*, the term is used with great fluidity: it describes many, very different, situations. Contributing labour to a food-for-work scheme is participation in a way, but clearly the choices of the participants are more limited than for those who participate in devising their own development project – or reject the project of development itself. What are people participating in? Does merely asking people's opinion constitute participation, or is something more fundamental required? In a sense these are impossible questions to answer but, for those actively involved in development intervention, there is a need to find practical ways of making sense of the new development orthodoxy. One of the most common of these is to focus on the way 'locals' organize themselves.

From within academia, this focus has most recently been manifested in calls for support to 'grassroots movements', community-based organizations, and indigenous movements (Ferguson 1990; Escobar 1995). Such support makes obvious sense – while the participation of all individuals cannot be ensured, presumably working through and with groups that represent them is the next best approach. In South/Central America especially, but elsewhere too, there are numerous well-documented examples of people organizing together, occasionally in opposition to the state, but always reflecting a strong sense of mutual interests. The feminist groups we described in Chapter 3 are an obvious example, but there are many others. For example, heroes inspired in part by ecological principles, such as Chico Mendes and Vandana Shiva, and environmental movements have emerged the world over (see Redclift 1989; Pearce 1991). Support for such movements entails an acceptance of potentially contentious agendas, whether feminism, ecology, the rejection of capitalism or socialism, or opposition to international business.

Acceptance of contentious agendas does not, however, sit comfortably with the neutral language of planning. For many international donors, the support of 'local groups' is a win–win situation: it does not imply dangerous radicalism, but rather reflects the donors' own views of how 'communities' could or should be organized. Women's groups are an important case in point. For international donors, women's groups are seen as efficient vehicles for smaller-scale and project-based attempts at poverty alleviation. They are thought to be particularly good at reaching 'vulnerable groups' – among which women are persistently included. Thus, while macro-level sectoral reform has generally been blind to its gendered effects, remedial and direct measures are specifically targeted at women and women's groups. Associated with this is a widespread assumption that women have a particular proclivity to work collectively, while men are more individualistic. In recent years, the focus on women's groups has shifted from an early concern with welfare to the objective of increasing the price and productivity of women's labour in the short term (Buvinic 1989). This has involved vocational training, credit for micro-enterprises, and income generation for women who otherwise worked outside of the cash economy. This instrumental objective is often combined, in name at least, with more nebulous ones concerned with 'empowerment'.

This tendency to work with women's groups has come under scrutiny. On the one hand, donors themselves question the effectiveness of working with localized groups whose achievements are necessarily on a small scale and which are often riven by dispute and mismanagement. On the other hand, the achievements of widespread and sometimes even apparently successful attempts to empower of women are doubtful. As Goetz and Sen Gupta (1996) have shown with a range of group-based approaches to credit in Bangladesh, high rates of loan repayment may disguise considerable inequities between men and women in control over those loans.

Despite doubts about effectiveness, this interest in women's groups has grown, in parallel with economic liberalization and support to non-governmental organizations in general. In Sub-Saharan Africa, the kind of groups with which donors work varies in form and purpose. Some, such as the women's self-help group movement in Kenya, are part of a wide network, established for decades (Kabira and Nzioki 1993; Karega 1996). They are also strongly supported by the government, so the relationship between donor and government influence is not necessarily transparent. Others, such as a number of groups in Zambia, are of more recent origin, and not apparently linked into a larger structure.

While various assessments have been made of the measurable achievements of such women's groups, far less attention has been paid to the meanings associated with the groups for those involved. Why are they formed as women's groups rather than given any other organizational identity, such as one linked to their main occupation (as many other groups are)? This question is pertinent because the groups we are interested in here are not those that are formed for explicitly feminist reasons. Feminist groups originate from an awareness of how interests are gendered. These interests are more significant, within at least the context of the group, than other aspects of differentiation such as class or ethnicity. Of course, no women's group transcends the other differences contributing to identity, but there is a prioritization in principal.

Women's groups must thus be viewed within the wider social and cultural contexts in which they are created. As von Bulow (1995) argues, the donor interest in women's groups rests on simplified images of these groups and insufficient knowledge of women's own motives for forming them. The same might be said of other types of group (fish-farming groups, farmers' collectives, bee-keeping societies, credit associations). However, women's groups are special in that a particular characteristic – gender – is apparently prescribed in advance as a basis for all the other things that the group might do. Understanding the nature of the motives for forming them is therefore important, especially if there is no productive benefit. To discover this requires not only noting what people claim, but their practices.

First, who are in the groups and on what terms? A limited number of studies have examined the role of 'elite' women in women's groups in Sub-Saharan Africa (for example Buvinic 1989; Sörensen 1990; Touwen 1990; Sylvester 1995; von Bulow 1995). They tend to argue that elite women construct alliances to gain access to material and symbolic resources, but that shared gender identity is seldom an important basis for such alliances. Dorthe von Bulow, in a study of women's groups in Kilimanjaro, Tanzania (1995), argues that modern, income-generating women's groups may contain elements of empowerment and solidarity, but that within many, the dominant feature is that a few women use the groups as part of personal strategies to obtain access to power, prestige, and economic resources. The women who do this tend to be building on existing positions of prestige and respectability. In the case of Kilimanjaro, the influence of Christianity is important – WaChagga women use women's groups to signal modernity and development-mindedness at the same time as maintaining the image of good Christian wives and mothers. 'Hence ideologies about female and maleness ... can also be used by women to enhance their position in society. However, it is a strategy which is only open to a minority of women, whose position in society depends on the fact that prevailing patriarchal gender relations are continued' (von Bulow 1995: 13).

In contrast to the work on elite women in women's groups, there is far less evidence or discussion regarding how men fit into this, as husbands and even as group members. The fact that women's groups have only women in them is virtually taken for granted. It does, however, need to be scrutinized. If there are male members, the need to question why the official identity is that of 'women's group' rather than any other becomes more acute.

Second, to what extent do the form and structure of women's groups reflect prevailing social organization? This question is closely related to the first. It arises from the presumption that the highly formal bureaucratic structure of many women's groups is partly the product of the legacy of donor (and probably colonial) intervention, and may have less to do with other modes of social organization with which it coexists.

March and Taqqu (1986: 106) suggest that the widespread attention of donors to cooperatives and groups in their support for development is 'based on a rationalist western model of political decision making which is not uniformly intelligible throughout the world'. In other words, donor models of bureaucratic organization are fed back to the people who are expected to be participating. Clearly, this is somewhat of a caricature: much PRA explicitly endeavours to discover rather than create local forms of organization. Nevertheless, as we argue below, the bureaucratization of rural life provides strong evidence against any unproblematic categorization of 'the locals'.

## Men in women's groups

People's responses to development are informed by their own history as well as their experience of, or at least the reputation of, development intervention. When people appear to be cooperating, adapting to, or resisting externally driven development projects, they are not merely reacting to outsiders. They may be reinterpreting development concepts – such as 'tradition', 'progress' and 'modernity' – but their actions are meaningfully understood only within the context of their own social, economic, and political positions, and the ideologies that arise from these.

The formation of groups is another important way in which development agendas are adopted. In Luapula, although there is a general apathy towards party politics (except in so far as some people wish to distance themselves from earlier UNIP connections), the status of being an 'office-holder' is none the less important. This is indicative of a widespread bureaucratization of village life. As one man explained: 'It is important to have a post – like now, I am choir secretary. It is good to have a post because then you can go to meetings and be a leader. You have more respect as a top leader.'

Organizations take diverse forms: from church-based working groups to clubs arising out of external assistance, school parent–teacher associations, and groups formed for mutual assistance. What they all have in common is their strict bureaucratic structure: a group must be properly constituted, with elected office-holders and a committee. In one village a mutual farming group had seven office-holders (chairman, vice-chairman, secretary, vice-secretary, treasurer, organizer, trustee) – and only one member. What is interesting about this stress on the importance of bureaucratic organization is its derivation from outside influences such as the government and aid organizations, and the fact that it has now been internalized as a key part of village life – for some. The office-holders in one group often appear as office-holders in another – and all of them are those who in some sense identify themselves with modernity and 'being developed'.

Of course, diverse groupings are made for a wide range of productive and distributive purposes. They may be, for the farmers concerned, the most effective means of using restricted resources. People are also aware of the strategic importance of connections to clubs. In Monga area, when word got around that UNICEF was now going to be diverting resources away from the women's clubs and towards education, there was a sudden scramble for places on the executive of the Parent-Teacher Association. A UNICEF-supported vegetable-growing group also attracted people other than those intended. UNICEF's official target for members of the group was the 'poorest people' in Monga. The group was to be given seed, fertilizer, and advice on marketing. However, the eventual membership of the group did not reflect initial objectives:

> They made a census and then they fed the names into the computer. But the original people selected did not respond. They were suspicious. They did not know why their names were picked and anyway old people were mainly selected and they were not interested. So out of 24, only eight responded. So the gaps were filled by the available people who were chosen by the agricultural assistant (pers. comm. 1992).

Those who filled the gaps included teachers, and others who had a high profile in the area. The executive consisted of: chairman (also vice-chairman of the fish-farming group and headman); secretary (also contact farmer for FAO, member of the fish-farming group, and trials farmer for ARPT); treasurer (a woman, also secretary of the women's group and wife of the fish-farming group's vice-treasurer); and vice-treasurer (wife of the chairman, and daughter of one of the few tractor-owners in the area). Of the original people chosen for membership, none was involved in the executive, with its direct access to UNICEF funds and resources.

As was illustrated in Chapter 7, a limited number of people present themselves as 'progressive' and reinforce the developers' notions of the social context within which they are operating. At the same time, some people are excluded. For a number of reasons, women and older people face specific constraints, arising from problems in access to land and labour. However, while group membership may reflect particular mechanisms of exclusion, these do not follow strictly gendered lines. Clearly this is partly because of the fact that women are not an undifferentiated category. It is also the result of the parallel processes in which women suffer subordination in development processes, yet are a high-profile 'target group'.

In Luapula, there are indications that both women and men have internalized the possible importance to them of adopting a gender agenda that has filtered down to them through the promotion of women's and other groups. This promotion permeates into 'village' understandings of developers' priorities in diverse ways. There are the regular (often expatriate) visitors from development organizations. They are apparently interested in talking primarily to women, and may bring promises of resources, particularly when women show an ability to work together. As groups are recognized by many as a means of access to development assistance, it is not surprising that women's groups are popular. In one village, which had received at least four researchers asking questions about women, an ALCOM information officer taking photographs of women, a German-funded nutrition project for women, a Swedish-funded health clinic with a focus on women and children, a Danish-supported sewing project, and an ALCOM-supported 'mutual feeding centre', women come together as groups at the least encouragement (see Harrison 1995). A group of women demanded to be 'registered' as a club. When asked what they meant one explained: 'We are women. We have dug ponds. We must be a club now. We need to be registered.'

They said that they had received many visitors who had promised them a club but that still nothing had happened. When asked what the value of being part of a club was the women were perplexed. They said, 'But you want us to have women's clubs.' But why women's clubs? Again, 'That is what you want.'

In addition, though, local-level bureaucrats who are the 'front-line' representatives of these development organizations convey models about village gender relations – models that may reflect reality only remotely, but are replicated by some members of rural communities. An aspect of this is the connected ideas that women are weak, that they need men, and that they need to work together. The source of these ideas is uncertain. It is at least partly influenced by the fact that applications for agricultural loans by women must be guaranteed by their husbands. This in turn reflects a legacy of colonial, development donor, and government attitudes in which women are seen as marginal and secondary to men. At a seminar for 'fish-scouts' (extensionists) organized by ALCOM, one scout explained: 'Traditionally, women are known to be weak to men. This therefore puts them off most of the activities, for instance, fish-farming. In short, inferiority complex is a big hindrance to women.'

In Luapula, there is considerable female autonomy in specific aspects of decision-making, particularly related to farming. Married women and men often have separate fields, and control the products from these separately. Nevertheless, the ideas of female powerlessness, and relatedly of the need for women to work together, are partially adopted within rural communities – by both women and men.

Thus it is not only women who have responded to the gender agenda. The Monga women's farming group, which was also supported by UNICEF, had a number of male members. The chair of the women's group was a man. His wife was the treasurer, and the granary for storing the maize grown by the group was kept on his land. He explained that he was just helping the women with contacts and collecting the various forms that they needed from town. This man was also chairman of the fish-farmers' group, and contact farmer for most agencies working in the area, including FINNIDA, ARPT, and FAO. Other male members of the group were married to female members.

The participation of the men in the women's group prompted certain questions, particularly regarding how other members viewed it. Was there any sense of anomaly, or that the men were impostors? Why was it a women's group rather than just a farming group? Such questions were dismissed by the members as if they were irrelevant. They stressed that male membership of women's groups in the area was in no way unusual. Two messages were reiterated: that the women needed the men, and that UNICEF wanted to support women this year – why should this mean that men should not take part?

The ideas that 'men and women need to work together' and that 'women are too weak without men' were repeatedly emphasized. They are, however, not as straightforward as they appear. As noted, the separation of economic activities between women and men is varied in Luapula – some married men and women have a wide range of autonomous activities, while other couples have much greater inter-dependence. Those who work most closely together tend to be the resource-poorest, farming cassava and maybe groundnuts or beans and having minimal income to pool. Conversely, those with clearly separate economic activities and decision-making are also rather better off, largely because of their more diverse sources of income – whether from vegetable growing, trading, maize-farming, or brewing (Harrison 1993). In Monga, these people were also the most active members of the women's group. Nevertheless, however separate their other activities, they were willing to articulate the externally reinforced ideology of female dependence when it came to the workings of the group.

Apparently, then, the women's group illustrated an alliance between some women and men in which aspects of an outside gender agenda were selectively internalized. This does not necessarily mean that there were substantial material benefits. The women's group was nominally involved in a wide range of activities – fish-farming, maize-farming, vegetable-growing, training in domestic skills. They had plans to take up chicken- and maybe rabbit-rearing. However, the benefits derived from any of these activities and who controlled these, were seemingly few. Meetings were held, a fish-pond had been dug but not stocked, vegetables were harvested, but nobody knew who was controlling the proceeds. There was no evidence that anybody was misappropriating funds. This might have been taking place, but would not anyway repudiate the broader proposition that membership of the group was as much about the meanings associated with it as the reality of material gain – indeed, the fact that this material gain is hard to identify indicates the significance of the symbolic aspects of this internalization of 'development' values.

For the majority of the women in Monga area, the women's group was an irrelevance. These women did not speak English, were not *au fait* with bureaucratic structures, and instead emphasized the individualistic nature of production in the area. While distribution of what they produced took place according to reciprocal, generally kin-based, relationships, production was invariably limited to the conjugal unit, with a degree of negotiation over the gender division of labour. For poorer women, especially those without access to male labour, the struggle to pay or 'beg' people to clear land for planting was not relieved by access to women's groups – or any other kind of group. This isolation and apparent alienation from the externally induced development process was reinforced by two combined factors: the pressure of material imperatives (principally less time to attend meetings), and the more nebulous sense of consequence and social standing that members, both men and women, attributed to their own role in these groups.

It is clear that behind the nominal women's group, a number of complex processes were going on, in which strategic alliances between some men and some women transcended what donors assumed would be strategic alliances between women. The phenomenon of men as members of women's groups in Sub-Saharan Africa is not well documented. Sylvester (1995) notes that in Zimbabwe a number of women's farming groups were chaired by men and that where this was the case, women tended to 'authorize' the men in terms of their indispensability and ability in meetings. Njonjo et al. (1985) reports that in Kenya, 7 per cent of the membership of women's groups was male. Sörensen (1990) suggests that this is largely because of male skills in marketing and book-keeping, but argues that the fact that men are drawn in and that better-off and elite women, who identify strongly with their men's interests, are members 'seriously undermines the collective potential of female solidarity across houses' (1990: 18). Although we found in western Kenya that even better-off Luo women's groups members articulated an opposition between their interests and those of their husbands, they also explained that they were under pressure to give the impression to their husbands that they too would benefit from the activities of the group. They would, for example, buy presents for their husbands out of the income they accrued through producing stoves as a group. Furthermore, one women's group was chaired by a man because, members reported, he had useful local political contacts, and most groups tended to be dominated by the higher-income, better-connected households.

These findings are only indicative. They point to the need for caution in assuming that women's groups, however successful, are a means towards, or an indicator of, women's empowerment. Greater attention needs to be paid to the differences as well as the similarities between women, to how gender relations are mediated by class and other aspects of stratification, and to how people selectively adopt or internalize occasionally contradictory values. In particular, the simplistic equation of women with poverty needs to be reassessed and replaced by a more thorough analysis of how gender relations are actually played out. Certainly, many women are among the poorest, but in Luapula poorer women apparently had few interests in common with the richer members of the groups.

Buvinic (1989) notes the donor tendency to support activities, including clubs, that increase women's status and income-earning potential rather than changing the power relations between men and women in the family. Such an approach assumes that benefits for women will cost men nothing – unlikely to be the case when differentials in power are at issue, as we argued in Chapter 3. This is an important criticism, but needs to be reinforced by an attempt to understand the complex ways in which alliances between women and men are created, sustained, and undermined.

## Villages, communities, locals

Unpacking the relationships within women's groups provides an indication that 'putting locals in the driving seat' is not as straightforward as simple calls for participation imply. Some locals are more able or willing to learn to drive than others – and some have already built their own cars. This cannot be neatly predicted according to class, age, or gender, but understanding the interaction of these variables is none the less important. Clearly, too, a distinction between donors' 'partners' and the ultimate beneficiaries – the real 'locals' – is impossible to sustain. We suggested in Chapter 4 that the language of partnership tends to be used to describe relationships between donors and the organizations that act as intermediaries between them and the ultimate beneficiaries. There is an implied (though false) equality between the partners. Also, though, negative associations often emerge about partners who fail to make the grade – the kind of associations that are made much less frequently with 'locals' or 'local communities', who are also less likely to be portrayed as equals. However, membership of such categories is not mutually exclusive or static. Is the head of a village-based farming group simply a 'local', or, from somebody else's perspective, including her own, could she instead be seen as a developer? And what about the local partners, whose identity may be simultaneously (or consecutively) that of developer, farmer, Zambian, knowledge-holder, and powerless?

Villareal (1992) sheds light on the position of local partners, or frontline workers, in development projects by pointing out that they have to work out appropriate strategies, possibilities, and constraints. They are faced with the task of presenting a package and making it work. Although strategies and standards for action are created outside,

> the implementor's practical analysis cuts through these categories, as he or she now has to face people and their interests, their different understandings, their constraints, their abilities etc. Here is the crucial moment of decision making, of actual accomplishment of projects, which mostly turn out to be drastically different from written plans (1992: 251).

The fish-scout who was the representative of the ALCOM project and the Department of Fisheries in Chibote area illustrates this clearly. He was, nominally at least, ALCOM's partner. Posted there against his will while nearing retirement, expected to cover an area of 930 square kilometres on a moped with insufficient petrol or spare parts, forced to live in a poor-quality thatched hut with his wife and seven children, in some ways part of the village, but in other ways not – his position as local partner is worthy of examination as it illuminates further the fluidity of apparently simple categories.

The DoF fish-scout had to contend with both his relative powerlessness at the bottom of a departmental hierarchy and in relation to ALCOM, and his slightly ambiguous position in relation to farmers. He claimed that his seniors never visited him or read his reports. He was a potential distributor of largess, but had limited practical ability to do this. In material terms he was no better off than many of the farmers with whom he worked. At the same time, his position as a representative of the government distanced him. In this respect he is similar to a Zambian agricultural extension worker whose experiences are described by Hedlund (1984). Hedlund argues that interaction between the extensionist and the villagers was sporadic because his ideology and ambitions were so totally in contrast to the villagers' point of view. At the same time as being at the bottom of the extension hierarchy, he saw himself as the representative of the government and the nation in the village. He was keen to assert formal difference, particularly because of his youth and the fact that his education was not significantly above that of many of the villagers. 'To the agricultural extension officer villagers represented disorder, irrational values, conservatism and not least an indifference to his own development ideology' (Hedlund 1984: 242).

However, for the fish-scout in Chibote, opposition between himself and the village was not straightforward. He had to manage a number of competing priorities: doing what ALCOM and DoF had designated in his work-plan (visiting and training farmers, rehabilitating Mission-built breeding-ponds and carrying out a census of fish-farmers); supervising the construction of a new house for himself; getting on with the people among whom he lived. Coming originally from the neighbouring district, he was not a stranger to the area. His wife had many relatives nearby and was enmeshed in social relations in Chibote. Thus the need to assert difference was tempered by the need to belong.

Given these circumstances there were a number of outcomes that were, if not inevitable, then not surprising. He concentrated on what he perceived to be both ALCOM's priorities and a way of making allies: a limited number of 'model farmers' and the Mission ponds. ALCOM was conducting on-farm 'trials' with two contact farmers. It was these farmers who were visited: 'they understand easily, and we want to work with those who understand, then others will copy'. Extension work with others was sporadic at best, but predominantly non-existent. The rehabilitation of the Mission ponds enabled him to make friends through his control over resources – the ponds were to be repaired using pieceworkers. Given the lack of employment opportunities in the area, working for the fish-scout was a potentially valuable source of income. When the banks of two of the ponds collapsed, releasing all of the fish, the scout claimed that they had been broken by the villagers, so they could be employed to rebuild them. ALCOM and DoF blamed poor construction.

Although in 1988 ALCOM had identified Chibote as a flourishing site of fish-farming, by 1992 the project was deemed to have been a fiasco. Very little extension had taken place, there was no visible evidence of improved pond management, and the village hatcheries did not look promising. In ALCOM most of the blame was unofficially pinned on the personal failings of the fish-scout. However, these personal failings could also be seen as a fairly reasonable response to the situation he found himself in. With personal motivation and commitment lacking, there was little that was likely to engender them. As Arce and Long argue, although it might seem that the particular strategies of an individual are highly idiosyncratic, 'in fact they are shaped by the possibilities for manoeuvre and discourse that already exist' (1993: 181).

In many ways, the fish-scout should be seen as a local. He lived as a local, he was part of village relations of exchange and negotiation, and he took part in, as well as being the subject of, local gossip. But his position was more complicated than this. He was simultaneously an insider and an outsider whose primary affiliation adapted with circumstances. Similarly his friends, the model farmers, did not unambiguously see themselves as 'villagers'. Their association with the project and with the fish-scout meant that other identities were also important. However, once we begin to accept the fluidity of such identities, clearly the whole idea of the village and the local becomes contestable.

The implications of this for simple notions of participation and resistance are obviously problematic. Reification of the 'village' or the 'local community' is pervasive. However, a recent criticism of participatory approaches (Brown 1997) suggests that participation is likely to be an alliance between local elites. This is echoed by Mosse (1994), who argues that the public nature of most attempts at participation naturally precludes many (usually women) from taking part. Brown's argument goes further. He derides the trend in what he sees as 'neo-populism' undermining the 'legitimacy of the development professional in favour of a growing faith in the power of the rural poor themselves' (1997: 2). This, he says, results in a paradoxical alliance between those who espouse the primacy of the marketplace, whatever its social consequences, and those neo-populists who claim to demand equity but who are suspicious of 'professionals' who might want to play any role in this. Because no arbitration between competing interests is offered, the result is a dearth of political analysis and the likelihood that participation will be partial at best. Structural inequalities are ignored.

The populist alternatives to mainstream development illustrate the tension between individual agency and those analyses that privilege the importance of structure. Much populist writing is individualistic. For example, Chambers argues that 'fundamentalisms are profoundly divisive and weaken any sense that individuals can make a difference ... Caricatured in their vulgar forms, both neo-classical and Marxist theory render the individual virtually powerless to change the course of human affairs ... The key is personal choice' (Chambers cited in Brown 1997: 6). Brown argues that this approach is 'as sceptical of the conditioning influence of society as the most hardened Thatcherite' (1997: 6). He takes exception to the way the argument is consistently diverted from structural relationships to individual responsibilities.

To explain why particular individuals in the same economic or political position as each other behave differently, some account has to be taken of individual histories. For example, while one relatively low-income Kenyan potter decided to take part in the stoves programme because she had a positive experience of development projects, another declined because her past contact with foreign aid agencies had wasted her time and brought nothing. Even so, those individual histories are not unconnected to political and economic structures or shared symbolic systems. Rather than polarizing individual choice and structures, the relationship between these levels deserves more investigation. Choice takes places within the confines of structures at various levels and is not, therefore, merely 'personal' but expresses past and present social relationships. Thus structures do not merely restrict behaviour: they leave plenty of room for manoeuvre and offer opportunities for some. Furthermore, since those structures are the product of individuals' actions, and new actors keep entering the fray, they are under continual revision.

While recognizing the power structures between those giving and receiving aid, we have tried to show that the portrayal of 'beneficiaries' as either passively obedient or defiantly resisting the 'developers' does not fit with reality. We have seen in this chapter that inclusion and participation in 'development' do indeed lead to some people, whom we might call 'elites', putting themselves forward, and increasing their visibility. This may be through forming groups, through associating themselves with the local extensionists, or through accepting development projects. Almost by definition, the excluded are less visible, if not silent. Those putting themselves forward may be celebrated for their ability to organize themselves, or even resist. However, it is also clear that the construction of interests and identity is more complicated than simple opposition between 'the village and the outside world': people create, cross, and re-create such boundaries. The balance between this and the structural determinants of their room for manoeuvre is the subject of the concluding chapter.

# CHAPTER 9

# The Cohesive Machine

Resilient constructs are embedded within development organizations: social evolutionism, a belief in the magical nature of technology, faith in economic rationality, and androcentrism continue to thrive. We have argued that these are expressed in the speech, documents, and actions of development practitioners and theorists. The origins of such constructs can be traced back to the European Enlightenment and beyond and received a boost during colonialism. For some writers on development there is a certain determinacy about such processes. Thus the discourses and practices of development are analogous to a machine whose actions seem predictable or inevitable. The image of social change being driven solely by such a bundle of European ideas is, however, a distortion.

First, cultures outside Europe plainly developed their own parallel or hybrid versions of these constructs long before the Enlightenment. Second, ideas alone cannot drive the development 'machine', any more than they can determine behaviour in other contexts. Third, the 'machine' analogy becomes unconvincing when you look at the relationships between its supposed components. The claim that development discourses and practices are entirely controlled by developers, predominantly from Europe and America, is becoming increasingly tenuous in the face of globalized communication systems. National boundaries are becoming irrelevant to the processes of information dissemination and even knowledge construction. Even long before globalization, Europe had been hugely influenced by Africa and Asia, far more than is usually acknowledged: 'the real frontiers between Europe and non-European worlds have been much more blurred and porous than the rhetoric and imagery of "European civilisation" suggest. European culture developed in the context of several forms of osmosis' (Pieterse 1994: 131).

This influence continues even more obviously within European countries today, partly as a result of migration. Research with British migrants, many of whom have moved from former British colonies, shows that many have complex, hybrid identities. For example, a young British-born Gujarati living in Wellingborough recently said: 'I'm Indian at home and once I'm out the back door I'm British' (Kothari and Crewe 1997: 18). It might be argued that since he was born in a British town, both non-European identity and development are irrelevant to him. Since the white majority in Wellingborough have not, however, found it easy to incorporate Indian identity into their idea of Britishness (or Europeanness), his Britishness is far from straightforward.

Other members of his community (and other black groups in the town) are running community development projects that face many of the same kinds of problems as international development projects. How to do participatory needs assessment, provide better access to services for women, greater accountability of voluntary and statutory organizations to communities, and so on, are also endlessly debated by black and white community organizations in Wellingborough. This work is, of course, a continuation of a long history of community development in Britain. So, since development plainly has taken place in Britain for some time, geographically bounding the development 'machine' makes little sense.

Furthermore, machine analogies, and in fact most models of development, rely on a number of apparently straightforward dichotomies that dissolve as soon as you scrutinize them. We have tried to show in Chapters 5 to 7 how developers/recipients, local/non-local, traditional/modern, culture/economics, state/NGO, expert/non-expert, us/them all merge when explored in context. The central dichotomy – developer/recipient – is plainly not the only, or even the most important, way that people are classified in the day-to-day thinking of development practitioners. Significant differences in attitudes between different continents, and the countries within them, prevail. For example, a former staff member of a large British NGO reported that project staff approached NGOs in South/Central America and those in Africa (excluding South Africa) with completely different sets of presuppositions:

> In Latin America NGOs are run by intellectuals with a much more sophisticated discourse than the British NGOs. They are almost in awe of them. They work with trade unions there, and treat them with great respect. In Africa, they patronize people. They see the situation as hopeless. Four hundred work in the Gambia, but virtually none (except for VSO) work in Nigeria. It has oil, but that is not a reason for not working there. After all, the way it's distributed means that there is great poverty there. They do not work there because it is difficult and people are far from deferential (anonymous pers. comm. 1997).

This woman, now a consultant, reveals that assumptions about particular groups of 'recipients' vary dramatically. People fuse a mixture of historically based racist stereotyping (for example, Indians are not capable of governing themselves), and individual experience that appears to them to confirm or deny the stereotype (for example, one NGO committee member reported that 'Indians cannot cope with finance'). No one is merely influenced by the 'developers' versus 'recipients' dichotomy alone. As we argued in Chapter 4, the attributions to particular groups may be derogatory, or even racist. The point we wish to stress here is that those working in development behave with an awareness of differentiation within each category. And yet both practitioners and theorists often fall back on the developers/recipients duality in certain contexts.

For example, while acknowledging complexity and hybridity, the expanding literature on the anthropology of development still tends to make use of simplifying dichotomies, such as the one between 'us' (developers ) and 'them' (recipients). A number of writers (notably Hobart 1993) have presented the difference between these as acute and, ultimately, irreconcilable. He speaks of the various discourses of development (of governments, developers, and local people) as being incommensurable. As Grillo has pointed out, such thinking borders on cultural solipsism. He argues that it implies that '"local" knowledges are grounded in such different philosophical foundations from "Western" knowledge that communication between them is in fact impossible; rationalities are not shared or share-able' (1997: 14).

While we agree that development encounters involve the meeting of people with different philosophies, morals, and systems of meanings (a fact that is often overlooked in the employment of 'cultural translators'), a position of inevitable incommensurability is untenable. On the one hand, philosophies within the 'West' diverge as much as they do between the 'West' and elsewhere. Fundamentalist Christianity can be found, for example, in common between some Americans and some Brazilians, while the views of atheists and Christians within America are sometimes deeply opposed. On the other hand, as Lévi-Strauss pointed out, all systems of knowledge are similarly designed to create order and different systems require the same mental operations even if they are applied to different phenomena (1972: 13). Intuitively too, as Aristotle argued: 'one may observe in one's travels to distant countries the feelings of recognition and affiliation that link every human being to every other human being' (cited in Nussbaum 1995).

The problem for us is not that there are no shared meanings; it is one of identifying how these are created and sustained by material circumstances. All those participating in development projects are under pressure to communicate so that they can fulfil their respective roles. Thus, in the context of rural Luapula, in some circumstances there was a shared discourse between some farmers and some developers that was stronger than a shared discourse between these farmers and their neighbours. Associations between modernity and digging ponds are reconstructed through relationships between some farmers and developers, as we described in Chapter 7. As a student undertaking research in Sri Lanka, Emma Crewe had more in common with Sri Lankan social scientists working in development than with visiting British engineers, who seemed to talk a different language of development. Although those Sri Lankan social scientists were 'developers' in most contexts, one in particular became the 'recipient' of Emma's supposed expertise in monitoring and evaluation. The fact that we are able to identify such shared discourses across the apparent developers/ recipients divide undermines any arguments of complete incommensurability. The confusion about whether Sri Lankan development practitioners are developers or recipients challenges the very division itself. And yet, to be able to talk about power relations and material inequalities within development, categories are necessary. The tension between deconstruction and the analysis of power and inequality is a central theme of this chapter, and one to which we will return below.

Escobar, particularly in his 1995 book *Encountering Development*, also works with the categories of developers and those who are developed, but adds a third, idealized category of those who resist development. We argued in Chapter 8 that reification of the 'local' is problematic and that much of what is labelled resistance may overstate the intention involved. Sherry Ortner has criticized what she calls 'resistance studies' – when a poor man steals from a rich man, is this resistance or simply a survival strategy? (1995: 175). Furthermore, creating a category out of those who engage in resistance ignores contextuality and change. If it were fixed in membership, where would we place the farmers, potters, or stove-users who comply with project staff's demands on some occasions and then ignore their advice on others?

We have seen that NGOs on different continents are seen as deficient in different ways. There are even more pronounced differences in attitudes towards people in NGOs and the so-called direct beneficiaries, local 'community' members. Institutional partners tend to be denigrated – they lack skills and usually require training and capacity-building. The members of the beneficiary category are more consistently celebrated. Anthropological studies have long focused on discrete, identifiable 'communities', frequently paying attention to the effects of their interaction with the outside world. As we have seen in this book, anthropologists have been joined (or even influenced in some cases) by what Richards calls the 'priests of humanistic plurality' (cited in Grillo 1997: 8). These priests espouse bottom-up, participatory approaches to development, but with a romantic, even naive, view of the formation and articulation of interests. 'Local truths' are thus given prominence and romanticized with little sense of the variability and normative nature of such truths.

The romantic view of the 'local' (in this context within 'communities' rather than formal institutions) as unsullied, simple, and unitary was never historically correct. Implicitly, the celebration of the 'local' perpetuates such misunderstandings and confusion about what local means. We are not saying that locality does not exist, rather that it is not an objectively verifiable physical entity with fixed membership. As Appadurai suggests, 'space and time are themselves socialized and localized through complex and deliberate practices of performance, representation and action' (1995: 206).

If identification of 'them' (for example, locals) is problematic, then is the category 'us' any easier to characterize in terms of aspirations, discourses, assumptions, or practices? At an obvious level, of course it is. Institutions of development, such as the UN agencies, the World Bank, bilateral donors, and international NGOs are all part of the development establishment, as are academics concerned with development, international consultants, and civil servants in the donor countries. But is this establishment composed of donors? No: Intermediate Technology is both a donor (to partners in other countries) and a recipient of funds from other donors. All organizations, including governments, are involved in endless money transactions that form international and national networks of exchange rather than flows in one repeated direction. And what about recipient governments, who may be both the agents of development for their countries, and subject to the strictures and controls of international development? Are they part of establishment, servants, or opposed to it? And indigenous NGOs who may both promote particular ideologies of development and see an opposition between themselves and the ultimate beneficiaries: are they recipients of development? Clearly, classifying organizations is not as straightforward as it initially appears.

Equally, though, there are differences even within apparently homogeneous organizations. In *The Anti-Politics Machine*, James Ferguson draws an analogy between the 'development apparatus' and Foucault's writings on the prison. Foucault argued that, while the prison had failed to reduce crime, it had succeeded in producing delinquency, which was politically and economically less dangerous: 'so successful has the prison been that, after a century and a half of "failures", the prison still exists, producing the same results, and there is the greatest reluctance to dispense with it' (cited in Ferguson 1990: 20). In Ferguson's case, the 'development apparatus' in Lesotho is a machine for reinforcing and expanding the exercise of bureaucratic state power. But is the machine such a monolith?

In Chapter 4 we stressed that the rhetoric of partnership often disguises considerable inequalities in the power and choices of supposed institutional 'partners'. At an obvious level, the development apparatus is fragmented: not only is there a great diversity in types of organization, but the ways they work, the histories of individuals within them, and their political contexts vary greatly. The apparent power of one set of actors, for example the promoters of a technology, is not simple or unitary. Different actors act under variable constraints, making power more fluid than it might at first seem. As Quigley (1993) points out in his analysis of caste relations in India and Nepal, there is no one rigid hierarchical system where people's rank is generally agreed. Caste is relational, and status is negotiated in context between particular groups. Similarly, social groupings in development do not constitute a linear hierarchy on racial or national lines. Rather, development encompasses people positioning themselves in relation to other groups, especially the dominant one, in a particular context. Colombo-based NGO staff are dominant in some contexts (in relation to potters), subordinated in others (when dealing with donor representatives). Some stove-making potters are dominant when employing other poorer household members as labourers, but subordinate when evaluators (expatriate or national) visit and investigate how successful they have been.

Chapter 4 suggested that there is often a significant failure to take account of the diverging priorities of institutional 'hosts' or partners. The ALCOM project was conceived in Rome. It apparently took scant account of the incentives, priorities, or resources of its institutional hosts, the governments of the SADC region, and their employees. Intermediate Technology's partners in Sri Lanka and Kenya had a much more curtailed ability to decide the course of events than the rhetoric of partnership might seem to imply. However, differences among both 'us' and 'them' go further than this. In Chapter 8 we described how, in the face of decentralization, people in Intermediate Technology headquarters both negotiated according to individual priorities and accepted a transformation that reduced their power at the same time. This was also the case within the ALCOM project. At the same time, individual 'recipients' respond differently to opportunities presented by development and some are warmly embraced into the 'us' category. As in any hierarchical system, different people's motivations and priorities are partially influenced by their relative position within that hierarchy at any one moment, as we illustrate below.

## One of us?

ALCOM's pilot project in Luapula was small for a donor-funded development project with limited financial input, modest objectives, and the posting of three young expatriates over the space of three years. However, even in such a small case, the differences between individuals had profound effects. The three expatriate Associate Professional Officers (APOs), who were the 'face' of ALCOM during the life of the project, were in complex positions. They were involved in three contrasting, but not necessarily compatible, worlds: the demands of Rome and Harare, the needs of the local department, and the farmers with whom they were supposed to be working. The evolution of the project was strongly influenced by their abilities to negotiate their positions within these worlds.

APOs are the most junior among FAO's 'expert' staff. Many APOs have considerable knowledge in their area of technical specialization, though not necessarily any direct knowledge of the countries where they go to work. They are in part trainees, but the notion of training and supervision was hard to put into practice in the context of the Luapula pilot project – the APOs were at least two days' journey from their supervisor in Harare. This meant that they had to interpret their work-plan as best they could. The first two APOs left before the end of their contracts, partly because relations with the local department (DoF) were awkward (perhaps in turn due to the department's disappointed expectations).

The APO who arrived in 1991 (we shall call him Peter) had to pick up the threads of the project and the legacy of ill-feeling that had developed between ALCOM and DoF. He was trained principally in marine biology, but had also studied aquaculture, and it was his first posting in Africa. From Rome and Harare, two messages were clear: the importance of the correct adoption of procedures, and the need to show evidence of work, particularly the production of fish. Equally, though, he needed to respond to the donor agendas influencing the direction of ALCOM, the most significant one being the concern with gender and the need for participation and interaction with farmers. At the same time, the resources with which he was to work were limited: an office, one four-wheel-drive vehicle, and restricted funds for diesel and equipment. Nominally, Peter's role was the provision of 'technical support' to the Department of Fisheries, with the assumption that DoF would be supporting its own extension activities.

Peter was faced with a complicated set of problems. On the one hand, the notion of technical support to a non-functioning extension service was meaningless. On the other, he was aware of the main criticism of the first phase of the pilot project – essentially that 'nothing happened', and that he had a limited period of time (three years at most) in which to make his mark. Making things happen fast and effectively was, he knew, not necessarily in the spirit of participation. He needed to find a way of resolving top-down and bottom-up. His response was to try to steer the project away from its previous emphasis on studies and station-based trials, towards training, monitoring, and trying to improve relations with extensionists. For Peter, what he perceived as the apathy and lack of commitment of the extensionists was a serious challenge. He believed that an important part of his job was to engender greater commitment. Finally, he paid scrupulous attention to the reporting demands of his employers, realizing that, ultimately, the quality of his reports would be how he would be judged in Rome and Harare.

The work with farmers met some obvious criteria for participation. The training courses, for example, took place close to farmers' homes, practical activity was stressed, and particular efforts were made to involve women farmers. However, there were other pressures. There was no time to adapt the courses to the specifics of each group, so, for instance, a group who had already built ponds were instructed in how to do so. The efforts to include women generally failed: a very small proportion attended. The fact that others did not because they did not have the time was generally accepted. Most importantly, perhaps, for the extensionists who were meant to adopt a 'participatory' approach to the training, this was an alien concept. They were used to instructing, not learning with the farmers. As a result, despite good intentions, participatory workshops became lectures.

The wish to bring the extensionists on board was hampered in other ways. In March 1992, all of the Luapula fish-scouts were invited to a seminar in Mansa, organized and funded by ALCOM. Fish-scouts were asked to present papers on their views concerning constraints on fish-farming and encouraged to use a 'problem-solving' approach to addressing those constraints. Peter intended that through sharing ideas, mutually advantageous solutions could be reached. For the fish-scouts this approach was incomprehensible. Notions of group decision-making and problem-solving were alien in the hierarchical context with which they were familiar and with which ALCOM was closely associated. This is understandable: the request for their opinions took place at the same time as reminders of the very clearly defined boundaries of expression of 'inferiors' in relation to their 'superiors'. Thus at meals a 'high table' was set aside for ALCOM, the Provincial Fisheries Development Officer and the visiting national fish culturist. Speeches were given in order according to the importance of the people concerned, following an accepted institutional format. It was repeatedly stressed (by their departmental superiors) that fish-scouts are not involved in planning, that their job was simply the collection of data and teaching farmers. The scouts themselves were therefore understandably unwilling to venture opinions on possibilities for improved aquaculture development other than those relating to the provision of items of equipment.

In the evaluation of the pilot project, Peter's energy was applauded. The list of his activities was impressive. However, it was also suggested that the pilot project had moved away from what it should have been: 'methodology development' ('we were never meant to be doing extension'), and thus might have created demands that could not be met. Peter had acted reasonably, given the situation he had to live with. This did not, however, tie in with objectives elsewhere in the project (his seniors in Harare). They, in turn, were not in a position to dispute the Rome-derived pressure for 'results'.

We can see that aspirations towards participation, however genuine, take place in the context of existing relations of power and hierarchy. But a division between powerful developers and powerless recipients does not do justice to the complex power relations involved. The participation of both fish-scouts and farmers was superficial at best. At the same time, like the fish-scout in Chibote (as described in Chapter 8), the ALCOM expatriate workers did not command dominance over the fish-scouts/farmers; they too had to make the best of the situation they found themselves in.

So far we have highlighted differences between people's situations in this case study. Commonality was also significant, for a reason that is overlooked in documentation about development. All three of the expatriates posted in Luapula between 1990 and 1993 formed long-term relationships with local Zambians – two got married and the third (although not married) has a child with a Zambian man. These expatriates were certainly not leading separate, incommensurable lives caught in a cocoon of European isolation. Their experiences are not so unusual (although perhaps ALCOM's 100 per cent record in this respect is). The prevalence of marriage, sexual relationships, and friendships between 'developers' and 'recipients' is widely acknowledged (at least informally) among development practitioners, but they rarely appear in development studies literature. More generally, the ways in which personal relationships intersect with professional ones, influenced for example by race and gender, are ignored by policy-makers despite their importance to understanding power relations and decision-making in development.

## One of 'them'?

One of the first potters who produced improved stoves in a particular programme was a likeable and energetic woman whom we shall call Alice. In 1987 Intermediate Technology approached her women's group, along with three other groups, and explained that it would teach them to make ceramic stoves. For two years her group was the only one that gradually established a stove-making business. The other three 'promised' that they would start any time, but explained at the end of the project that they never did because they thought other enterprises would be more profitable. Alice's neighbours asked her: 'What is the point in these stoves, you can't eat them?' It was difficult to sell the stoves – they were bulky, easily breakable, and difficult to transport to market. Convincing people to buy a new untested product proved hard work; even so, Alice, and the other members of the women's group, continued because they said that they trusted the project staff. They made only tiny amounts of money out of the business, but they pursued the project in the cause of 'development'. In particular, Alice developed a friendship and rapport with the British Intermediate Technology representative who acted as Project Manager of this stoves programme for about five years. She also got on well with one of the many British evaluators of the programme; they corresponded and exchanged presents by post.

During the second phase of the stove programme (from 1989), a national was recruited as Project Officer by Intermediate Technology and it was planned that she would take over from the British Project Manager by the end of the new two-year project. She clashed with many people involved in the project, including Alice. Alice's stories about her unacceptable behaviour were instrumental in the Project Officer's dismissal at the end of this phase of the programme. As the third phase began, a new Project Officer was recruited, a former government employee who had been involved in disseminating the stoves and had already established a good relationship with Alice. By this time Alice's group had begun earning a small but reasonable income from stove production and she was overwhelmingly the most energetic producer. Intermediate Technology often hired her on a consultancy basis to teach other potters how to make stoves; she travelled to neighbouring countries to advise other stove programmes as well.

Alice's success created tensions within her household and with her neighbours. In the early 1990s, after her domestic problems reached a crisis, she moved to the main town where Intermediate Technology had a small office. At the same time, Intermediate Technology offered her a job with a regular salary. She became a technical assistant to the Project Officer, mainly training new women's groups to make stoves, check the quality of those made, and give technical assistance. She travelled to England and publicized Intermediate Technology's work on the radio and in a play seen by numerous development agencies. In the space of five years, she had left her village and transformed her life, her work, and her identity. She had moved from being a farmer/potter/women's group member living in a small wattle-and-daub house in a village to being a salaried development worker living on her own in a brick house in a large town. She had surely become a 'developer'.

The decisions to choose Alice's group, to recruit and dismiss Project Officers, and to employ Alice as a technical assistant, were all made by the British Intermediate Technology manager and her boss in the UK. Although Alice had a few useful local political contacts (along with other members of her group), this would have ensured only Intermediate Technology's initial introduction to the group. Alice had no greater access to wealth than other women's group members and no qualifications; she was not, therefore, in a straightforward position of power within her group. She did have, on the other hand, unusual intelligence, charisma, and energy. Also, as a woman with no children, possibly already in a difficult household situation, she may have been unusually motivated to seek independence from her community. Her particular history and circumstances account for her special relationship with key Intermediate Technology personnel and, consequently, with her transition from 'beneficiary' (them) to 'developer' (us). At the same time, she is probably that programme's most significant beneficiary in financial terms.

These two case studies point to the fuzziness of the 'developers' and 'recipients' categories. They also illustrate that all actors are constrained by various pressures and limits but create their own space for man-oeuvre when they can. Weak versus powerful individuals are not so easy to identify.

## The gap between promise and practice

A number of accounts aim to avoid presenting 'images of local people as weak, powerless, and dependent, and unable to create their own futures' (Porter et al. 1991: 210). However, stress on 'local' (meaning villagers/farmers) diverts attention from dynamic agency at other levels and in other spheres. Benhabib (1995) discusses this in relation to the work of Richard Rorty, who also makes continual references to 'us' and 'them' as if such terms were simple and uncontested. She points out that the lines between us and them do not necessarily correspond to the lines between one culture and another: 'I think where "we" are today globally is a situation in which every "we" discovers it is in part a "they", that the lines between "us" and "them" are continuously redefined through the global realities of immigration, travel, communication, the world economy, and ecological disasters' (1995: 244).

Benhabib suggests that rather than looking at such relationships in terms of discrete cultures, we might call them 'communities of conversation'. These communities have shifting identities and no discrete boundaries. They do not necessarily coincide with ethnic boundaries: 'we are all participants in different communities of conversation as constituted by the intersecting axes of our different interests, projects, and life situations' (1995: 247). This concept may be a useful way of addressing the permeable relationship between us and them. It reinforces the notion that people in very diverse settings do in fact speak the same language. It also leaves space to acknowledge that another necessary part of this is the exclusion of certain groups.

The development 'machine' too is comprised of a number of parts which are clearly capable of independent action, and whose identities are not fixed or rigid but capable of adapting to circumstances to some extent. This is a recurring theme in some studies of development. Porter et al. argue against the idea that development is something that is done by us to them because of competing and sometimes conflicting objectives among us. In their case of a resettlement project in Kenya, there were different objectives ascendant at different times within the donor agency itself. The gulf between these objectives and those of the host government was even greater. Tim Morris tells a similar story for a primary health care project in Yemen, where 'none of the other players in our aid game ... shared our vision' (1993: 208).

In much analysis of development, the greatest anti-heroes are the developers themselves, as if they were part of a conspiracy. But this assessment is too simple; a more measured critique is warranted. Porter et al. (1991) argue that the project staff they met in Kenya had two things in common: their passion about their experiences with the project, and their sincere wish to improve the lives of the project beneficiaries. One of our objectives in this book is to inquire into why and how so many good intentions can lead to such poor outcomes. Porter et al. advocate greater humility as critics of development than, for example, Hancock does in his polemic against the *Lords of Poverty* (1989) or Sachs does in his *Development Dictionary* (1992). The people with whom we have worked in Rome, Zambia, Rugby, Sri Lanka, and Kenya, who were, nominally at least, part of the 'machine', all had good intentions.

There is no coordinated conspiracy in the development industry, and not all projects obviously 'fail'. Rew argues that there is no certainty of failure or that projects will always consolidate national or international power relations (1997). Similarly, he points out, with reference to Ferguson's work, that as much as there are projects that extend the nation state, there are others that weaken it. Where projects do successfully expand the power of the state, we argue, a government-led conspiracy is not necessarily at work. The idea that individuals anticipate the impact of their actions and organize their behaviour accordingly makes little intuitive sense and is neither empirically nor logically verifiable, as we tried to show in Chapter 6. Similarly, Bloch argues that the ritual of the royal bath in Madagascar demonstrates the legitimation of the monarch's authority but that this function does not explain the ritual (1989a: 208). Thus the impact of a ritual, institution, or even industry (in our case organized for development) cannot be assumed to be its cause.

Still, a yawning chasm remains between the stated goals of development and its practices and outcomes. Ambitious aims of partnership and gender sensitivity, recognizing indigenous knowledge and decentralized decision-making, often appear disappointingly empty. But they are clearly related to practices and material conditions, a point that is often peripheral to or even absent from the arguments of much post-modernist criticism of development. As Jackson points out, the post-modernist stress on discourse, particularly on words, narratives, and texts, is often worryingly silent on material conditions, particularly with regard to poverty: 'the shift from materialism is a feature of postist understandings of poverty, where culture, ideas, and symbols are discursively interesting and constitutive of power, whilst materiality is of questionable status and at least suspect' (1997: 147). Even Escobar, who pays great attention to the monolithic power of the 'West', does not give a substantive account of how this relates to material conditions and outcomes.

Similarly, Sylvester (1995) stresses the unsettled, unfixed, and negotiated nature of gender identity in Zimbabwe. She argues that it is sensible to view Zimbabwean women as 'women', 'that is, as bearers of an unsettled, unfixed, and indeterminate subject status that the people thus labelled may or may not embrace' (Sylvester 1995: 185). She argues that we should problematize this category of meaning, not taking it as given, especially in the context of competing and conflicting messages. While the device of sitting back critically, even from such an apparently straightforward category as woman, succeeds in drawing attention to the fact that meanings vary, the refusal to accept any one meaning has worrying implications. In a sense, what it does is to deny the concrete conditions under which women clearly are women, and have shared experiences of both material and symbolic subordination, in access to resources, to land, to control over their own bodies, and so on. Interestingly, Sylvester is drawn back to this herself towards the end of the piece, when she asks 'where's the truth?' and answers 'no one questions gender as a meaningful identity: there are men and there are women and everyone knows who is who' (1995: 201).

The balance between materialist 'grand theory' certainties, and post-modern insights into nuance and complexity, is a difficult one to strike. Benhabib has argued that the methodological sophistication of many recent writers, 'their contextualist scruples and post modern hesitations' (1995: 236), runs into a variety of cultural relativism that can be both callous and indifferent to human suffering and injustice. This is a point echoed by Jackson (1997), who is also concerned by an apparent trend away from the acceptability of saying anything substantive about inequality or injustice. On the other hand, there is a problem with much grand theory that continues to place the powerful at the centre of the stage while the meek merely respond.

In this book we have not marshalled empirical evidence about the material outcomes of aid at an aggregate level. We have, however, asserted repeatedly that aid has specific material effects that are often at odds with the rhetoric. For example, ambitions for gender sensitivity are often translated into a focus on women. The corollary of this is that the concrete conditions of gender inequity are not always challenged and women continue to have, for example, less control over decision-making and resources (see Chapter 3). Rhetoric about equality in partnership, meanwhile, tends to translate merely into attempts to elicit the views of staff in partner agencies. There is a gloss over the dominance that donors retain through their control of finance and the construction of public knowledge about development (see Chapter 4). Participatory aspirations, meanwhile, whereby 'locals' are supposed to be in the driving seat, should be viewed in contrast to the practices that continue to leave material inequalities unchanged. Not only are 'locals' reaffirmed in their subordinate position to those bringing aid but wealthy elites among the 'local' category are often legitimized or strengthened in the process (see Chapter 8).

Why is there such a disjunction between what is claimed for development and practice? A number of explanations have emerged from the anthropology of development that are rather less deterministic than the work of people such as, for example, Escobar and Sachs. These focus on the 'control orientation' of development organizations and the pressure for simplification within them (as examples, Porter et al. 1991; Morss 1984; Nindi 1990). Control orientation is the assumption that social and physical environments characterized by a high degree of uncertainty must be rigorously controlled (Porter et al. 1991: 4). It partly accounts for the persistence of projects (Morss 1984). The orientation leads people to make assumptions about the capacity of local institutions that are at best heroic. Any decisions to refine the control orientation – for example, by trying to leave greater room for local determination of priorities (encouraging participation) – are made by people who have little awareness of the paradox implied in trying to put this into practice. Arguably, intervention by hierarchical organizations through project aid is antithetical to releasing control.

Quarles van Ufford (1988) also considers a gap between rhetoric and reality in a Dutch development project in Indonesia. He focuses on the nature of bureaucratic organization, arguing that the dominance of Weberian models of bureaucracy serves to perpetuate theoretical distinctions between rational policy and politics. In practice, though, the segmentation of roles within bureaucracies means that there is increasingly little connection between policy and what happens once policies have been made. Indeed, much development policy is undertaken in ignorance of what goes on once funding decisions have been made. This certainly echoes much of what we have found: segmented bureaucracies such as FAO and Intermediate Technology do not function as Weberian integrated wholes. Rather policies are reinterpreted according to the rationales, predilections, and positions of the individuals concerned. Equally, those creating the policies, even if they have had 'field experience' at some point in their careers, are physically, as well as conceptually, separated from those charged with carrying out their policies.

A related aspect of segmentation and the nature of bureaucratic organization is a tendency towards simplification and categorization. The pressures for this can be irresistible for a number of reasons. First, professionalism is often associated with activities that are seen to be technical or scientific. In the apparently non-technical subject of gender, matrices, dichotomies, and models proliferate to convey the impression of professionalism (see Chapter 3). Second, donor agencies shy away from giving funds for pre-project work, for example carrying out research to discover what local needs are. They need a mechanism for decision-making and aim to give the impression of rationality and coherence in their choices. Their staff and board members have their own preferences for environmental management, health care, population control, or whatever. They formulate their own policies and allocate funding according to their set criteria. Open-ended needs assessment, for example, is difficult to assess according to sector-based criteria. The result is that fund-seeking agencies often have to fabricate the 'needs' of their intended beneficiaries or, at the least, grossly simplify and homogenize their social, economic, and political situations.

Third, international development agencies are under pressure to present simple messages. Whether they are raising funds, influencing other agencies, or explaining their work to 'beneficiaries', the complexity of their experience has to be simplified for communication purposes. This partly reflects the extraordinary ambition and optimism of many international agencies in working with huge numbers of different cultural and occupational groups, in different countries or even continents, and/or across many so-called sectors. While national voluntary agencies, whether in Britain or Tanzania, tend to specialize in one topic or region, many international agencies appear to assume that working in 'developing' countries requires less specialization. Their simplification of many issues perhaps partly reflects their assumption that generalizations about certain people in certain countries can be more easily made because their problems, needs, or cultures are simpler.

On another level, we should not expect anything other than a gap between rhetoric and practice. Aspirations for equality are sometimes expressed in Utopian plans for reversing power relationships. Since these plans are written by those in a position of power, their relationship with reality is bound to be remote. In this respect, the processes of projects bear a remarkable resemblance to many rituals. The performance of various aspects of development intervention can be highly regulated: all projects tend to be divided into set stages (appraisal, planning, implementation, evaluation); training, seminars, and workshops often have standard components (plenary, small group sessions, single-speaker presentations); and reports tend to have the same headings according to their function (evaluation reports often cover inputs, outputs, achievements, impact).

Viewing development as ritualized may help us to fill a gap in our picture of how development ideologies are produced and reproduced. Bloch claims, with particular reference to Merina rituals in Madagascar, that rituals are important for explaining how ideology is created (1989a: 124). In the same way that Merina rituals reaffirm that women naturally give birth and bring up children (among other things), development ideologies are re-created and communicated through the various stages of projects. For example, within a project plan it is reiterated that it is 'local communities' in particular parts of the world that have the social, economic, and technological problems while the 'developers' have the solutions. This is symptomatic of the evolutionist ideology that we described in Chapter 2. The ways in which projects are implemented also express numerous ideological constructs, some of which we have explored in this book. Finally, during the ritual of evaluation, a donor is advised to continue funding (but perhaps shift objectives) or switch its attention to other schemes. Through evaluation, then, the ideological constructs are reconfirmed and the idea of the legitimacy of the donor as benign benefactor is consolidated. As Bloch puts it, 'ideology appears as a picture of the world where specific power-holders are the source of all good things' (1989a: 133).

Projects may not be the only way in which such ideologies are created. Education, literature, and the media, for example, undoubtedly play a part in rebuilding ideas that retain currency in development. Development also consists of much more than mere projects. But projects are an important way in which these ideas, and those that apparently challenge them, are negotiated between the various groups involved in development. Role reversals, as advocated in PRA for example, are typical of many rituals and can act to confirm rather than challenge the status quo. Thus ideologies expressed in the ritual of projects legitimize the power of aid-givers without posing a real threat to the existing social order.

Even if we accept the analogy with ritual, we still have not explained why these ideologies persist. More specifically, why do aid-receivers participate in development if the ideologies underlying it legitimize the power of their benefactors? In addition to some people being motivated by material gain (actual or expected), the answer lies partly in fragmentation. There is no clear identifiable group of aid-receivers, as we explained earlier in the chapter. Many of those so-called 'locals' who participate see themselves as 'developers' rather than the 'poor' or 'recipients' or the 'exploited'. There is not a monolithic machine with one single group exploiting another single group, so resorting to ideas such as 'false consciousness' in explaining why any individual participates does not help.

Nevertheless, inequalities, injustices, and poverty remain unchallenged by development and it is perplexing why actors apparently participate in this process, especially when many lose out. Even if it is not a matter of powerful versus powerless, or even a linear hierarchy with powerful/rich/donors at the top and powerless/poor/recipients at the bottom, hierarchies clearly prevail. Of course aid does not reproduce hierarchies on its own. Terms of trade and debt are far more significant in perpetuating poverty and inequality. For example, the Multi-Fibre Arrangement costs Asia, Africa, and South/Central America about $50 billion a year in lost export earnings, roughly equivalent to the total global flow of development aid (Simmons 1995: 19).

Power relations within the aid industry are plainly intimately bound up with the global capitalist system. Those working in development tend to ignore this, although unusually Clare Short, secretary of state for international development, said soon after the Labour government won the British general election: 'It is very important that those interested in development should widen their interest to include trade, debt, agricultural policy and so on. Otherwise the aid budget – however large – can be simply a charitable sop that helps lessen the impact of other policies which create impoverishment' (1997). Aid-receiving countries are already locked into trade relations with donor countries, who tend to be the same countries who negotiate and benefit from the international terms of trade. Although tying aid to trade has become politically difficult to justify, the two international systems of exchange cannot be disentangled.

In theory even the subordinate participants in aid, that is, those on the receiving end, have the opportunity to gain dominance over non-participants by allying themselves to modernity (for example, through modern technology). It might be argued that this is their main motive for seeking aid. This would imply, however, a simpler view of intentionality than we require, whether we are concerned with national governments or individuals. We have established that motivation cannot be reduced to materialism alone. At the same time, we have no wish to replace the quest for material gain or social status with ideology as an explanation of motivation. Rather, we would question the idea of motivation itself because it assumes that individuals are capable of making choices irrespective of their culture. There are two problems with individualistic theories about motivation. The relative consistency of behaviour within a particular culture remains unexplained, and there is confusion about how human behaviour works in relation to time.

Ideology does not drive action in the present, but is used in patterned ways to explain or make sense of the past. Ideology rationalizes what has happened and then acts as a legitimation of the present social order, but does not determine what people do. Those ideologies that are particularly effective as a rationalization of the social order are more likely to survive. A powerful affinity or resonance is needed between the two. The same ideologies can survive with other realities (for example, evolutionism has continued through colonialism and development), so the two do not have a necessary relationship. But the idea, for example, of superior 'modern' technology invented by 'modern' men has survived because it works well for rationalizing the dominance of 'modern' men in the development industry. The idea of low-capital-intensive technology being superior on occasions (as suggested by some within Intermediate Technology) has been singly unsuccessful (even within Intermediate Technology at times) because it has no resonance with the existing wider social order.

Thus the connections between ideology and power become clearer. The 'powerful' are not aiming to consolidate their position as individuals by propagating ideas that favour their social position. Rather all actors learn about how the world is ordered through their practical experience of it. Ideological constructs and practical experience, including the material realities about who is wealthy, depend upon each other. Ideology survives because people inherit it, try it out as a way of explaining the past, and usually find it makes sense. That does not mean it is true, of course; it simply means that it legitimizes the dominance of particular groups effectively because it resonates with people's experience of domination. The groups in the social order are plainly not fixed, in either position or membership. According to context, they contain completely different people at different times and so one individual will dominate in some contexts and not in others. Thus it is important to emphasize that power is not a commodity invested in particular people, but expresses the relationship between classificatory groups into which actual people come and out of which they go.

Among the people who have been the focus of this book there are no obvious heroes or villains. Our aim was not to identify failure, attach blame, or flush out scapegoats. Rather we have tried to question various orthodoxies, including ideas about success and failure, from different perspectives. Accordingly, we have presented no simple solutions. Those who are busy with the day-to-day rush of problems, targets, and meetings that characterizes much development work may understandably feel that time is short, too short to be merely asking questions. And yet challenges to some of development's fundamental assumptions are already gaining momentum. Perhaps some of the ideas underlying development, like any system of knowledge, will change as the disjunction between assumptions and experiences becomes too large to accommodate.

# References

Ackerley, B. (1995) 'Testing the tools of development: credit programmes, loan involvement and women's empowerment', *IDS Bulletin*, vol. 26, no. 3.

Adams, A. (1979) 'An open letter to a young researcher', *African Affairs, Journal of the Royal African Society*, vol. 78, no. 313.

Ahmed, I. (ed.) (1985) *Technology and Rural Women: Conceptual and Empirical Issues*, George Allen and Unwin, London.

Aitken, J., S. Joseph, and P. Young, (1989) 'Evaluation of the Sri Lanka urban stoves programme', unpublished report, Intermediate Technology Development Group, Rugby.

Appadurai, A. (1995) 'The production of locality', in R. Fenton (ed.), *Counterworks, Managing the Diversity of Knowledge*, Routledge, London.

Appleton, H. (ed.) (1995) *Do it Herself. Women And Technical Innovation*, Intermediate Technology Publications, London.

Apthorpe, R., and D. Gasper (eds) (1996) *Arguing Development Policy: Frames and Discourses*, Frank Cass, London.

ALCOM (Aquaculture for Local Community Development) (1989a) Second advisory committee meeting report, GCP/INT/436/SWE/REP/3, FAO, Rome.

— (1989b) Pilot project document, Aquaculture and Rural Development, Luapula Province, unpublished.

— (1992a) *ALCOM News*, no. 6, ALCOM, Harare.

— (1992b) *ALCOM News*, no. 5, ALCOM, Harare.

— (unpublished) Formulation document.

Arce, A., and N. Long (1993) 'Bridging two worlds: an ethnography of bureaucratic–peasant relations in western Mexico', in M. Hobart (ed.), *An Anthropological Critique of Development: The Growth of Ignorance*, Routledge, London.

Asad, T. (1973) *Anthropology and the Colonial Encounter*, Ithaca Press, London.

— (1979) 'Anthropology and the colonial encounter', in G. Huizer and B. Mannheim (eds), *The Politics of Anthropology*, Mouton, The Hague and Paris.

Asia Regional Cookstove Program (1995) *Fifth Annual Report, January–December 1995*, ARECOP, Yogyakarta.

Basu, A. (ed.) (1995) *The Challenge of Local Feminisms: the Women's Movement in Global Pespective*, Westview, Boulder, CO.

Baylies, C. (1984) 'Luapula province: economic decline and political stagnation in a rural UNIP stronghold', in C. Gertzel, C. Baylies and M. Szeftel (eds),

196 · *Whose development?*

The Dynamics Of The One-Party State In Zambia, Manchester University Press, Manchester.

— (1995) 'Political conditionality and democratisation', *Review of African Political Economy*, vol. 22, no. 65: 321–37.

Becker, G. (1981) *A Treatise on the Family*, Harvard University Press, Cambridge, MA.

Benhabib, S. (1995) 'Cultural complexity, moral independence, and the global dialogical community', in J. Glover and M. Nussbaum (eds), *Women, Culture and Development: A Study of Human Capabilities*, Clarendon, Oxford.

Bennett, K. (1990), 'Technical objectives of donor-funded biomass energy programmes', in P. J. G. Pearson (ed.), *Energy Efficiency in the Third World*, Surrey Energy Economics Centre, University of Surrey.

Bhagavan, M. R., and S. Karekezi (1992) *Energy Management in Africa*, Zed and AFREPREN, London.

Bierschenk, T. (1988) 'Development projects as arenas of negotiation for strategic groups: a case study from Benin', *Sociologia Ruralis,* vol. XXVIII.

Bloch, M. (1989a) *Ritual, History and Power, Selected Papers in Anthropology*, The Athlone Press, London.

— (1989b) 'The symbolism of money in Imerina', in J. Parry and M. Bloch (eds), *Money and the Morality of Exchange*, Cambridge University Press, Cambridge.

— (1991) 'Language, anthropology and cognitive science', *Man*, vol. 26, no. 2.

Bloch, M., and J. Parry (1989) Introduction, in J. Parry and M. Bloch (eds), *Money and the Morality of Exchange*, Cambridge University Press, Cambridge.

— (1989) *Money and the Morality of Exchange*, Cambridge University Press, Cambridge.

Boserup, E. (1970) *Woman's Role in Economic Development*, St. Martin's Press, New York.

Bourdieu, P. (1977) *Outline of a Theory of Practice*, Cambridge University Press, Cambridge.

— (1984) *Distinction. A Social Critique of the Judgement of Taste*, Routledge and Kegan Paul, London, Melbourne, and Henley.

Braidotti, R., E. Charkiewicz, S. Hausler, and S. Wieringa (1994) *Women, the Environment and Sustainable Development: Towards a Theoretical Synthesis*, Zed in association with INSTRAW, London.

Brandt, W. (1980) *North–South: A Programme for Survival*, Pan, London.

Brewster, C. (1991) *The Management of Expatriates*, Kogan Page, London.

Brokensha, D., D. M. Warren, and O. Werner, (1980) *Indigenous Knowledge Systems and Development*, University Press of America, Lanham.

Brown, A. (1995) *Organizational Culture*, Pitman, London.

Brown, D. (1997) 'Professionalism, participation and the public good: issues of arbitration in development management and the image of the neopopulist approach', paper presented to Conference on Public Sector Management for the Next Century, University of Manchester, 29 June–2 July 1997.

Bulow, D. von (1995) 'Power, prestige and respectability: women's groups in Kilimanjaro, Tanzania', Centre for Development Research Working Paper 95. 11, Centre for Development Research, Copenhagen.

Burne, S. (1985) 'Seeing the wood through the trees. Woodstoves in Kenya', unpublished report, Intermediate Technology Development Group, Rugby.

Bush, C. G. (1983) 'Women and the assessment of technology: to think, to be, to unthink', in J. Rothschild (ed.), *Machina Ex Dea*, Pergamon, New York.

Buvinic, M. (1986) 'Projects for women in the Third World: explaining their misbehaviour', in *World Development*, vol. 14, no. 5.

— (1989) 'Investing in poor women: the psychology of donor support', *World Development*, vol. 17, no. 7

Cancian, F. (1980) 'Risk and uncertainty in agricultural decision making', in P. Bartlett (ed.), *Agricultural Decision Making: Anthropological Contributions To Rural Development*, Academic Press, New York.

Carloni, A. (1997) 'Women in FAO projects: cases from Asia, the Near East and Africa', in K. Staudt (ed.), *Women, International Development and Politics: The Bureaucratic Mire*, Temple University Press, Philadelphia.

Chambers, R. (1986) 'The crisis of Africa's rural poor: perceptions and priorities', in *The Challenge of Employment and Basic Needs in Africa*, International Labour Organization, Nairobi.

— (1988) 'Sustainable rural livelihoods: a key strategy for people, environment and development', in C. Conway and M. Litvinoff (eds), *The Greening of Aid: Sustainable Livelihoods in Practice*, Earthscan, London.

— (1994) 'All power deceives', in S. Davies (ed.), *IDS Bulletin*, vol. 25, no. 2

— (1996) *Whose Reality Counts?*, Intermediate Technology Publications, London.

Charity Projects (undated), Information Pack, Charity Projects, London.

Christian Aid (1987) 'British Council of Churches, Christian Aid, working group on project applications and reports', unpublished, Christian Aid, London.

Clark, J. (1992) *Democratizing Development: The Role of Voluntary Organizations*, Kumarian Press, West Hartford, CT.

Clifford, J. (1986) 'On ethnographic allegory', in J. Clifford and G. E. Marcus (eds), *Writing Culture: The Poetics and Politics of Ethnography*, University of California Press, California.

Cline-Cole, R. A., H. Main, and J. E. Nichol (1990) 'On fuelwood consumption, population dynamics and deforestation in Africa', *World Development*, vol. 18, no. 4.

Coche, A., B. Haight, and M. Vincke (1994) 'Aquaculture development and research in Sub-Saharan Africa', FAO CIFA Technical Paper no. 23, FAO, Rome.

Collinson, D., and J. Hearn (1996) *Men as Managers, Managers as Men: Critical Perspectives on Men, Masculinities, and Management*, Sage, London.

Cornea, G., R. Jolly, and F. Stewart (eds) (1987) *Adjustment with a Human Face*, Clarendon, Oxford.

Cornwall, A., I. Guijt, and A. Welbourn (1994) 'Acknowledging process: challenges for agricultural research and extension methodology', in I. Scoones and M. Thomson (eds), *Beyond Farmer First*, Intermediate Technology Publications, London.

Crehan, K., and A. von Oppong (1988) 'Understandings of development: an arena of struggle', *Sociologia Ruralis*, vol. XXVIII.

Crewe, E. (1989) 'Women's potter training project, Kenya, evaluation report', unpublished, Intermediate Technology, Rugby.

— (1993) 'Size isn't everything. An anthropologist's view of the cook, the potter, her engineer, and his donor in appropriate technology development in Sri Lanka, Kenya and the UK', unpublished thesis, University of Edinburgh.

Crush, J. (ed.) (1995) *Power of Development*, Routledge, London

Cunnison, I. (1959) *The Luapula Peoples Of Northern Rhodesia*, Manchester University Press, Manchester.

Dalton, G. (1961) 'Economic theory and primitive society', *American Anthropologist*, vol. 63: 1–25.

Davidson, O., and S. Karekezi (1993) 'A new environmentally sound energy strategy for the development of Sub-Saharan Africa', in S. Karekezi and G. A. Mackenzie (eds), *Energy Options for Africa*, Zed, London.

Davies, S. (ed.) (1994) *IDS Bulletin*, vol 25, no. 2.

DFID (Department for International Development) (1997) 'Eliminating world poverty – a challenge for the 21st century: summary', White Paper on international development, presented to parliament by the secretary of state for international development, HMSO, London.

DoF (Department of Fisheries, Luapula Province) (1990) 'Annual report 1989–90', unpublished.

Dixon-Mueller, R. (1985) *Women's Work in Third World Agriculture*, International Labour Organisation, Women, Work and Development, no. 9.

EPA (Economic Planning Associates) (1992) 'Triennial review of Intermediate Technology development group submitted to Overseas Administration, main report', unpublished, EPA, London.

Edwards, M., and D. Hulme (eds) (1995) *Non-Governmental Organisations: Performance and Accountability*, Earthscan, London.

Ellen, R. F. (1986) 'What the black elk left unsaid. On the illusory images of Green primitivism', *Anthropology Today*, vol. 2, no. 6: 8–12.

Eliot, T. S. (1940) 'Choruses from "The Rock"' I, *The Wasteland and Other Poems*, Faber and Faber, London.

Elson, D. (1995) 'Male bias in macro-economics: the case of structural adjustment', in D. Elson (ed.) *Male Bias In The Development Process*, Manchester University Press, Manchester.

ESMAP (Energy Sector Management Assistance Program) (1990) 'ESMAP in the nineteen-nineties. The findings of the Commission to Review ESMAP', ESMAP (World Bank/UNDP), Washington, DC.

ESMAP/UNDP (1991) 'An Evaluation of Improved Biomass Cookstoves Programs: Prospects for Success or Failure', a joint ESMAP/UNDP report,

Industry and Energy Department, World Bank, Washington, unpublished report, October.

Escobar, A. (1984) 'Discourse and power in development: Michel Foucault and the relevance of his work to the Third World', *Alternatives*, vol. 10, no. 10: 377–400.

— (1991) 'Anthropology and the development encounter: the making and marketing of development anthropology', *American Ethnologist*, vol. 18, no. 4.

— (1995a) *Encountering Development: The Making and Unmaking of the Third World*, Princeton University Press, Princeton, NJ.

— (1995b) 'Imagining a post development era', in J. Crush (ed.), *Power of Development*.

Esteva, G. (1992) 'Development', in W. Sachs (ed.), *The Development Dictionary*.

Evans, A. (1989) 'Women: rural development, gender issues in rural household economics', IDS Discussion Paper no. 254, IDS, Brighton.

Evans-Pritchard, E. E. (1937) *Witchcraft, Oracles and Magic among the Azande*, Oxford University Press, Oxford.

Ferguson, J. (1990) *The Anti-Politics Machine: Development, Depoliticization and Bureaucratic Power in Lesotho*, Cambridge University Press, Cambridge.

Folbre, N. (1994) *Who Pays For The Kids? Gender and the Structures of Constraint*, Routledge, London.

Foley, G., and P. Moss (1983) *Improved Stoves in Developing Countries*, Earthscan, London.

Foley, G., P. Moss, and L. Timberlake (1984) *Stoves and Trees. How much wood would a wood stove save if a woodstove could save wood?* Earthscan, London and Washington.

FAO (Food and Agriculture Organization) (1987) 'Women in aquaculture: proceedings of the ADCP/NORAD workshop on women in aquaculture', FAO, Rome.

— (1989) *Farming Systems Development: Concepts, Methods, Applications*, FAO, Rome.

— (1993) 'Enhancement of the role of women in inland fisheries and aquaculture development project. Project Findings and Recommendations' (unpublished), FAO, Rome.

FAO/NORAD (1987) *Thematic Evaluation of Aquaculture*, FAO, Rome.

Fowler, A. (1988) 'Non-governmental organizations in Africa: achieving comparative advantage in micro-development', Discussion Paper no. 249, IDS, Brighton.

— (1992) 'Building partnerships between Northern and Southern NGOs: issues for the nineties', *Development*, vol. 1: 16–23 (Journal of the Society for International Development, Rome).

Gardner, K. and D. Lewis (1996) *Anthropology, Development, and the Postmodern Challenge*, Pluto, London.

Gasper, D. (1996) 'Essentialism in and about development discourse', in R. Apthorpe and D. Gasper (eds), *Arguing Development Policy*.

Gatter, P. (1990) 'Indigenous and institutional thought in the practice of rural development: a study of an Ushi chiefdom in Luapula, Zambia', unpublished PhD thesis, School of Oriental and African Studies, University of London.

— (1993) 'Anthropology in farming systems research: a participant observer in Zambia', in J. Pottier (ed.), *Practising Development*.

Goetz, A. M. (1994) 'From feminist knowledge to data for development: the bureaucratic management of knowledge on women and development', *IDS Bulletin*, vol 25, no. 2: 27–36.

Goetz, A. M., and S. Baden (1997) 'Who needs [sex] when you can have [gender]? Conflicting discourses on gender at Beijing', in K. Staudt (ed.) *Women, International Development and Politics*.

Goetz, A. M., and R. Sen Gupta (1996) 'Who takes the credit? Gender, power, and control over loan use in rural credit programmes in Bangladesh', *World Development*, vol. 24, no. 1.

Goody, J. (1982) *Cooking, Cuisine and Class: A Study in Comparative Sociology*, Cambridge University Press, Cambridge.

Gould, J. (1989) *Luapula: Dependence or Development?*, Zambia Geographical Association/Finnish Society for Development Studies, Finland.

Gould, S. J. (1977) *Ever Since Darwin: Reflections in Natural History*, Penguin, London.

Gregory, C. A. (1982) *Gifts and Commodities*, Academic Press, London.

Grillo, R. (1997) 'Discourses of development: the view from anthropology', in R. Grillo and R. Stirrat (eds), *Discourses of Development*, Berg, Oxford.

Grillo, R., and A. Rew (eds) (1985) *Social Anthropology and Development Policy*, ASA Monographs no. 23, Tavistock Publications, London.

Guyer, J. (1986) 'Intra-household processes and farming systems research: perspectives from anthropology', in J. L. Moock (ed.), *Understanding Africa's Rural Households And Farming Systems*, Westview, Boulder, CO.

Hancock, G. (1989) *Lords of Poverty*, Macmillan, London.

Harrison, E. (1993) 'My pond has no fish', research report, University of Sussex, Brighton.

— (1995) 'Fish and feminists', *IDS Bulletin*, vol. 26, no. 3.

Harrison, E., J. Muir, A. Stewart, and R. Stirrat (1994) 'Fish farming in Africa: what's the catch?', research report, University of Sussex, Brighton.

Hayward, P. (1987) 'Socio-cultural aspects', in ALCOM, *Socio-Cultural, Socio-Economic, Bio-Environmental, and Bio-Technical Aspects of Aquaculture in Rural Development*, ALCOM GCP/INT/436/SWE.1, Harare.

Hedlund, H. (1984) 'Development in action: the experience of the Zambian extension worker', *Ethnos*, vol. 49.

Hess, D. J. (1995) *Science and Technology in a Multicultural World: the Cultural Politics of Facts and Artifacts*, Columbia University Press, New York.

Himmelstrand, K. (1997) 'Can an aid bureacracy empower women?' in K. Staudt (ed.), *Women, International Development and Politics*.

Hobart, M. (1993) *An Anthropological Critique of Development: The Growth of Ignorance*, Routledge, London.

Hofstede, G. (1991) *Cultures and Organizations: Software of the Mind*, McGraw-Hill, London.

Holy, V., and M. Stuchlik (1983) *Actions, Norms and Representations: Foundations of Anthropological Inquiry*, Cambridge University Press, Cambridge.

Howorth, C. (1992), 'Energy transitions in Africa', *Boiling Point*, no. 27, Intermediate Technology Development Group, Rugby.

Hulme, D. and M. Edwards (eds) (1997) *NGOs, States and Donors*, Macmillan, Basingstoke.

Hulscher, W. S. (1997) 'The fuel ladder, stoves and health', *Wood Energy News*, vol. 12, no. 1, Regional Wood Energy Development Programme in Asia, Bangkok.

ICLARM/GTZ (1991) *The Context of Small Scale Integrated Aquaculture Systems in Africa: A Case Study of Malawi*, ICLARM, Manila, Philippines.

Illich, I. (1976) *Limits to Medicine. Medical Nemesis: the Expropriation of Health*, Penguin, London.

Intermediate Technology (1993) 'Towards a gender strategy: draft notes', unpublished policy note, Intermediate Technology, Rugby.

— (1997a) 'Traditional knowledge explored', *IT News*, no. 1, Intermediate Technology, Rugby.

— (1997b) 'Making the future work: ethics and technology, development, not aid', unpublished paper, Intermediate Technology, Rugby.

Jackson, C. (1992) 'Gender, women and environment: harmony or discord?', discussion paper, GAID, no. 6, School of Development Studies, UEA.

— (1997) 'Post poverty, gender and development', *IDS Bulletin*, vol. 28, no. 3.

Jahan, R. (1997) 'Mainstreaming women and development: four agency approaches', in K. Staudt (ed.), *Women, International Development and Politics*.

James, W. (1973) 'The anthropologist as reluctant imperialist', in T. Asad (ed.), *Anthropology and the Colonial Encounter*, Ithaca Press, London.

Jensen, K. (1997) 'Getting to the Third World: agencies as gatekeepers', in K. Staudt (ed.) *Women, International Development and Politics*.

Kabeer, N. (1991) 'Gender, production and well being: rethinking the household economy', IDS Discussion Paper no. 288, IDS, Brighton.

— (1994) *Reversed Realities: Gender Hierarchies in Development Thought*, Verso, London.

— (1997) 'Tactics and trade-offs: revisiting the links between gender and poverty', *IDS Bulletin*, vol. 28, no. 3.

Kabira, W. M., and E. A. Nzioki (1993) *Celebrating Women's Resistance: A Case Study of the Women's Group Movement in Kenya*, African Women's Perspective, Nairobi.

Kajese, K. (1987) 'An agenda of future tasks for the international and indigenous NGOs: views from the South', *Development Alternatives: The Challenge for NGOs*, special issue of *World Development*, vol. 15.

Kardam, N. (1991) *Bringing Women In: Women's Issues in International Development Programes*, Lynne Rienner, Boulder, CO.

Karega, R. (1996) 'Women's groups: from welfare to small-scale business in Kenya', *Small Enterprise Development*, vol. 2, no. 1: 13–19.

Kartzow, A. de, P. van der Heijden, and J. van der Schoot (1992) 'Integration of fish farming into the farm household system in Luapula province, Zambia', ALCOM field document no. 16, ALCOM, Harare.

Kent, G. (1988) 'Improved use of fisheries resources: alleviating malnutrition in Southern Africa', *Food Policy*, vol. 13, no. 4: 341–58.

Kirk, C. (1983) 'Pottering with incorporation: social change and the Sinhalese potters of Ratmalagahawewa', in H. Heringa, U. L. J. Perera, and A. J. Weeramunda (eds), *Incorporation and Rural Development*, Unversity of Colombo, Colombo.

— (1984) 'Ratmalagahawewa: occupation and social organisation in a Sinhalese potter village. Sociological aspects of rural and regional development', Colombo Research Paper Series no. 2, Netherlands Universities Foundation for International Cooperation Project, Colombo.

Kothari, U., and E. Crewe (1997) 'Migration, work and identity. Gujaratis in Wellingborough', unpublished research report, Institute for Development Policy and Management, Manchester.

Kuper, A. (1983) *Anthropology and Anthropologists: The Modern British School 1922–72*, Allen Lane, London.

Leach, G., and R. Mearns (1988) *Beyond the Woodfuel Crisis: People, Land and Trees in Africa*, Earthscan, London.

Lévi-Strauss, C. (1972) *The Savage Mind*, Weidenfeld and Nicoloson, London.

Long, A. (1992) 'Goods, knowledge and beer: the methodological significance of situational analysis and discourse', in N. Long and A. Long (eds), *Battlefields of Knowledge*.

Long, N. (1992) 'From paradigm lost to paradigm regained? The case for an actor-oriented sociology of development', in N. Long and A. Long (eds), *Battlefields of Knowledge*.

Long, N., and A. Long (1992), *Battlefields of Knowledge: The Interlocking of Theory and Practice in Social Research and Development*, Routledge, London.

Long, N., and J. van der Ploeg (1989) 'Demythologizing planned intervention: an actor perspective', *Sociologia Ruralis*, vol. XXIX, no. 3/4.

Lukes, S. (1974) *Power: A Radical View*, Macmillan, London.

McCormack, C., and M. Strathern (1980) *Nature, Culture and Gender*, Cambridge University Press, Cambridge.

McRae, S. (1991) 'Making equality work for women', *New Scientist*, vol. 1330, no. 1770, 25 May.

Maar, A., M. Mortimer, and I. van der Lingen (1966) *Fish Culture in Central East Africa*, FAO, Rome.

Malinowski, B. (1927) 'The life of culture', in G. E. Smith et al. (eds), *The Diffusion of Controversy*, Norton, New York.

Manzo, K. (1995) 'Black consciousness and the quest for a counter-modernist development', in J. Crush (ed.), *Power Of Development*.

March, K., and R. Taqqu (1986) *Women's Informal Associations in Developing Countries: Catalysts for Change?* Westview, Boulder, CO, and London.

Marchand, M., and J. Parpart (1995) *Feminism/Postmodernism/Development*, Routledge, London.

Marglin, F., and S. Marglin (1990) *Dominating Knowledge: Development, Culture and Resistance*, Clarendon, Oxford.

Markoff, J., and V. Montecinos (1992) 'The ubiquitous rise of economists', *Journal of Public Policy* 13; 37–66.

Marx, K. (1976) *Capital: A Critique of Political Economy*, Volume One, Penguin, Harmondsworth.

Mauss, M. (1924) *Essai sur le don*, L'Année Sociologique, Seconde Serie. 1923–24.

— (1970) *The Gift: Forms and Functions of Exchange in Archaic Societies*, Routledge, London.

Mbozi, E. (1991) 'Integration of gender issues into fish farming in Chibote, Zambia', ALCOM field document GCP/INT/436/SWE. 17, Harare.

Meadows, D. H., D. C. Meadows, W. Behrens III, and J. Randers (1972) *Limits to Growth*, Universe Books, New York.

Merchant, C. (1980) *The Death of Nature: Women, Ecology, and the Scientific Revolution*, Wildwood House, London.

Mies, M., and V. Shiva (1993) *Ecofeminism*, Zed, London.

Mishra, S. (1994) 'Women's indigenous knowledge of forest management in Orissa (India)', *Indigenous Knowledge and Development Monitor*, vol. 2, no. 3: 3–5.

Moehl, J. (1989) 'Consolidation et réorientation du programme de vulgarisation piscicole en République Centrafricaine', FAO, working paper FI:DP/CAF/85/004.

Mohanty, C. (1988) 'Under Western eyes: feminist scholarship and colonial discourses', *Feminist Review*, no. 30: 61–8.

Molnar, J., B. Duncan, and L. Upton Hatch (1987) 'Fish in the farming system: applying the FSR approach to aquaculture', *Research in Rural Sociology and Development*, vol. 3: 169–93.

Molyneux, M. (1985) 'Mobilisation without emancipation? Women's interests, state and revolution in Nicaragua', *Feminist Studies*, vol. 11, no. 2.

Moore, H., and M. Vaughan (1994) *Cutting Down Trees: Gender, Nutrition and Agricultural Change in the Northern Province of Zambia, 1890–1990*, James Currey, London.

Morgan, D. (1996) 'The gender of bureaucracy', in D. Collinson and J. Hearn (eds), *Men as Managers*.

Morris, T. (1993) 'Eze-Vu – success through evaluation: lessons from a primary health care project in north Yemen', in J. Pottier (ed.), *Practising Development*.

Morss, E. (1984) 'Institutional destruction resulting from donor and project proliferation in Sub-Saharan African countries', *World Development*, vol. 12, no. 4: 465–70.

Moser, C. (1989) 'Gender planning in the Third World: meeting practical and strategic gender needs', *World Development*, vol. 17, no. 11.

— (1993) *Gender Planning and Development: Theory, Practice and Training*, Routledge, London.

Mosse, D. (1994) 'Authority, gender and knowledge: theoretical reflections on the practice of participatory rural appraisal', *Development and Change*, vol. 25, no. 3: 497–526.

Mouzelis, N. (1988) 'Sociology of development: reflections on the current crisis', *Sociology*, vol. 22, no. 1.

Mpande, R., and N. Mpofu (1995) 'Survival skills of Tonga women in Zimbabwe', in H. Appleton (ed.), *Do it Herself.*

Mudimbe, V. Y. (1988) *The Invention of Africa*, James Currey, London.

Nagabrahmam, D., and S. Sambrani (1980) 'To keep the home fires burning: women's drudgery in firewood collection', unpublished report, Institute of Rural Management, Anand.

Nash, C. (1986) *Observations on International Technical Assistance to Aquaculture*, FAO, Rome.

NLCB (National Lottery Charities Board) (1996) 'International grants programme for UK-based agencies working abroad', application pack, unpublished, NLCB, London.

Niamir, M. (1995) 'The indigenous systems of natural resource management among pastoralists of arid and semi-arid Africa', in D. M. Warren et al., *The Cultural Dimension of Development*.

Nindi, B. (1990) 'Experts, donors, ruling elites and the African poor: expert planning, policy formulation and implementation – a critique', *Journal of Eastern African Research and Development*, vol. 20: 41–67.

Njonjo et al. (1985) *Study on an Integrated Approach to Women's Programmes in Kenya*, Business and Economic Research Co. Ltd/Danida, Nairobi.

Norman, D. W., and D. Baker (1986) 'Components of farming systems research, FSR credibility and experiences in Botswana', in J. L. Moock (ed.), *Understanding Africa's Rural Households And Farming Systems*, Westview, Boulder, CO.

Nussbaum, M. (1995) 'Human capabilities, female human beings', in M. Nussbaum and J. Glover (eds), *Women, Culture and Development: A Study of Human Capabilities*, Oxford University Press, Oxford.

Oakley, P. (1991) *Projects with People: The Practice of Rural Development*, International Labour Organization, Geneva.

Olivier de Sardan, J. P. (1988) 'Peasant logics and development project logics'; *Sociologia Ruralis*, vol. XXVII, no. 2/3.

OECD (Organization for Economic Cooperation and Development) (1996) *Shaping the 21st Century: The Contribution of Development Cooperation*, OECD, Paris.

— (1997) *Development Cooperation: Efforts and Policies of the Members of the Development Assistance Committee, 1996 Report*, OECD, Paris.

— (1998) *DAC Guidelines For Gender Equality Women's Empowerment In Develop-*

*ment Co-Operation*, Development Co-operation Guidelines Series, OECD, Paris.

Ortner, S. (1995) 'Resistance and the problem of ethnographic refusal', *Comparative Studies in Society and History*, vol. 37, no. 1.

ODA (Overseas Development Administration) (1990) *British Overseas Development*, no. 14, November, ODA, London.

— (1992) *Checklist for the Participation of Women in Development Projects*, ODA, London.

— (1995a) 'Progress report on ODA's policy objectives, 1992/93 to 1993/94', unpublished report, ODA, London.

— (1995b) *ODA Fundamental Expenditure Review* by Suma Chakrabati, Roger Wilson, Peter Rundell, assisted by Helen Wilson, main report, unpublished report, London.

— (undated) *The Joint Funding Scheme: Guidelines and Procedures*, ODA, East Kilbride.

Pacey, A. (1983) *The Culture of Technology*, Basil Blackwell, Oxford.

Pearce, F. (1991) *Green Warriors: The People and the Politics Behind the Environmental Revolution*, Bodley Head, London.

Perera, J. (1997) 'In unequal dialogue with donors: experiences of the Sarvodaya Shramadana Movement', in D. Hulme and M. Edwards (eds), *NGOs, States and Donors*, Macmillan, Basingstoke.

Pieterse, J. N. (1994) 'Unpacking the West: how European is Europe?', in A. Rattansi and S. Westwood (eds), *Racism, Modernity and Identity on the Western Front*, Polity, Cambridge.

Pigg, S. L. (1992) 'Inventing social categories through space: social representation and development in Nepal', *Comparative Studies in Society and History*, vol. 34, no. 3.

Poewe, K. (1978) 'Matriliny in the throes of change: kinship, descent and marriage in Luapula, Zambia', *Africa*, vol. 48, no. 3.

— (1981) *Matrilineal Ideology: Male–Female Dynamics In Luapula, Zambia*, Academic Press, London.

Polanyi, K. (1977) *The Livelihood of Man*, Academic Press, New York.

Porter, D., B. Allen, and G. Thompson (1991) *Development in Practice: Paved With Good Intentions*, Routledge, London.

Pottier, J. (ed.) (1993) *Practising Development: Social Science Perspectives*, Routledge, London.

Quarles van Ufford, P. (1988) *The Hidden Crisis of Development: Development Bureaucracies*, Free University Press, Amsterdam.

Quigley, D. (1993) *The Interpretation of Caste*, Clarendon, Oxford

Quiroz, C. (1994) 'Biodiversity, indigenous knowledge, gender and intellectual property rights', *Indigenous Knowledge and Development Monitor*, vol. 2, no. 3: 12–15.

Rabinow, P. (1986) 'Representations are social facts: modernity and post-modernity in anthropology', in J. Clifford and G. E. Marcus (eds), *Writing*

*Culture: The Poetics and Politics of Ethnography*, University of California Press, California.

Ranger, T. (1983) 'The invention of tradition in colonial Africa', in E. Hobsbawm and T. Ranger, *The Invention of Tradition*, Cambridge University Press, Cambridge.

Razavi, S., and C. Miller (1995) 'From WID to GAD: conceptual shifts in the women and development discourse', UNRISD Occasional Paper No. 1, Geneva.

Redclift, M. (1989) *Sustainable Development*, Routledge, London.

Redclift, M., and T. Benton (1994) *Social Theory and the Global Environment*, Routledge, London.

Rew, A. (1997) 'The donor's discourse: official social development knowledge in the 1980s', in R. Grillo, and R. Stirrat (eds), *Discourses of Development*, Berg, Oxford.

Richards, P. (1985) *Indigenous Agricultural Revolution*, Allen and Unwin, London.

— (1993) 'Cultivation: knowledge or performance?', in M. Hobart (ed.), *An Anthropological Critique of Development.*.

Rogers, B. (1980) *The Domestication of Women: Discrimination in Developing Societies*, Routledge, London and New York.

Roper, M. (1994) 'Gendering organisational studies', *Anthropology in Action, Journal for Applied Anthropology in Policy and Practice*, vol. 1, no. 2.

Ruddle, K. (1991) 'The impacts of aquaculture development in socio-economic environments in development countries: towards a paradigm for assessment', in R. Pullin (ed.), *Environment and Aquaculture in Developing Countries*, ICLARM Conf. Proc. 31, ICLARM, Manila.

Sachs, W. (ed.) (1992) *The Development Dictionary: A Guide To Knowledge and Power*, Zed, London.

Saha, S. (1998) 'A colonial spectre amid the groves', *Times Higher Educational Supplement*, 23 January.

Sahlins, M. (1976) *Cultural and Practical Reason*, Chicago University Press, Chicago.

Sanderson, S. K. (1990) *Social Evolutionism: A Critical History*, Blackwell, London.

Schmitz, G. J., and D. Gillies (1992) *The Challenge of Democratic Development: Sustaining Democratization in Developing Societies*, North–South Institute, Ottawa.

Schumacher, E. F. (1971) 'Industrialisation through "intermediate technology"', in *Developing the Third World: The Experience of the Nineteen-Sixties*, Cambridge University Press, Cambridge.

— (1973) *Small is Beautiful: A Study of Economics as if People Mattered*, Abacus, London.

— (1975) *The End of An Era*, The Iona Community, Iona.

Schwartzman, H. B. (1993) *Ethnography in Organizations*, Qualitative Research Methods Series 27, Sage, Newbury Park.

Scoones, I., and M. Thompson (1994) *Beyond Farmer First: Rural People's Know-*

*ledge*, Agricultural Research and Extension Practice, Intermediate Technology Publications, London.

Scott, J. (1977) 'Patronage or exploitation?', in E. Gellner and J. Waterbury (eds), *Patrons and Clients in Mediterranean Societies*, Duckworth, London.

— (1985) *Weapons of the Weak: Everyday Forms of Peasant Resistance*, Yale University Press, New Haven, CT.

Seddon, D. (1993) 'Anthropology and appraisal: the preparation of two IFAD pastoral development projects in Niger and Mali', in J. Pottier (ed.), *Practising Development*.

Sen, A. (1979) 'Rational fools', in F. Hahn and M. Hollis (eds), *Philosophy and Economic Theory*, Oxford Readings in Philosophy, Oxford University Press, Oxford.

— (1995) 'Gender inequality and theories of justice', in M. Nussbaum and J. Glover (eds), *Women, Culture and Development: A Study of Human Capabilities*, Oxford University Press, Oxford.

Sen, G. and C. Grown (1985) *Development Crises and Alternative Visions: Third World Women's Perspectives*, Monthly Review Press, New York.

Sen, S., E. Seki, and J. van der Mheen-Sluijer (1991) *Gender Issues in Fisheries and Aquaculture, including Proceedings of the Workshop on Enhanced Women's Participation in Fisheries Development*, ALCOM GCP/INT/436/SWE/REP. 7, Harare.

Shekar, P. (1995) 'Manual silk reeling in India', in H. Appleton (ed.), *Do it Herself*.

Shiva, V. (1989) *Staying Alive*, Zed, London.

Shore, Chris (1993) 'Inventing the "people's Europe": critical approaches to European Community "cultural policy"', *Man*, vol. 28, no. 4.

Short, C. (1997) Speech by the Right Honourable Clare Short MP, secretary of state for international development, School of Oriental and African Studies, London, 28 May 1997.

Simmons, P. (1995) *Words into Action: Basic Rights and the Campaign against World Poverty*, Oxfam, UK and Ireland.

Smith, B. H. (1987) 'An agenda of future tasks for the international and indigenous NGOs: views from the North', *Development Alternatives: the Challenge for NGOs*, special issue of *World Development*, vol. 15.

Smith, J. (1983) 'Women and appropriate technology: a feminist assessment', in J. Zimmerman (ed.), *The Technological Woman: Interfacing with Tomorrow*, Praeger, New York.

Smith, K. R. (1992) 'The case for stove programmes', unpublished summary of a paper, Programme on Environment, East–West Centre, Honolulu.

Snape, E. G. (1990) 'The human infrastructure requirements of technicians, in appropriate development for survival – the contribution of technology', Workshop Notes, 9–11 October, Institute of Civil Engineers, London.

Sörensen, A. (1990) 'Women's organisations and changing gender relations among the Kipsigis of Kenya', CDR Project Paper 90. 5, Copenhagen.

Stamp, P. (1989) *Technology, Gender, and Power in Africa*, International Development Research Center, Canada.

208 · *Whose development?*

Staudt, K. (ed.) (1997) *Women, International Development and Politics: The Bureaucratic Mire*, Temple University Press, Philadelphia.

Stirrat, R. L. (1989) 'Money, men and women', in J. Parry and M. Bloch (eds), *Money and the Morality of Exchange*, Cambridge University Press, Cambridge.

— (1997) 'Cultures of consultancy', unpublished manuscript.

Stirrat, R., and H. Henkel (1997) 'The development gift: the problem of reciprocity in the development world', *Annals of the American Academy of Political and Social Science*, vol. 554: 66–80.

Stromgaard, P. (1985) 'A subsistence society under pressure: the Bemba of Northern Zambia', *Africa*, vol. 55, no. 1.

SIDA (Swedish International Development Authority) (1989) *Fish Farming for Rural Development. An Evaluation of SIDA Supported Aquaculture in Southern Africa*, SIDA, Stockholm.

Sylvester, C. (1995) '"Women" in rural producer groups and the diverse politics of truth in Zimbabwe', in M. Marchand and J. Parpart (eds), *Feminism/Postmodernism/Development*.

Toren, C. (1989) 'Drinking cash: the purification of money through ceremonial exchange in Fiji', in J. Parry and M. Bloch (eds), *Money and the Morality of Exchange*, Cambridge University Press, Cambridge.

Touwen, A. (1990) 'Socio-economic development of women in Zambia: an analysis of two women's organisations', *African Studies Research Reports*, no. 42, Leiden, The Netherlands.

Ulluwishewa, R. (1994) 'Women's indigenous knowledge of water management in Sri Lanka', *Indigenous Knowledge and Development Monitor*, vol. 2, no 3: 17–19.

United Nations (1995) Beijing Declaration and Platform for Action Adopted by the Fourth World Conference on Women: Action for Equality, Development and Peace. Beijing, September 1995.

UNDP (United Nations Development Programme) (1995) *Human Development Report 1995*, UNDP, New York.

USAID (1982) 'The gender information framework pocket guide. A set of guidelines and resources for incorporating gender considerations in AID development activities', unpublished, Bureau for Program and Policy Coordination, USAID, Washington, DC.

Usinger, J. (1991) 'Limits of technology transfer', *Boiling Point*, no. 26, Intermediate Technology Development Group, Rugby.

Villareal, M. (1992) 'The poverty of practice: power, gender and intervention from an actor oriented perspective', in N. Long and A. Long (eds), *Battlefields of Knowedge*.

Warren, D. M., L. J. Slikkerveer, and D. Brokensha (1995) *The Cultural Dimension of Development: Indigenous Knowledge Systems*, Intermediate Technology Publications, London.

Wekiya, I. F. (1995) 'Nkejje fish in Lake Victoria', in H. Appleton (ed.), *Do it Herself*.

White, S. (1994) 'Making men an issue: gender planning for the "other half"', in M. Macdonald (ed.), *Gender Planning in Development Agencies: Meeting the Challenge*, Oxfam, Oxford.

Whitehead, A. (1981) 'I'm hungry mum: the politics of domestic budgeting', in K. Young, C. Wolkowitz, and R. McCullagh (eds), *Of Marriage and the Market: Women's Subordination in International Perspective*, CSE Books, London.

— (1985) 'A conceptual framework for the analysis of the effects of technological change on women', in I. Ahmed (ed.), *Technology and Rural Women.*

— (1990) 'Food crisis and gender conflict in the African countryside', in H. Bernstein, B. Crow, and M. Mackintosh (eds), *The Food Question: Profits Versus People?* Earthscan, London.

Wieringa, S. (1994) 'Women's interests and empowerment: gender planning reconsidered', *Development and Change*, vol. 25, no. 4.

Wieviorka, M. (1994) 'Racism in Europe: unity and diversity', in A. Rattansi and S. Westwood (eds), *Racism, Modernity and Identity on the Western Front*, Polity, Cambridge.

Wijkstrom, U. (1991) *How Fish Culture can Stimulate Economic Growth: Conclusions from Fish Farmer Surveys in Zambia*, ALCOM GCP/INT/436/REP. 9, Harare.

Wijkstrom, U., and E. Jul Larsen (1986) 'Aquaculture: tackling the main constraints', *Ceres* 112: 19–22.

Wijkstrom, U. and K. Wahlstrom (1992) *Tilapia Culture by Farmers in Luapula Province*, Zambia, ALCOM Field Document no. 9, ALCOM, Harare.

Woodford Berger, P. (1987) *Gender, Rural Development and Aquaculture In Southern Africa: Factors Affecting the Representational Involvement of Women*, Development Study Unit, Department of Social Anthropology, University of Stockholm, Report no. 14.

Woodward, A. (1996) 'Multinational masculinities and European bureaucracies', in D. Collinson and J. Hearn (eds), *Men as Managers.*

World Bank (1989) *World Development Report 1989*, Oxford University Press, Oxford.

— (1994) *A Global Partnership for Development*, World Bank, Washington, DC.

— (1996) *The World Bank's Partnership with Nongovernmental Organizations. Participation and NGO Groups*, World Bank, Washington, DC.

Young, K. (1993) *Planning Development with Women: Making a World of Difference*, Macmillan, London.

Young, M. (1991) *An Inside Job: Policing and British Culture in Britain*, Clarendon, Oxford.

Yturregui, L. P. (1995) 'Coping with a lack of electricity in marginal urban areas', in H. Appleton (ed.), *Do it Herself.*

# Index

159 (adoption of, 113; and Information Technology, 11–14; decision-making about, 128–31; designed by men, 34; development process of, 32; impact on women, 101; in Sri Lanka, 83–4; manufacture of, 38; non-functioning of, 44; non-use of, 99; payback period for, 37, 128; preference for, 127; production of, 86; reasons for using, 125–8; unpopularity of, 12, 159); *Megan Chula*, 103; sawdust-burning, 104; traditional, 104

structural adjustment programmes, 69
SUTRA organization, India, 53
swidden farming, assessment of, 105
Sylvester, C., 170, 188–9

technology, 32, 48, 176; and expertise, 91–112; appropriate, 31, 33, 57, 110; as solution for poverty, 23; associated with men, 34, 92; associated with professionalism, 34; assumed neutrality of, 91, 92; culturally acceptable, 110; definition of, 92; development of, 27 (male domination in, 47); evolution of, 25; gendered effects of change in, 93; indigenous, 92; ladder of, 30–6; non-neutrality of, 34; traditional, 102–6; usefulness to women, 34

theory, construction of, 104
tilapia, raising of, 119
time, important to women, 128
tools, distinction between, 35
tradition, 25, 45, 153, 156; triumph over modernity, 132–54; viewed as constraint, 43; *see also* culture, traditional
traditional: definition of, 103; use of term, 30
tribal identities, 134
tribe, categories of, 139

Uganda, fish preserving in, 107
underdevelopment, 17, 91
United Nations (UN), 14, 49, 71, 93
UN Development Project (UNDP), 31; gender issues within, 63
UNICEF, 157, 158, 167, 169
UNIFEM, and stove projects, 102
UN World Women's Conferences, 49, 52, 54
United Nations Development Project (UNDP), 31
USAID, 51, 100; gender issues within, 63

vegetable gardens, growing of, 158
village, reification of, 174

voluntary sector workers, motivations of, 130

Water Wells Trust, 157
Weber, M., 50, 152
witchcraft, 134, 135, 138, 144, 145, 153; belief in, 45
women: affected by poverty, 51; African, assumptions about, 30; and agriculture, 107, 117; and fishing, 122; and innovation, 92, 93, 106–9; and ownership of fish-ponds, 116; as collective workers, 163; as cooks, invisibility of, 108; as engineers, 64, 109; as potters, 85, 116, 118, 175 (socialization of, 160; training of, 89); as social scientists, 58; concealment of time-savings, 128; elites, 165; excluded (from bureaucracies, 50; from technical development, 106); focus on, 189; importance of time to, 128; inclusion of, 183; inequalities between, 35; involvement in fish-farming projects, 60, 61; key in environmental management, 51; marginalized in technology development, 22; needs of, 54, 55; oppressed by science and technical applications, 35; refusal to make stoves, 127; relationship with nature, 36; reproductive work of, 51; responsibility for household work, 101; seen as weak, 168, 169; self-help movement in Kenya, 164; subordination in development process, 51; technical expertise of, 34; 'Third World', viewed as passive victims, 52; treated as separate category, 59; use of technology, 34
women in development (WID), 51, 53, 56
women's groups, 163, 164, 168, 170; and men, 166–71; in Kilimanjaro, Tanzania, 165
women's work, 61, 118, 163; invisibility of, 51, 101; reduction of, 93; unpaid, 14 (reduction of, 13)
women's workload, increase of, 12
World Bank, 5, 14, 17, 57, 59, 64, 71, 72, 99, 160, 180
World Health Organization (WHO), 3, 4
World Vision, 157
Worldwide Fund for Nature (WWF), 82, 157

Zambia, 20, 21, 60, 80, 81; number of donor-financed projects in, 90
Zimbabwe, 60, 170; women's agriculture in, 107